By the Editors of Consumer Guide

Amazing Prophecies of the Bible

Timothy J. Dailey, Ph.D.

David M. Howard, Jr., Ph.D., Consultant

Publications International, Ltd.

Timothy J. Dailey earned his doctorate in theology from Marquette University and studied at Wheaton College and the Institute of Holy Land Studies, Jerusalem. He has taught theology, biblical history, and comparative religion in the United States and Israel including the Biblical Resources Study Center, Jerusalem, and Jerusalem Center for Biblical studies. He is author of *Mysteries of the Bible.*

David M. Howard, Jr., is professor of Old Testament and Hebrew at the New Orleans Baptist Theological Seminary and holds a Ph.D. in Near Eastern Studies from the University of Michigan. He is the author of *Fascinating Bible Facts, An Introduction to the Old Testament Historical Books,* and *The Structure of Psalms 93-100.* His other writing credits include contributions to *The International Standard Bible Encyclopedia, Anchor Bible Dictionary,* and *Peoples of the Old Testament World.* He is a member of the Society of Biblical Literature.

Louis Weber, C.E.O.
Publications International, Ltd.,
7373 North Cicero Avenue,
Lincolnwood, Illinois 60646.

Printed in U.S.A.

Consumer Guide is a trademark of Publications International, Ltd.

8 7 6 5 4 3 2 1

ISBN: 0-451-19902-2

Picture credits:
Front cover: **The Crosiers**
AP/Wide World Photos: 89, 102, 108, 203, 279; **Archive Photos:** 12, 69, 81, 96, 188, 197, 254, 277, 355, 375; **Art Resource:** Giraudon/ Musee du Petit Palais, Paris:153; Erich Lessing/ Sammlungen des Stiftes, Klosterneuburg Abbey, Austria: 8; The Pierpont Morgan Library, New York: 132 (m.644, f.248v), 379 (m.644, f.142v), 385 (m.644, f.190), 460 (m.524, f.21); Scala/Duomo, Orvieto: 328, 339; Scala/Sistine Chapel, Vatican State: 171, 192; Victoria & Albert Museum, London: 5; **Corbis-Bettmann:**15, 24, 122, 128, 136, 145, 172, 228, 230, 245, 323, 333, 345, 352, 409, 411, 413, 416, 420, 429, 449, 451, 465, 469, 471; Reuters: 9, 294, 299, 388; UPI: 272, 311, 467; **The Doré Bible Illustrations/Dover Publications, Inc. 1974:** 42, 53, 84, 104, 113, 142, 156, 179, 239, 262, 319, 364, 455; **The New Testament/ Dover Publications, Inc. 1986:** 281, 287; **Ann Ronan at Image Select:** 21, 58, 65; **SuperStock:** 30, 62, 78, 266, 362; Baptistry of the Cathedral, Padua: 349; Castel Capuano, Napoli: 442; Christie's Images: 36, 437; Civic Museum, Oderzo: 306; Civic Museum, Padua/ Mauro Magliani: 166; Correr Civic Museum, Venice/ET Archive, London: 10; ET Archive, London: 39, 220; The Grand Design, Leeds: 422; Pinacoteca, Volterra: 431.

Contents

The New Testament *continued*

Conclusion

A Holy Cow Named Melody

"We have been waiting 2,000 years for a sign from God, and now he has provided us with a red heifer." These words, spoken recently by an Israeli activist in reference to a calf named Melody, illustrate the growing belief in the appearance of mysterious, purportedly divine signs in our world that point to the end of the age.

Christ enthroned: Redemption for all Christians, and the underpinning of much biblical prophecy.

Many students of biblical prophecy believe that at the end of time the Jewish Temple in Jerusalem will be rebuilt and animal sacrifices resumed. Some are convinced that this event will usher in a Messianic age. Others believe it will mark the beginning of a series of cataclysmic, world-ending events. It is into this scenario that Melody neatly fits—one small part of an expansive landscape of biblical prophecy that this book, via numerous passages from Scripture, will address.

The Heifer and Holy Law

Many believe that an obscure requirement found in the Law of Moses must be met before the Temple is rebuilt: This is a statute of the law that the Lord has commanded: "Tell the Israelites to bring you a red heifer without defect, in which there is no blemish and on which no yoke has been laid. You shall give it to the priest Eleazar, and it shall be taken outside the camp and slaughtered in his presence" (Numbers 19:2-3). The ashes of this flawless red heifer are then to be carefully gathered and preserved "for the water for cleansing. It is a purification offering" (Numbers 19:9).

All sacrifices ceased after the destruction of the Temple in 70 A.D. by the Romans. The next two millennia were marked by a forlorn longing of the Jewish people. Many, however, believe that the old Chinese proverb, "May you live in interesting times," is being fulfilled in our day. After nineteen centuries, Jerusalem is once again the capital of a Jewish state, leading some to begin preparations for what they believe will be the eventual rebuilding of the Temple.

According to rabbinical teaching, no red heifer has been born within the biblical land of Israel since the destruction of the Temple. Hence in 1997 religious Jews followed with curiosity and growing excitement the discovery of Melody, a red heifer born on a kibbutz (agricultural commune) near the northern Israeli port of Haifa. A team of rabbinical experts confirmed that, despite a few white hairs, Melody met the biblical criteria for a genuinely holy cow.

Melody, if all goes according to plan, will be slaughtered when full grown and burned according to the stipulations found in the Mosaic Law. The ashes will be made into a liquid paste and used in a purification ceremony to enable religious Jews to enter the Temple site to begin building a new structure.

Rabbinic experts believe that the red heifer must be at least three years old before it is used in a ritual sacrifice. Melody's year of birth is 1997, indicating the year 2000 as the first possible date for this portentous event.

One Heifer, Many Indications

The discovery of the red heifer is heralded as one of an increasing number of prophetic signs in our day. Teachers of prophecy point out that Jesus warned of international conflicts, famines, earthquakes, and deadly pestilences at the end of time. In what other age, they ask, has each one of these signs been present in such abundance?

Skeptics deny that there is anything extraordinary about the days in which we live. They quote the words of the writer of Ecclesiastes: "What has been is what will be, and what has been done is what will be done; there is nothing new under the sun" (Ecclesiastes 1:9). Indeed, historians note that the same prophetic signs have been present in earlier ages, when

Twelfth-century enamel plaque depicting the twelve beasts of the Apocalypse.

Travail in the Middle East, as during the Gulf War of 1991, recurs in Scriptural prophecy.

speculation was rife about the end of human history. In the years leading up to the year A.D. 1000, for example, signs and wonders were reported in the heavens and on earth. Wandering preachers and prophets warned that the appearance of eclipses and comets, as well as wars, famines, and plagues, were omens of the end of the world.

Speculation about the imminent conclusion of human history also flourished at the end of the nineteenth century, when stories about the end of the world found an enthusiastic audience. The writer H. G. Wells caused a sensation with his apocalyptic novel, The *War of the Worlds,* published in 1897.

The Urge to Prophesy

Reflection about the future is in fact timeless. Throughout the ages, theologians, philosophers, and artists have sought in their own ways to, in the words of the Apostle John,

Poe's Revelation

In his story "The Conversation of Eiros and Charmion," Edgar Allan Poe drew upon the symbolism found in Revelation to portray Earth's final hour. The observer Eiros describes a deadly comet as it races toward the planet: "Its approach was not, at first, seemingly rapid; nor was its appearance of very unusual character. It was of a dull red, and had little perceptible train. For seven or eight days we saw no material increase in its apparent diameter, and but a partial alteration in its color. . . ." For a moment there was a wild lurid light alone, visiting and penetrating all things. Then—let us bow down, Charmion, before the excessive majesty of the great God!—then, there came a shouting and pervading sound, as if from the mouth itself of HIM; while the whole incumbent mass of ether in which we existed burst at once into a species of intense flame, for whose surpassing brilliancy and all-fervid heat even the angels in the high Heaven of pure knowledge have no name. Thus ended all."

Poe's violent end of the world.

"write the things which shall be hereafter," that is, to prophesy. Some attribute this well-established tradition of contemplation to the human need to experience an apex of human history that will allow people to make sense of everything. Others ascribe the fascination with the end of the world to an obsession with individual mortality. This line of reasoning holds that humans find it difficult to accept that the universe will continue indefinitely without them, and are anxious for insight into the meanings of their lives. People have searched for this insight not just in holy writings, but in poetry, essays, even fiction.

But before all prophetic speculation is attributed to the emotional yearnings of the human spirit, an account must be given for the startlingly precise biblical predictions that many believe have found fulfillment in history. For example, the Hebrew prophets accurately predicted centuries beforehand the rise of the great empires of Media, Persia, and Greece, as well as the falls of ancient Near Eastern cities such as Babylon and Tyre. Also, a thread of prophecies about the coming Messiah, said to be born in Bethlehem of the lineage of David, can be traced throughout Hebrew scripture.

Israel

Much biblical prophecy is based on phantasmagoric visions, such as this one beheld by Ezekiel.

One intriguing prediction claimed by some to signal the end of the age has piqued interest above all others: the re-establishment of the modern State of Israel. In his "Vision of Dry Bones," the prophet Ezekiel foretold the regathering of the Jewish people to their own land prior to a final cataclysmic battle at the end of time.

Whereas every age has had natural disasters, intractable diseases, and wars, many believe the existence of the State of Israel is the clearest evidence yet that we are living at the last stages of human history.

Ezekiel also described a rebuilt temple and the resumption of animal sacrifices. While scholars disagree as to the interpretation of this passage, some believe that today's celebrity cow, Melody the red heifer, may play a notable role in the re-establishment of those sacrifices.

Events Yet to Come

It is said that prophecy is history written in advance. If so, let us begin our journey through the amazing prophecies of the Bible in hopes that we may understand more clearly the prophecies given to the ancient oracles, who obeyed the divine command: "Now write what you have seen, what is, and what is to take place after this" (Revelation 1:19).

THE NAVEL OF THE EARTH

One of the most mysterious places in the ancient world lies some 300 miles from Athens at the foot of Mount Parnassus in central Greece. Here, overshadowed by the twin Shining Cliffs and perched on the edge of an ominous 600-meter gorge, is Delphi, whose oracles were consulted by kings and commoners for over a millennium.

Modern tourists follow the Sacred Way, which testifies to the extraordinary influence Delphi had in the ancient world. According to the Greek historian Herodotus, the Sacred Way was lined with 3,000 statues and treasuries built to house the offerings of pilgrims—and this was after the theft of 500 statues by the

People have long been fascinated by the art of prophecy. Pythia, the ancient world's famed oracle at Delphi, often utilized snakes to predict the future.

Roman emperor Nero, who was eager for retribution after an oracle censured him.

Modern-day pilgrims make their way to the Temple of Apollo, where the *Pythia,* or female oracle, awaited her visitors seated on a unique bronze tripod designed to protect her from injury when she entered the state of divine possession. The Pythia interpreted the future in a trancelike state induced, it is said, by the vapors emanating from a crevice below the temple. As the Byzantine-Roman emperor

Justinian wrote: "In a dark and narrow recess of a cliff at Delphi there was a little open glade and in this a hole, or cleft in the earth, out of which blew a strong draft of air straight up and as if impelled by a wind, which filled the minds of poets with madness."

Modern scientific testing assures us that no intoxicating fumes now exist, but the enigma surrounding this spectacular sacred place, whose story stretches back to the beginning of recorded history, remains. According to Roman mythology, Jupiter released two eagles to determine the central point of the earth. The birds flew in opposite directions from sunrise until sunset until they met at Delphi, which was honored with the title "the navel of the earth." It was here where Apollo is said to have triumphed over the earth goddess Gaea to establish the Dorians, the founders of Greece.

Moving from myth to legend, sometime in the late second millennium B.C. a shepherd named Coretas is said to have noticed his goats bleating and cavorting at a certain place overlooking the Delphi ravine. The legend relates that as Coretas approached the spot he saw a fissure in the rock and was seized with the spirit of the gods. The site soon attracted local interest and alarm: The people who visited there were gripped by a strange madness and attempted to hurl themselves into the gorge. In time a shrine, and later the Temple of Apollo, the primary oracular deity of the Greeks, was built over the supposed crevice.

For reasons not entirely clear, the medium—or Pythia—of Delphi was a woman at least 50 years of age, who was nevertheless dressed as a girl. This is perhaps to fulfill the idea of the Pythia as the bride of Apollo. Written questions were given to the attending male priests, who then presented them to the Pythia. The medium entered the temple, taking her seat on her bronze tripod over the sacred chasm. She then began to chew on a laurel leaf and drink from a chalice of spring water drawn from the Cassotis spring. Simultaneously, a crown of laurel leaves was placed on her head.

The Pythia then entered a trance. All eyes were on her as she began to speak—according to some sources in a voice different from her own. This state of altered consciousness convinced believers that the Pythia was a conduit to the spirit world, and thus capable of predicting the future. The incoherent mutterings of the Pythia were translated by the attending priests into hexamatic (six-part) verse that often defied comprehension.

The ancient Greeks accepted this ambiguity because of their belief that Apollo did not answer questions candidly. Rather, depending on the piety of the inquirer, Apollo could be expected to puzzle the rash questioner with ambiguous or even misleading replies. And the prophetic service was not without cost: The elaborate rituals cost the equivalent of two days' wages for an Athenian, in addition to the costs of free-will offerings and traveling expenses. Official state inquiries cost ten times the rate charged to private individuals.

As to the accuracy of the predictions given at Delphi, ancient sources are divided. The second-century writer Plutarch, who served at Delphi as a priest, claimed that not a single instance of a false prophecy given by the Pythia could be found. His judgment is supported by a prediction given at Delphi and recorded by the Greek historian Herodotus.

According to Herodotus, Croesus (563-546 B.C.), King of Lydia in Asia Minor, decided to test the veracity of six of the oracle sites in Greece, including Delphi. Croesus sent envoys with instructions to ask what the king was doing at a particular moment on a pre-determined date. Four of the oracles failed outright, and only Delphi was exactly correct. The reply of the Pythia is recorded by Herodotus:

> *I can count the sands, and I can*
> *measure the Ocean;*
> *I have ears for the silent, and know what*
> *the dumb man meaneth;*
> *Lo! on my sense there striketh the smell*
> *of shell-covered tortoise,*
> *Boiling now on fire, with the flesh of a lamb,*
> *in a cauldron,*
> *Brass in the vessel below, and brass to*
> *cover above it.*

In response, Croesus concocted a novel feast: cutting up a tortoise and a lamb and boiling them together in a covered brass cauldron.

Contrary to Plutarch's biased opinion, however, on other occasions the Pythia was known to have given misleading prophecies or ones that failed completely. One spectacular and costly example occurred when Croesus, duly impressed with the oracle's powers, inquired whether he should attack the Persians. He received the reply that if he were to do so, a great empire would be destroyed. Croesus wasted no time in attacking Cyrus II the Great of Persia, only to discover to his dismay that the empire to be destroyed was his own.

Later, as if attempting to compensate for its brash optimism, the Pythia urged caution in Greece's resistance to Persia. The result was another military setback, after which the oracle never regained its political power. Yet the site remained an important center for individual consultation. States going to war continued to promise a tithe of their booty to Delphi as a hedge to guarantee divine support.

After the fourth century B.C., when the Greek empire moved eastward under Alexander the Great, the rulers of his far-flung kingdom no longer dispatched emissaries to

Alexander the Great

Delphi. The decline of the oracle continued until the Roman empire became Christianized under Constantine. The oracle at last fell silent . . .

. . . But not without one last utterance, spoken during the rule (360-363 A.D.) of the Roman emperor Julian the Apostate, so named for his flagrant attempts to turn the empire once again back to paganism. Julian attempted to restore the shrine at Delphi, which had fallen into ruin. His emissary, sent to the site to inquire about his plan's chance of success, received the Delphi's last recorded prophecy:

Tell the king, the monumental hall has
fallen to the ground.
Phoebus no more has a hut, has no
prophetic bay,
No speaking stream.
Even the voice of the water is quenched.

A Global Phenomenon

Delphi is one of the most well-documented examples of the worldwide practice of divination—the obtaining of knowledge about the unknown or the future—which has played a central role in cultures, past and present, around the world. From the dawn of history men have consulted the gods, seeking protection against natural disaster, remedy for their troubles, and knowledge about the future. So great was the importance of understanding the supernatural forces affecting lives that no known culture has lacked those who communicated the divine will. Variously known as shaman, oracle, diviner, medicine man, priest, or priestess, each served as mediator between heaven and earth, placating malevolent spirits and discerning things to come.

Modern-day reliance upon divination can be seen most vividly in non-literary cultures, which exhibit a profound belief in the reality of evil spirits, ghosts, and various spiritual beings. All of these unseen malevolent forces require the intervention of the medium to interpret the reasons for droughts, danger, death, and manifold other calamities and fears—and, if possible, to appease the spirit beings and prevent evil from happening.

Many types of divination have been employed at different times and places, each of which involves the expert interpretation of phenomena that, to the untrained eye, might appear meaningless. As we shall see, the subtle variations in, say, the shape and color of the dissected liver of an animal can mean the difference between prosperity and poverty, victory and defeat, life and death. In the Greco-Roman world the flight and behavior of birds or the demeanors of sacrificial animals were scrutinized for portents about future events, as were the unusual symbolism or visions of dreams.

In Rome an official college of priests, numbering up to 16 diviners or augurs, was established to interpret the signs regarding future events sent by the gods. Virtually every decision of consequence was deferred to the priests, including the election of magistrates, the passing of laws, and going to war.

At night an appointed diviner would station himself on a hill outside the city to watch for omens, such as a flight of birds or flash of thunder. He would pitch a tent, cover his head, and ask a sign of the gods. He would be seated facing southward, having the favorable east to

Roman prophesiers known as augurs analyzed the behavior of birds to foretell coming events.

his left and the unfavorable west to his right. Thus positioned, the augur (official diviner) would carefully scan the horizon and listen for the sounds of the night. The callings of birds and animals were considered to have special significance and were duly noted.

The ancient Chinese used divination extensively, based on the Confucian idea of fate, which was thought to govern every aspect of life. Divining sticks and blocks were used to predict the future, as was the reading of palms (palmistry) and the natural marks on the shells of tortoises. Astrology was practiced by the Chinese at an early date. The practice persists to this day: Chinese buildings are properly situated and aligned in accordance with *yin* and *yang* factors and the "five elements." Further, the Chinese Book of Changes, or the *I Ching,* is still used to determine the future.

During the late Shang dynasty (1200-1050 B.C.) diviners used "oracle bones," more than 107,000 of which have been excavated, to discern future events. In Burma and Siam (present-day Thailand) an egg was pierced at each end and the contents blown out upon the ground; the resulting form was interpreted to discern future events.

Remarkably, many of the same practices were employed by medicine men and the priestly class in the New World. In ancient Mexico a college of augurs similar to that of Rome passed along the skills of divination from generation to generation. As in Rome, the Mexican augurs were responsible for observing birds and other animals.

In Peru, diviners observed the shape and colors of leaves of tobacco and maize, or the juice of coca. The paths of spiders and the direction of falling fruit had significance. In a more macabre variation the Peruvians, who practiced human sacrifice, scrutinized the forms in the smoke of their burning victims. Peruvian diviners practiced another unusual oracular method, called "making idols speak," which was thought to involve ventriloquism and a tree trunk the height of a man, which allegedly uttered the oracles of the Peruvian deity Jurupari.

Birds are constants in the oracular arts of many cultures. They had special significance for American Indian tribes, who strangely combined messages given by birds with those offered by serpents. Some tribes believed a bird was a spirit that, because of a powerful enchantment, had taken a visible form; others believed that the souls of the departed entered into birds. Naturally, close attention was paid to the movements of such creatures.

Indeed, throughout the Americas we find the same means of divination employed, based upon the central tribal figure of the medicine man or shaman. According to traditional accounts, the shaman would enter the tent or hut of the individual seeking assistance. It is said that when he began chanting his incantations, the entire lodge would tremble and rock, as if shaken by spirit forces. Following this, a terrifying noise, which seemed to emanate from the bowels of the earth, would fill the lodge.

Such accounts have been reported by missionaries working among North American native tribes. Shamans and medicine men who converted to Christianity have stated that they entered into a trancelike state and were unaware of the commotion their ministerings caused. While apparently in deep sleep they questioned the spirit and received generally ambiguous answers of a type similar to those given by the Pythia at Delphi. The hypnotic, trancelike state was also used by diviners in the Americas as a means to communicate with the dead.

The ability to see visions was an important role of the native American diviners, an ability enhanced by the use of coca leaves and the snake plant, as well as peyote and other hallucinogens. Numerous plants were cultivated by the tribes expressly for this purpose, and published accounts of startling predictions underscore the value placed on these cerebral intoxicants as revealers of the future.

In his biography, the famous Sac chief Black Hawk stated that his grandfather believed that at a certain date four years hence "he should see a white man, who would be to him as a father." At the appointed time he traveled to a certain place, where he met a Frenchman who was instrumental in forming an alliance between France and the Sac tribe.

In a similar instance in the 1860s, the white pioneer John Mason Brown and several other men were searching unsuccessfully for a band of Native Americans. After encountering numerous difficulties Brown and his men were about to abandon their hunt when they ran across a party of braves from the tribe they were searching for. The Indians explained that their tribal shaman had described Brown and his men in detail. Brown asked the medicine man how he knew they were coming and was able to describe them. The shaman, described as "a frank and simple-minded man," replied that he "saw them coming and heard them talk on their journey."

In Guatemala, a prophecy regarding the arrival of other white men meant death and destruction. The king of Kiche, Kicah Tanub, was informed that the race of white men that had conquered Montezuma's Mexico was headed their way. Kicah Tanub commanded four court diviners to foretell the outcome of the white men's arrival in Guatemala. The augurs took their bows and directed arrows at a rock. Upon examination, the arrows were seen to have made no impression upon the rock, which was taken to mean that the invaders would be triumphant. Not content with this dire prediction, Kicah Tanub consulted other augurs, who on the basis of the mysterious shattering of an ancient sacred stone, also accurately predicted the fall of Kiche.

Montezuma himself was the victim of a tragic misinterpretation of events as the Spaniards were advancing on his kingdom about 1520. A number of ominous signs appeared, including earthquakes, floods, strange lights in the sky, and mysterious voices heard in the air. Montezuma consulted the most famous diviner of his kingdom, who informed him that these were the signs preceding the return of the legendary divine-hero Quetzalcoatl to his people. The hesitation with which Montezuma awaited the Spaniards was a decisive factor in the latter's rapid conquest of Mexico.

Prophecy in Mesopotamia

Earliest records from the great river cultures of Mesopotamia, known as the Cradle of Civilization, confirm that divination was already an ancient art by the time of Abraham. The book of Genesis states that Abraham's family "went out together from Ur of the Chaldeans to go into the land of Canaan" (Genesis 11:31). Ur is the name of one of three major population centers in ancient Sumer and Babylonia in lower Mesopotamia. It is identified with modern Tel el-Muqayyar, about 220 miles southeast of Baghdad, Iraq.

The most important modern exploration of Ur was conducted by the renowned English

The ancient city of Ur has provided the modern world with physical evidence of the fascinating culture of Mesopotamia, notably religion.

archaeologist Leonard Woolley between 1922 and 1934. Woolley's excavation revealed that Ur was first settled in about 5500 B.C. and continued to be occupied for more than five thousand years.

The royal tombs tell us something about the religious milieu out of which Abraham was called by Yahweh, the name of the God of the Bible. The male and female attendants as well as animals of the king were killed, so that they might accompany him on his journey to the Netherworld, where he would continue his reign. This world view is similar to that of Egypt's and those of other ancient Near Eastern cultures that considered the king to be a divine being.

Woolley also uncovered a ziggurat, one of the massive stepped-pyramid-shaped structures that played an important role in the religion of ancient Mesopotamia. The ziggurat at Ur was dedicated to the moon god, the patron-god of the city, and contained chambers on its summit for a high priestess. It was there, in that lofty chamber at the juncture of heaven and earth, where the will of the gods was revealed. This is the stated purpose of the builders of another ziggurat, the primordial Tower of Babel: "Come, let us build ourselves a city, and a tower with its top in the heavens" (Genesis 11:4).

The ancient Near East was the home of the two great river cultures of Babylonia and Assyria, both of which practiced various forms of divination. Interpretation of the future was a highly developed art that was jealously guarded by a large and organized body of priests. The discovery of the library at the Assyrian capital city of Nineveh, with its large horde of cuneiform (wedge-shaped) clay tablets, inscribed with various portents, provided a wealth of information about Assyro-Babylonian divination.

One technique of discerning future events, divination by oil, is known to have been used at the earliest stages of recorded history. Urukagina, king of Lagash (c. 2800 B.C.), used this method, which consisted of pouring oil upon the surface of a pool of water. The resulting forms taken by the oil as it spread across the water were interpreted by professional diviners using arcane rituals to indicate the future course of events. Such was the potential for graft on the part of the priesthood that Urukagina abolished the exorbitant fees that had been demanded for the diviners' services.

Another means of divining the future was examination of the liver of a sheep. For the peoples of the ancient Near East the liver, not the heart, was the vital body organ. "Reading" the liver was a highly-developed art in which the organ of the sacrificed sheep was exposed by the priest. Archaeologists have discovered clay models of livers inscribed with notations that were consulted to determine the correct prediction. The shape and color of the organ, as well as markings on the veins and ducts, were all considered omens indicating what the future held.

To the mind of the ancients it would have been reckless for the king to make decisions of any significance without first consulting the gods. Unearthed cuneiform tablets contain appeals of the king regarding the outcome of military campaigns, the dispatch of envoys, the giving of daughters in marriage, and the outcome of sickness. The appearance of peculiar signs in the atmosphere or the heavens were thought to be evil portents. Unusual atmospheric conditions as well as eclipses and storms indicated divine displeasure, and it became a matter of urgency to determine what had offended the gods and to make appeasement.

In the face of heavenly phenomena, people—scholars and the uneducated alike—felt uncomfortably small and vulnerable. They grew eager for answers. The practice of looking to the heavens for indications about the future eventually developed into astrology, the belief that the movements of stellar bodies determine events on earth.

The ancient Babylonians looked to inner space to learn what the future held. One of the most important functions of that culture's professional diviners was the interpretation of dreams. In the seventh century B.C. the Assyrian king Ashurbanipal claimed that a vision of the goddess Ishtar was responsible for his victory over Elam. It is likely that the appearance occurred during sleep—and not to the king himself but to one of the court seers. Every detail of such a dream could have significance, requiring the services of a highly-trained diviner.

"Mad Over Idols": The Temples of Babylon

The diminutive Land of Israel inhabited a hilly region located far from the great cities and cultures of ancient Mesopotamia. Yet by the time of the prophet Jeremiah, the idolatrous practices of Assyria-Babylonia had already led to the military defeat of the northern kingdom of Israel in 722 B.C. As he observed the collapse of the southern kingdom of Judah in 586 B.C., Jeremiah recorded the divine condemnation of Babylon:

"A sword against the Chaldeans,
says the Lord,
and against the inhabitants of Babylon,
and against her officials and her sages!
A sword against the diviners,
so that they may become fools!
A sword against her warriors,
so they may be destroyed! . . .
A drought against her waters,
that they may be dried up!
For it is a land of images,
and they go mad over idols"

(Jeremiah 50:35-36, 38).

Archaeology and the annals of history confirm the idolatrous religion and widespread practice of divination of Babylon. King Nebuchadnezzar (who reigned 604-562 B.C.) recorded the numerous temples he built in Babylon. One of the gods he honored, Marduk, is known as Bel in the Bible, and is condemned by the God of Israel speaking through the prophet Jeremiah: "I will punish Bel in Babylon, and make him disgorge what he has swallowed. The nations shall no longer stream to him; the wall of Babylon has fallen" (Jeremiah 51:44).

The city from which Nebuchadnezzar ruled was the largest and one of the most important capital cities of ancient Mesopotamia. In later, classical times, the massive walls of the city and its renowned Hanging Gardens were listed among the Seven Wonders of the Ancient World. The Greek historian Herodotus reportedly visited the city in 460 B.C., claiming that "it surpasses in splendor any city of the known world."

Inside the massive walls were more than a thousand temples and religious structures that served a population of nearly 100,000. One ancient inscription provides details: "Altogether there are in Babylon 53 temples of the chief gods, 55 chapels of Marduk, 300 chapels

The awesome Tower of Babel was a potent symbol of Babylonian paganism and the power of the priestly class. Babylonia's worship of a multitude of gods is condemned by the Bible.

of earthly deities, 600 for the heavenly deities, 180 altars for the goddess Ishtar, 180 for the gods Nergal and Adad and 12 other altars for different gods."

The most prominent temple in Babylon was Esagila ("the temple that raises its head"), in which dwelled Marduk, the patron god of Babylon. More than 50 other temples and shrines were on the site. More than 6,000 figures and figurines testified to Jeremiah's comment that the city was "mad over idols."

Next to Esagila was the great staged tower or ziggurat called Etemenanki ("the foundation house of heaven and earth"), a structure thought to be similar to the biblical Tower of Babel. The tower was nearly 300 feet square and rose to a height of nearly 300 feet.

The magnificent glory of Babylon was a testimony to the might of the priestly class, who, with their divination, held enormous power and sway over events in the city.

The Beleagured Prophets of Israel

In stark contrast to the great river civilizations of Mesopotamia, Israel had no equivalent of an established, all-powerful priestly class whose dictates were respected and obeyed by the king. Israelite prophets were often isolated, beleagured figures drawn from the fringes of society. Typical among them was Amos, a shepherd from Tekoa, a dusty village ten miles south of Jerusalem on the edge of the wilderness. Amos made no claim to be a professional prophet: "I am no prophet, nor a prophet's son; but I am a herdsman, and a dresser of sycamore trees, and the Lord took me from following the flock, and the Lord said to me, 'Go, prophesy to my people in Israel'" (Amos 7:14-15).

Far from occupying an honored place in Israelite society, the prophets often stood in opposition to the apostasy and ethical corruption of the king and his ruling elite. It was a risky stance that was fraught with danger. The prophets proclaimed the word of the Lord, which had been given them through dreams, visions, or other means of inspiration, criticizing idolatrous practices and social injustice, calling the Israelites back to the faithful observance of the Law. For their efforts they were ignored, held in contempt, imprisoned, or worse. In his day Jesus referred to the abysmal treatment afforded the divine messengers of old:

> *"Woe to you! For you build the tombs of the prophets whom your ancestors killed. So you are witnesses and approve of the deeds of your ancestors; for they killed them, and you build their tombs. Therefore also the Wisdom of God said, 'I will send them prophets and apostles, some of whom they will kill and persecute, so that this generation may be charged with the blood of all the prophets shed since the foundation of the world'"*
>
> *(Luke 11:47-50).*

This statuette honored the pagan god Baal, who was worshiped by Phoenicians and others. Because Baal's powers were closely tied to nature, the golden-headed figure seen here may originally have wielded a lightning bolt.

Elijah was the archetypal miracle-working prophet who remains one of the most eminent and illustrious visionaries of Israelite history. He lived in the ninth century B.C. and prophesied to the northern kingdom of Israel during the rule of King Ahab and, later, during the rule of Ahab's son Ahaziah, a time when the foundations of Israelite religion were challenged by pagan idolatry.

Trouble visited Israel in the person of the Sidonian princess Jezebel, whom King Ahab married and brought to his capital city Samaria. Her name, which means "Baal is

Prince," indicates the struggle she would lead on behalf of Baal against Yahweh, the true God of Israel.

Jezebel had no use for Elijah, and sought to kill him and the other prophets in Israel, replacing them with prophets of Baal and his consort Asherah. To resort to pagan diviners, however, was in direct violation of the Mosaic Law:

> *"You must remain completely loyal to the Lord your God. Although these nations that you are about to dispossess do give heed to soothsayers and diviners, as for you, the Lord your God does not permit you to do so. The Lord your God will raise up for you a prophet like me from among your own people; you shall heed such a prophet" (Deuteronomy 18:13-15).*

The various cultures of the ancient Near East freely adapted each other's deities and religious practices. This was not, however, an option for the Israelites, who had been called apart by the one true God, Yahweh. At the very core of the Israelite religion was the worship of Yahweh in opposition to the pantheon of gods and goddesses of polytheistic ancient Near Eastern religion. For the Israelites to adapt practices of other religions would be to fatally compromise their own faith.

Baal, whose name means "lord, owner, master" was the supreme deity of Syro-Palestine. He was worshiped by the Phoenicians as well as the Philistines and other peoples of the region. Hence the various derivatives of Baal that are mentioned in the Bible, including the Philistine Baal-Zebub "lord of the flies" or "lord of the Prince"; the Moabite Baal-Meon "lord of the residence"; and Baal-Gad, "the lord of Gad" of the town in the valley of Lebanon.

Baal was the storm god as well as the god of fertility. His entourage included rain clouds, and he was believed to send the rains in their seasons. Lightning was his weapon, and he was often pictured with a lightning bolt in his upraised fist.

The temptation to worship a god of storm such as Baal was powerful for people of the parched land of Israel. Unlike the great river cultures of Egypt or Mesopotamia, whose great rivers such as the Nile, Tigris, and Euphrates provided abundant water, Israel had no year-long sources of water for irrigation. Instead, Israel was wholly dependent upon the winter rains to water its crops.

The biblical prophet Elijah was outraged by worship of the pagan god Baal, and engineered a violent, heavenly punishment of Baal's prophets at a brook called Kishon. 19th-century illustration by Gustave Doré.

But Baal's services came at a heavy cost. In return for supplying rain Baal demanded appeasement in the form of human sacrifice. In the Bible this form of sacrifice is termed "to pass through the fire." As the phrase suggests, the victims were burned alive, and such sacrifice was given as a primary cause for the fall of the kingdom of Israel: "They made their sons and their daughters pass through fire; they used divination and augury; and they sold themselves to do evil in the sight of the Lord" (2 Kings 17:17).

The degradation which Baal worship threatened—and eventually succeeded—to bring upon Israel prompted the prophet Elijah to force a confrontation with the prophets of Baal. Elijah challenged King Ahab, Jezebel's complicit husband, to assemble on Mount Carmel the four hundred fifty prophets of Baal and the four hundred prophets of Asherah, who eat at Jezebel's table (1 Kings 18:19).

Despite the odds, Elijah confidently proclaimed to all those present: "How long will you go limping with two different opinions? If the Lord is God, follow him; but if Baal, then follow him" (1 Kings 18:21). The people, however, "did not answer him a word." Undeterred, Elijah ordered that an altar be built, after which the prophets of Baal would call upon their god to send down fire to consume the bull that had been sacrificed upon it.

We read next the almost comical description of the prophets of Baal dancing around the altar, crying "O Baal, answer us!"—to no avail. At noon Elijah could not resist mocking them: "Cry aloud! Surely he is a god; either he is meditating, or he has wandered away, or he is on a journey, or perhaps he is asleep and must be awakened" (1 Kings 18:27).

The earthiness of Elijah's mockery is lost in the English translation. The phrase "[perhaps] he has wandered away" is in Hebrew a euphemism for stepping aside to a private place to relieve oneself. This impertinence enraged the prophets of Baal, who "raved on until the time of the offering of the oblation, but there was no voice, no answer, and no response" (1 Kings 18:29). Elijah then offers a brief yet eloquent prayer, after which we read that "the fire of the Lord fell and consumed the burnt offering, the wood, the stones, and the dust, and even licked up the water that was in the trench" (1 Kings 18:38). At the cost of their lives, the prophets of Baal realized that their god, like all gods of wood and stone, was incapable of answering their prayers.

Despite the unambiguous confirmation of Elijah as the true messenger of God, the Israelites continued to pursue other sources of prophetic inspiration. We read that at the beginning of his reign Israel's first king, Saul, "expelled the mediums and the wizards from the land" (1 Samuel 28:3). Mediums attempted to communicate with the dead, and wizards practiced the divining arts, both of which were expressly forbidden in the Law of Moses: "If any turn to mediums and wizards, prostituting themselves to them, I will set my face against them, and will cut them off from the people" (Leviticus 20:6).

Despite his prohibition of mediums, King Saul found himself driven to consult one not long before his death. He was about to fight his final battle against the Philistines, in the valley of Jezreel. The Israelite army was at the foot of Mount Gilboa while the Philistines were encamped across the valley at the town of Shunem on the hill of Moreh.

Saul was well aware that his position on relatively low ground put his army in a bad position vis-à-vis the Philistines. Tactics and strategy weighed heavily on Saul's mind. On the other side of Mount Moreh was the village of Endor, where a medium lived. Saul, overwrought with fear about the impending battle, sought divine guidance. He had, however, long been rejected because of his disobedience. We read that "the Lord did not answer him, not by dreams, or by Urim, or by prophets" (1 Samuel 28:6).

The Urim and Thummim were mysterious objects used in ancient Israel to determine God's will. Little is known about their composition or how they were used to predict the future. They are mentioned in the book of Exodus as being kept by the High Priest in a "breastplate of judgment." Moses entrusted their care to the tribe of Levi, and they were brought forth to receive divine guidance.

Early in his rule Saul used the Urim and Thummim to determine who had broken Saul's vow in a battle with the Philistines:

> *"Then Saul said, 'O Lord God of Israel, why have you not answered your servant today? If this guilt is in me or in my son Jonathan, O Lord God of Israel, give Urim; but if this guilt is in your people Israel, give Thummim.' And Jonathan and Saul were indicated by the lot, but the people were cleared. Then Saul said, 'Cast the lot between me and my son Jonathan.' And Jonathan was taken"*
>
> *(1 Samuel 14:41-42).*

This text indicates that the Urim and Thummim may have been objects drawn or shaken from a bag, with one object signifying a positive answer and the other a negative response.

Determined to obtain supernatural knowledge about what would befall him on the battlefield the next day, Saul disguised himself and went with two companions under cover of night to Endor, a dangerous journey requiring a considerable detour around the Philistine forces.

At Endor, Saul asked the medium to conjure up Samuel, who, as we have already read, has died. The woman does as he asks but something goes frightfully awry. When she sees Samuel the medium becomes terrified.

It seems that the medium did not expect to see what she saw. Does this imply that she was a fraud who intended to perform her usual chicanery but was shocked to see the venerated prophet? Possibly, though another likely reason for her terror would have been the presence of Samuel, who during his ministry faithfully stood against the practice of witchcraft, idolatry, and all challenges to the God of Israel.

Saul, who apparently cannot see the apparition, tries to assuage her fears and asks her to tell him what she sees. The woman replies that she sees a "divine being" coming out of the ground, which she describes "as an old man" who is "wrapped in a robe" (1 Samuel 28:14).

The reference to being wrapped in a robe may indicate Samuel's burial cloths. In any case, we read that Saul now realizes he is speaking with the prophet. He bows with his face to the ground and describes his plight to the apparition.

This passage has fascinated scholars, who disagree as to whether Samuel was actually conjured by the medium. Many theologians believe that the departed are not available to be "called up" by mediums, and that the practice of mediumship is inherently false and deceptive. They cite the prohibitions of mediumship in the Old Testament, and explain the alleged appearance of Samuel as a beguiling apparition that Saul mistakenly took to be the prophet. Others believe that the passage unmistakingly states that Samuel was roused from his "rest" to address Saul, and that this does *not* imply any recommendation of what is clearly considered a forbidden practice.

Whatever the actuality of the apparition confronting Saul, the news could not have been worse. In this final prophecy Saul is informed that he has been rejected by the Lord and that on the morrow Israel will be defeated, and Saul and his sons will die on the battlefield.

Upon hearing the dreaded news, Saul was "filled with fear because of the words of Samuel; and there was no strength in him" (1 Samuel 28:20). His terror was justified, for the next day would indeed be his last, and he and his sons would fall in battle on Mount Gilboa.

The Advent of Messiah

Throughout the ebb and flow of the Old Testament, in the midst of the triumph and the tragedy of Israel, runs a continuous thread of prophecies concerning a unique personage who possesses divine powers. This individual is referred to in the Hebrew Scriptures as the Messiah, a word that means "anointed one." Various figures from the Old Testament, including prophets and kings, are recorded as having their heads anointed with oil to signify that they have been set apart as God's representatives, each charged with a unique task or service. As time passed, however, prophecies began to emerge from one individual who soon towered above all others, a divine figure who was destined to bring salvation and deliverance to the children of Abraham.

The sheer volume of references in the Hebrew Bible to the Messiah (scholars have isolated more than 400 related texts) attests to the importance of this coming King and Savior, an interest reflected also in hundreds of messianic passages in the ancient Jewish rabbinical texts written after the Old Testament. It has been pointed out that the concept of a Messiah is unique in the ancient Near East. While the Assyrians, Babylonians, Egyptians, and others probably held messianistic concepts superficially similar to the notion as expressed in the Hebrew Bible, none seems to have grasped the Israelite concept of a divine figure who would bring about the final culmination of history.

Indeed, the very idea of history meant something radically different for Israel than it did for the other cultures of the Near East. The ancient Mesopotamians and Egyptians had a cyclic view of history, what the eminent philosopher Etienne Gilson called "the myth of the eternal return." In short, like the four seasons that follow one after another year after year, century after century, the ancients viewed life as a cycle that repeats itself endlessly.

In such a world view there is little room—or need—for what we moderns call progress. Indeed, if the whole of life is simply following an eternally ordained pattern, then there can be no real change or development. Hence, for periods of time lasting literally thousands of years, with civilizations rising and falling, we see remarkably little substantive material or cultural progress in the ancient Near East. People went about their everyday lives in much the same way as their ancestors: Farmers used the same agricultural techniques; cities were built using time-tested construction methods; and nations fought wars using much the same weapons and tactics as had been used in the past.

By contrast, the Hebrew notion of the world consisted of more than the recurrent cycles of nature. The Hebrews viewed time as linear. History had a goal and a termination point. History began with the creation of the world by Yahweh, the God of Israel, and would end with the eternal Messianic kingdom. In between these vast poles the battle between good and evil would be played out in events of history, in kingdoms, and in men's hearts.

The first biblical indication of this cosmic struggle is found in the third chapter of Genesis, where, after the primordial Adam and Eve were cast out of the garden, a series of enigmatic prophecies are recorded. One of these is directed toward the serpent, who represented the forces of evil: "I will put enmity between you and the woman, and between your offspring and hers; he will strike your head, and you will strike his heel" (Genesis 3:15).

This verse is traditionally known as the *protoevangelium,* the first proclamation of the good news of salvation. It refers to the enmity between the forces of evil and the woman, or Eve, along with "her offspring." As Eve is spoken of a few verses later as the "mother of all living," the reference to her "offspring" would mean her descendants. The same is true of the serpent, whose human minions have done his bidding throughout history.

Both of these offspring point us once again to the linear Hebrew view of time and history.

The expulsion of Adam and Eve from the Garden, depicted here by Gustave Doré, is a key event in the Hebrew saga of the titanic struggle between good and evil.

The evil seed will find its ultimate representation in the antichrist while the good seed will culminate in the Messiah. At the end of time these two personages and their forces will join in a battle so titanic as to eclipse all others.

We see also in this passage an indication of the *outcome* of that final confrontation. Many commentators have seen the ultimate victory of the forces of God in the image of the mortal wound to the serpent's head as opposed to the superficial injury to the foot of the woman.

A second clue as to the nature of the coming Messiah is found several chapters later, when Noah issues blessings and curses for his sons, Shem, Japheth, and Ham (here represented by his son Canaan): "Blessed by the Lord my God be Shem; and let Canaan be his slave. May God make space for Japheth, and let him live in the tents of Shem; and let Canaan be his slave" (Genesis 9:26-27).

Some scholars have seen in this passage an intimation that one day God will come and dwell among His people. The later Hebrews, for whom Yahweh was utterly transcendent and unapproachable, would have been amazed at this revelation. Had not Moses been told by the Lord Himself that "you cannot see my face; for no one shall see me and live" (Exodus 33:20)? Also, the reference to Shem possibly indicates a narrowing of the lineage of this future divine personage to the descendants of Noah's son Shem, the ancestor of the Hebrew people. The prophecy has grown more focused than before.

According to the Messianic genealogy found in the Gospel of Luke, Abraham was tenth in the lineage of Shem. When Yahweh called Abraham's family out of Ur he gave him the following promise: "I will make of you a great nation, and I will bless you, and make your name great . . . and in you all the families of the earth shall be blessed" (Genesis 12:2-3). With Abraham's wife, Sarah, seemingly unable to bear children, Abraham must surely have pondered how "a great nation" would issue from him. Finally, in advanced age, Sarah bore Isaac, called the "son of promise" because he would fulfill the prophecy given to his father. Biblical interpreters see the reference to the nations of the earth being blessed as finding fulfillment in the Messiah, who would bring salvation to mankind.

But Abraham's testing concerning God's promise was not yet over, for in Genesis 22 we read a curious incident in which he is called upon to take his son "to the land of Moriah and offer him there as a burnt offering on one of the mountains that I shall show you" (Genesis 22:2). Although Abraham understood that it was to be through his son that divine blessings would come, it nevertheless was a supreme act of faith for Abraham to obediently take Isaac for sacrifice atop the mountain. He had no guarantee that Isaac would be spared.

Abraham had full confidence that God's promises would not fail, for when he left his servants behind he instructed them: "Stay here with the donkey; the boy and I will go over there; we will worship, and then we will come back to you" (Genesis 22:5). Though he must not have fathomed how, he evidently fully expected his son to return from the mountain with him. Abraham's faith was rewarded, for at the last moment, as he was poised to slay his son, an angel stayed Abraham's upheld arm. A ram caught in a nearby thicket was substituted.

Another aspect of the coming Messiah was revealed to Abraham: The kingdom of the future and eternal King of Israel was not only spiritual but earthly as well. Though the rule of Messiah would extend to the ends of the earth it would be centered on the land of Canaan, which was promised to Abraham:

"The Lord said to Abram, after Lot had separated from him, 'Raise your eyes now, and look from the place where you are, northward and southward and eastward and westward; for all the land that you see I will give to you and to your offspring forever.'" (Genesis 13:14-15)

Because of passages like this, the land of Israel has continued to be the focus of much speculation, as students of the Bible look forward to the fulfillment of numerous specific prophetic events centered in the Holy Land. Some of these prophecies refer to events surrounding the end of history, and others provide specific information about the life of the coming Messiah.

One of the most specific details concerning the Messiah is given in the book of Micah: "But you, O Bethlehem of Ephrathah, who are one of the little clans of Judah, from you shall come forth for me one who is to rule in Israel, whose origin is from of old, from ancient days" (Micah 5:2).

Ephrathah is thought by many to be the name of a clan associated with the town of

Abraham so loved God that he was willing to sacrifice his son, Isaac, on God's order. Abraham's test of faith ended when an angel intervened, sparing the boy's life.

Bethlehem. While this passage was clearly understood by the Gospel writers to refer to the Messiah, the ancient Israelites must have found puzzling that their Anointed One would come from Bethlehem. Though indeed the birthplace of King David some 300 years before, the little farming hamlet had long been passed over in importance by the cultic centers of the Jewish nation. David himself had chosen to establish his capital not in his hometown but in the Jebusite city of Jerusalem, and it was from there that the royal lineage of Judah continued.

Even more perplexing was the manner of the coming Messiah's birth, which was foretold in the book of the prophet Isaiah as a miraculous event: "Therefore the Lord himself will give you a sign. Look, the young woman is with child and shall bear a son, and shall name him Immanuel" (Isaiah 7:14). This passage, understood by the Gospel writers as referring to the Virgin Birth of Jesus, has been hotly disputed by many biblical scholars, with some denying it has any direct reference to the Messiah.

Indeed, the Hebrew word translated "young woman" is not the technical term for virgin but rather means a young woman of marriageable age. However, it is equally true that in Hebrew culture it would have been understood that any young unmarried woman would be a virgin. The Greek Septuagint, the single most important translation of the Old Testament in ancient times, in fact confirms the obvious by translating the Hebrew word as "virgin." The title given to the child, "Immanuel," which means "God with us," also indicates that something greater than an ordinary human is at issue here.

Other messianic passages confirm that the Messiah is to be a divine figure who would of necessity require some kind of unique or supernatural origin. One of the most unambiguous references to the divine nature of the Messiah occurs just two chapters later in the book of Isaiah: "For a child has been born for us, a son given to us; authority rests upon his shoulders; and he is named Wonderful Counselor, Mighty God, Everlasting Father, Prince of Peace" (Isaiah 9:6).

Fundamental to the Hebrew world view was the inviolable distinction between God and the created order. Divine titles as we see here, such as "Mighty God" and "Everlasting Father," would never be applied to a mere mortal, and indeed never are in the Bible.

The ninth chapter of the book of Isaiah offers further geographical information about the Messiah. In a prophecy concerning Galilee of the nations we read: "The people who walked in darkness have seen a great light; those who lived in a land of deep darkness—on them light has shined" (Isaiah 9:2).

The reference to the Messiah coming from Galilee must have baffled many Israelites, as the region had been largely denuded of Jews, who had been sent into exile and replaced by foreign colonists after the Assyrian conquest of 722 B.C. All that would change with the rise of the Jewish Hasmonean kingdom in the mid-second century B.C., when many foreigners were expelled from Galilee, and Jewish towns were re-established there.

Among these new settlements was the obscure village of Nazareth, nestled in the hills on the edge of the Plain of Jezreel. Nazareth is not mentioned in the Old Testament or in any ancient Jewish sources save, curiously, documents found at the Essene community of Qumran at the shores of the Dead Sea. Archaeological excavation has determined that the population of Nazareth never exceeded about two hundred people. It remained a tiny settlement. The name Nazareth is derived from the Hebrew word for "shoot" or "branch," which

The book of Isaiah proclaims that the Messiah has been born in Galilee (above), a place that in biblical times had little more than a token Jewish population.

is used in relation to the Messiah in passages such as Isaiah 11:1: "A shoot shall come out from the stump of Jesse, and a branch shall grow out of his roots." Jesse is the father of King David, through whom the promised Messiah would come.

Interestingly, it has been suggested that Nazareth was settled by a clan that considered itself to be the rightful descendants—or messianic branch —of King David. Whatever the validity of this theory, it is at the very least coincidental that the earthly parentage of Jesus came from Nazareth, a town whose very name invokes messianic symbolism.

A confrontation recorded in the Gospels between Jesus and the people of Nazareth illustrates the fact that by the first century many Jews conceived of the Messiah as a political liberator. In a Jewish writing called the *Psalms of Solomon,* dated between 70-40 B.C., the Messiah is presented as a warrior-prince who would defeat the hated Romans from Palestine and usher in a Jewish kingdom whose power would extend to the whole world.

Likely Candidates?

Several Messiah candidates are mentioned in the New Testament and in the writings of the contemporary Jewish historian Josephus. The first of these was John the Baptist, who began preaching and baptizing in the region of the Jordan River. We read that the crowds of people that came out to see him were "filled with expectation, and all were questioning in their hearts concerning John, whether he might be the Messiah" (Luke 3:15).

John steadfastly denied that he was the Messiah, telling the people: "I baptize you with water; but one who is more powerful than I is coming; I am not worthy to untie the thong of his sandals" (Luke 3:16).

Another Messiah figure, Theudas, appeared on the scene after the time of Jesus and during the rule of the procurator Cuspius Fadus (44-46 A.D.). According to Josephus, Theudas led a large crowd to the Jordan, where he promised to repeat Joshua's miracle by commanding the river to dry up, and then lead his followers across.

Fadus sent a squadron of cavalry against the fanatics, who were gathered on the riverbank waiting for the miracle. Many were taken prisoner. Worse, Theudas was killed, his severed head brought back to Jerusalem.

This episode is mentioned also in the book of Acts, where the Pharisee Gamaliel cautions his fellow members of the Sanhedrin against taking extreme action against the Apostle Peter: "Fellow Israelites, consider carefully what you propose to do to these men. For some time ago Theudas rose up, claiming to be somebody, and a number of men, about four hundred, joined him; but he was killed, and all who followed him were dispersed and disappeared" (Acts 5:35).

In his speech Gamaliel gave another example of a false Messiah: "After him Judas the

It was felt by some that John the Baptist, shown here baptizing Christ, was the Messiah. Although a cult of devotees developed around John, he denied that he was the Messiah, making clear that that person was far greater than he. Illustration by Doré.

Galilean rose up at the time of the census and got people to follow him; he also perished, and all who followed him were scattered" (Acts 5:37). Josephus mentions Jacob and Simeon, the sons of Judas the Galilean, who attempted to lead a revolt against the procurator Tiberius Alexander (46-48 A.D.). Alexander captured the sons of Judas and ordered them crucified.

· Josephus records that under the procurator Felix (52-59 A.D.) an unnamed Egyptian gathered thousands of disciples who followed him up to the Mount of Olives, where he promised to bring down the walls of Jerusalem and deliver the Roman garrison into their hands. The Egyptian promised to subsequently rule as king over the nation. Felix sent soldiers who massacred many of the disciples, but their leader managed to escape, never to be heard from again.

This event is mentioned in Acts, when the Apostle Paul is arrested in the courtyard of the Temple. The Roman commander suspects Paul is the Egyptian who got away. Then, after hearing Paul speak Greek, the commander remarks: "Then you are not the Egyptian who recently stirred up a revolt and led the four thousand assassins out into the wilderness?" (Acts 21:38).

Finally, Josephus also reports that during the rule of the procurator Festus an anonymous, self-styled prophet promised salvation to all who would follow him into the desert. Soldiers were dispatched to dispel the gathered crowds with force, killing the prophet along with a number of his followers.

The Role of Jesus

Throughout Jesus' ministry many hoped that Jesus would be the political Messiah they were waiting for. The Gospel of John records what happened when Jesus explained the profoundly spiritual nature of his ministry: "Because of this many of his disciples turned back and no longer went about with him" (John 6:66).

It is likely that many of Jesus' fellow citizens of Nazareth dared to entertain the hope that perhaps their own native son, who had already made a reputation for himself as a teacher and miracle worker throughout Galilee, might be the promised Messiah. Throughout his ministry, however, Jesus took pains to disavow the role of political liberator. Later, when he was specifically asked this as he stood before Pilate, Jesus' answer was unambiguous: "My kingdom is not from this world. If my kingdom were from this world, my followers would be fighting to keep me from being handed over to the Jews. But as it is, my kingdom is not from here" (John 18:36).

The issue arises in the fourth chapter of the Gospel of Luke, when Jesus is asked to read the Scriptures in the synagogue at Nazareth. The passage to be read on that Sabbath day happened to come from yet another messianic passage in the book of Isaiah:

"The Spirit of the Lord is upon me, because he has anointed me to bring good news to the poor. He has sent me to proclaim release to the captives and recovery of sight to the blind, to let the oppressed go free, to proclaim the year of the Lord's favor" (Luke 4:18-19).

The fact that Jesus was asked to read the Scriptures in the synagogue indicates that he was well-respected in Nazareth. His audience, evidently keying in on the references to released captives and freedom for the oppressed, responded favorably to him. But then Jesus turned the situation on its head by deliberately rejecting the nationalistic re-making of the Messiah as Israel's political liberator:

> *"Truly I tell you, no prophet is accepted in the prophet's hometown. But the truth is, there were many widows in Israel in the time of Elijah, when the heaven was shut up three years and six months, and there was a severe famine over all the land; yet Elijah was sent to none of them except to a widow at Zarephath in Sidon. There were also many lepers in Israel in the time of the prophet Elisha, and none of them was cleansed except Naaman the Syrian"*
>
> *(Luke 4:24-27).*

To suggest that the blessings of the divine would fall upon Gentiles, such as the Sidonian

Jesus Christ, the Messiah. Although many of his followers hoped he would be a political king as well as a spiritual one, he was firm in his assertion that his kingdom "is not from here."

widow and the Syrian Naaman, instead of upon Israel was tantamount to blasphemy in the minds of Israelites. Their violent response, then, is scarcely surprising:

"When they heard this, all in the synagogue were filled with rage. They got up, drove him out of the town, and led him to the brow of the hill on which their town was built, so that they might hurl him off the cliff. But he passed through the midst of them and went on his way" (Luke 4:28-30).

There is no indication in the Gospels that Jesus ever returned to Nazareth after this decisive rejection on the part of his own townspeople. Instead, we are told that he makes his home in the fishing village of Capernaum on the shores of the Sea of Galilee, west of the borders of modern-day Syria and Jordan.

The idea of the Messiah as a king or ruler, while certainly present in numerous Old Testament texts, stands alongside another seemingly contradictory aspect: that of a Suffering Servant:

> *"Here is my servant, whom I uphold, my chosen, in whom my soul delights;*
> *I have put my spirit upon him; he will bring forth justice to the nations.*
> *He will not cry or lift up his voice, or make it heard in the street; a bruised reed he will not break, and a dimly burning wick he will not quench; he will faithfully bring forth justice"* *(Isaiah 42:1-3).*

This image of a humble Messiah is hardly in keeping with the conception of a warrior-king willing to liberate the downtrodden from political oppression.

In perhaps the most famous Messianic passage of all, the 53rd chapter of Isaiah, the coming King of Israel is portrayed in terms which many must have found astonishing: as someone who would be held in contempt and who would suffer a humiliating death:

> *"He was despised and rejected by others; a man of suffering and acquainted with infirmity; and as one from whom others hide their faces he was despised, and we held him of no account. Surely he has borne our infirmities and carried our diseases; yet we accounted him stricken, struck down by God, and afflicted. But he was wounded for our transgressions, crushed for our iniquities; upon him was the punishment that made us whole, and by his bruises we are healed"*
>
> *(Isaiah 53:3-5).*

The early Christians used these Old Testament prophecies as a powerful tool to demonstrate to others their conviction that Jesus of Nazareth was the promised Messiah. The success of the early evangelists testifies to the potency of their arguments. Their detractors, however, considered Jesus as merely another pretender who attempted to manipulate events to make him appear to be the Messiah. It was suggested by some that Jesus managed to be put to death because of some perverse, messianic wish fulfillment.

On the other hand, the early Christians pointed out that it was quite impossible that someone could manage to be of the required Davidic lineage, as was his earthly father Joseph; be born in Bethlehem in fulfillment of the messianic prediction; and arrange to be raised in a Galilean village—all in fulfillment of Old Testament messianic prophecies. The prophecies concerning the Messiah have occasioned deep religious divisions among faith traditions that remain to this day.

Other types of prophecy also are found in the Hebrew Scriptures, including remarkable predictions of the fall of great empires. Let us examine two examples of powerful kingdoms and city-states, the demise of which could scarcely have been predicted without the aid of divine foreknowledge.

The Fall of Mighty Babylon

The clattering hoofbeats echoed against the distant hillsides as the horses raced across the gravel plains of what is now Syria and northern Iraq. It was a curious-looking entourage, by today's standards, that hurried south toward the magnificent capital city of Babylon in about 607 B.C. One man in his twenties, Nebuchadnezzar, stood out among the riders. A look of steadfast determination spurred him onward to his destiny. The ancient world had just been rocked by a violent, decisive confrontation between the superpowers of the day. The once-powerful kingdom of Assyria, already in irreversible decline, now

King Nebuchadnezzar (above left) was a great military leader and a key figure in biblical prophecy. His ascension to the throne of Babylon in 605 B.C. reestablished that land as a world power.

lay mortally wounded, and the world marveled at the apparent rebirth of a civilization called Babylon, which had its origins in hoary antiquity.

In the South, the Egyptian empire, fearful of the emerging new order, had sent its army to support its old adversary Assyria. Moving north through the kingdom of Judah, the forces of Pharoah Neco II were challenged by King Josiah, who was determined to stop the Egyptian advance. Despite assurances from Neco regarding his intentions, King Josiah and his greatly inferior army chose to stand and fight. That fatal decision led to the destruction of the Judean army and the death of the Judean king.

The battle took place at the junction of a key pass through the Carmel range. The city of Megiddo, already ancient by the time of Josiah, stood overlooking that vital intersection. It would lend its name to numerous battles, both past and, according to the Bible, yet in the future. In the Greek language of the Apocalypse (the book of Revelation), this future battle will take place at a site called Armageddon, which means "the mountain of Megiddo."

The defeat of Josiah was little more than a footnote in the annals of history when regarded against another battle that would take place a few years later, far to the north at Carchemish, on the Euphrates. Located on what is now the border between Syria and Turkey, Carchemish marked the northern boundaries of the Assyrian empire. It was there, in August 605 B.C., that the young vice-regent Nebuchadnezzar defeated another combined Egyptian and Assyrian force in one of the pivotal battles of Syrio-Palestinian history.

At his moment of triumph Nebuchadnezzar received word that, back in Babylon, his infirm father had died. At once another crisis was in the wind. If Nebuchadnezzar could not quickly establish his right to claim the throne, it would be lost to him. He sped to Babylon and ascended the throne before three weeks had passed. His reign was vigorous and long, lasting until his death in 562 B.C. Nebuchadnezzar succeeded in raising an enigmatic civilization from the sleep of a thousand years. Historians later called the rejuvenated civilization the neo-Babylonian Empire.

The Land Between the Rivers

Babylon has a long and illustrious history and plays a significant role in biblical prophecy. The Greeks called the ancient land ruled by Nebuchadnezzar Mesopotamia, meaning "between the rivers." The two rivers, the Tigris and the Euphrates, flow through a region of astonishing fertility. It is here that the earliest civilizations known to man were nourished.

Mesopotamia has been a battleground since the dawn of recorded civilization, as one empire replaced another in an endless cycle of conquest. It was here that many innovations of ancient warfare were developed. Battles were won with high-tech weapons of the day: the chariot, bronze ax, the bow and arrow, and iron-bladed spear were, each in turn, radical inventions that proved decisive on the ancient battlefield.

Thousands of years later, the same cauldron of war would play host to weaponry undreamed-of by the ancients. A besieging army from distant lands would use vastly superior computerized weapons to defeat the modern heirs of ancient Mesopotamia.

The civilization of Babylon ranks among the world's greatest, with a history spanning two millennia. It dominated the region in the eighteenth century B.C., when King Hammurabi and his army of 50,000 men—a huge force at that time—conquered Mesopotamia.

Hammurabi's army was famous for its mounted archers who, along with chariots and infantry, posed a formidable threat to any foe.

More than 50 major pagan temples stood in ancient Babylon; nearly a third were built by Nebuchadnezzar. The temple ruin seen here is at Hatra, in present-day Iraq.

Hammurabi's reign, marked by material prosperity and a sophisticated social structure, was followed by a long period of decline. But Babylon's fortunes were revived in the late seventh century B.C. by the aforementioned Nebuchadnezzar.

It is this neo-Babylonian Empire that the Bible knows. During Nebuchadnezzar's long reign, Babylon experienced the pinnacle of its power and prosperity. From the beginning of his rule, Nebuchadnezzar sought to control the whole of Syria-Palestine, including the Kingdom of Judea. After 18 years of piecemeal advance, Jerusalem was conquered and destroyed in 586 B.C., as foretold by the Hebrew prophets.

It is because of this single event that we find Babylon haunting the pages of Scripture, until it reappears in the Apocalypse of St. John. As the first city mentioned in the Bible, and with more than 275 references from Genesis to Revelation, Babylon dwarfs the attention given to another great city, Rome, which is mentioned just 14 times. Only Jerusalem receives more attention than the capital city ruled by Nebuchadnezzar.

Jerusalem and Babylon present a fundamental contrast in Scripture. Jerusalem was the heart of true worship where the God of Israel dwelled in His holy Temple. It is light and truth and all things good; the Psalms are full of its praise: "Great is the Lord and greatly to be praised in the city of our God. His holy mountain, beautiful in elevation, is the joy of all the earth, Mount Zion, in the far north, the city of the great King" (Psalm 48:1-2).

Babylon, however, was unparalleled in ancient Mesopotamia as a religious center. According to extant Babylonian texts, at least 50 major temples stood in Babylon, at least 15 of which were built by Nebuchadnezzar. In an extraordinary record of religious continuity, some of those pagan temples remained in continual use for nearly two millennia. Cuneiform texts also mention hundreds of shrines and daises (raised platforms for idols) located throughout the city.

The Tower of Babel

The most famous of the religious monuments of ancient Babylon was the Tower of Babel, described in the eleventh chapter of Genesis. The foundations of an impressive tower believed by many scholars to be the biblical Tower of Babel may still be viewed in Babylon today. Known as the Temple Tower, or the Ziggurat of Babylon, it was a stepped structure whose heights, like the biblical edifice, reached to the heavens.

The Fall of the City of Conquerors

Babylon, with its ring of three massive defensive walls, was considered impregnable. However, in 539 B.C., 23 years after the death of Nebuchadnezzar, the city fell without a struggle. The victor was the army of Persia, which, thanks to an ingenious plan, was able to circumvent Babylon's immense fortifications. Laboring upstream, the Persians

Babylon was conquered in 539 B.C. by the Persian king Cyrus. Some 200 years later, the Macedonian Alexander the Great (above) won his turn as Babylon's conqueror and leader.

diverted the course of the Euphrates River and dried up Babylon's system of defensive moats. Persian troops infiltrated the city by a nighttime crossing of the river bed. As recorded by the book of Daniel, Babylon's leader, Belshazzar (whose name is not known outside the Bible), lost both his kingdom and his life that very night.

At the same moment as the famous predictive handwriting was appearing on the walls of Belshazzar's palace, the Persian army was marching into the city. Sixteen days later the Persian monarch Cyrus the Great entered Babylon amid much public acclaim, thus bringing an end to the Chaldean dynasty—a conclusion that had been predicted by the Hebrew prophets (Isaiah 13:21). Cyrus, enchanted with the city, chose to rule his vast Persian empire from Babylon rather than return to his own capital, Susa.

Cyrus was succeeded many years later by the conquering Macedonian, Alexander, who marched to Babylon in 331 B.C. The defending garrison chose not to fight, laying down its arms instead and giving Alexander a triumphant welcome. Like Cyrus before him, Alexander chose to make Babylon the center of his empire. He offered sacrifices to the Babylonian god Marduk and set in motion elaborate plans to rebuild the city. He envisioned the construction of a new port, as well as the restoration of the ancient monuments. The Temple of Bel, for example, which had been destroyed by the Persian ruler Xerxes, was ordered restored. Interestingly, the Jewish historian Flavius Josephus reports that the Jews who fought in Alexander's army refused to participate in the restoration of the pagan temples.

Alexander continued on to India, where he forged a great empire that eventually stretched from Libya to the Punjab. After conquering the known world, his army decimated by its long, punishing march back from India, Alexander returned once again to Babylon. Though himself weakened by illness, he seemed captivated by this city with its spirit of occultism.

The primordial Tower of Babel was one of the monuments that captured Alexander's interest most keenly. Perhaps he envisioned it as a magnificent symbol of his unified world empire. He began to clear the rubble from the base of the great ziggurat, intending to restore mankind's first boastful attempt to touch the heavens. That dream, as well as the other elaborate plans for the sacred city, were suddenly cut short. On June 13, 323 B.C., the greatest master of the ancient world, who wept bitterly when there was nothing left to conquer, succumbed in Babylon at age 33 to an infectious fever brought on by a minor wound.

While Alexander's empire was divided by his feuding generals, Babylon continued as a center of Hellenistic Greek culture. The city also hosted a large number of Jews who chose to remain in Babylon after many of their fellow countrymen returned from the exile to Judea. Indeed, by the first century A.D. the Jews of Babylon enjoyed self-government. It was in that city that some of the greatest works of Judaism, including the Talmud, were created.

The fascination with Babylon continued to draw conquerors with a thirst for temporal

Gustave Doré's representation of the fallen city of Babylon, whose fortunes had been diminished by pagan worship and topographical change, notably the gradual shifting of the Euphrates River.

power. The Roman Emperor Trajan fought his way east and entered the city in 115 A.D. His most significant act in the then-decaying city was to perform a sacrifice to Alexander's manes, or "divine spirit." Trajan doubtless aspired to the same measure of greatness as his illustrious predecessor.

Trajan was the last of the great leaders drawn to the city, which became a casualty of the gradual shifting of the Euphrates River. By 200 A.D. the site was deserted. However, Babylon would not remain buried in desert sands forever, a development that some Bible scholars view as a fulfillment of biblical prophecy.

A Nation Reborn

For centuries Babylon remained an undisturbed, indistinguishable mound of sun-dried bricks on the barren plains south of Baghdad. In 637 A.D. the new religion of Islam became dominant in the region, carried to eastern lands by Arabs with brandished swords. They were followed by Tamerlane and his Mongols and later by the Ottoman Turks, who ruled for 400 years. None of these conquerors paid attention to the ruins of what had been the greatest empire of ancient Mesopotamia.

By the early twentieth century, the Ottoman empire, dubbed "the sick old man of Europe," paid with its very existence for its support of Germany in the Great War (World War I). In 1918 the British Army occupied the territory of Iraq and organized a national government. It was out of this new nation that, two generations later, an obstinate ruler named Saddam Hussein would arise. He, too, would draw the attention of students of biblical prophecy.

The reason for the interest in Saddam in the early 1990s was an apparent reference to yet another fall of Babylon, which some believe is indicated by a prophecy found in the book of Jeremiah:

> *"Declare among the nations and proclaim, set up a banner and proclaim, do not conceal it, say: Babylon is taken, Bel is put to shame, Merodach is dismayed. Her images are put to shame, her idols are dismayed. For out of the north a nation has come up against her; it shall make her land a desolation, and no one shall live in it; both human beings and animals shall flee away. . . . For I am going to stir up and bring against Babylon a company of great nations from the land of the north; and they shall array themselves against her; from there she shall be taken. Their arrows are like the arrows of a skilled warrior who does not return empty-handed"*
>
> *(Jeremiah 50:2-3,9).*

For many students of the Bible, this passage appears to be a prophecy of the fall of Babylon that went unfulfilled in ancient times. As already noted, the city offered little or no resistance to the Persians and the Greeks. There was no carnage such as described in these verses: The land was not laid waste, and it was not abandoned until centuries later, and only then as a result of the shifting Euphrates.

Saddam's bombastic personality and boastfulness as he confronted the United States and the other coalition forces in 1990 fueled speculation that the apparent prophecy was about to be fulfilled in our day. References to a great company of nations coming against Babylon in Jeremiah were taken to refer to the multinational coalition forces.

Saddam himself began to take an interest in the ancient history of his country, and soon his interest apparently turned into an obsession. Saddam went to great lengths to cultivate parallels between himself and the rulers of ancient Babylon. Throughout Iraq stood huge monuments and murals showing him in the company of such notables as Hammurabi and Nebuchadnezzar. The Iraqi population was continually reminded of the key role the land of Babylon played in ancient history. Saddam's intent—to convince his people, and perhaps himself, as well, that Iraq was invincible—was clear.

Just as Nebuchadnezzar was a "world ruler" over the neo-Babylonian empire at the peak of its greatness, so also did Saddam Hussein aspire to become a latter-day Nebuchadnezzar who restored lost Arab glory. In honor of Iraq's "victory" over Iran in the punishing, stalemated war of the 1980s, Hussein went so far as to issue a medallion with his own likeness on one side—and Nebuchadnezzar's on the other.

Babylon Rises from the Sands of Time

To many students of the Bible, the connections between news events and biblical prophecy prior to the Gulf War seemed irrefutable. Astonishingly, for the first time in two millennia the mighty city of Babylon literally began to rise again, as Saddam directed the Iraqi Department of Antiquities to restore the ancient ruins. By the start of hostilities with Iran, part of the city wall and a major gate had been rebuilt. With typical immodesty, Saddam decreed that every fourth tile used in the reconstruction carry the inscription: "Built in the time of Saddam." This was an impertinent echo of Nebuchadnezzar, who ordered brickwork with a similarly boastful inscription.

Shortly before the outbreak of the Gulf crisis, Saddam ordered a gigantic image of himself, standing nearly ten stories high, erected over the restored gate of the city of Babylon. This huge image of Saddam Hussein looking down over the city is reminiscent of

Iraqi leader Saddam Hussein fancies himself a modern-day successor to Nebuchadnezzar. Murals and monuments throughout Iraq portray Saddam's (illusive) military prowess and sense of destiny.

the fate of Nebuchadnezzar as described in the book of Daniel:

> *"At the end of twelve months he was walking on the roof of the royal palace of Babylon, and the king said, 'Is this not magnificent Babylon, which I have built as a royal capital by my mighty power and for my glorious majesty? 'While the words were still in the king's mouth, a voice came from heaven: 'O King Nebuchadnezzar, to you it is declared: The kingdom has departed from you!'" (Daniel 4:29-31).*

Nebuchadnezzar's arrogant pride contributed to his downfall. We read that following the divine "decree" he was struck with a bout of insanity that lasted until he finally acknowledged the Most High God. Centuries later, as a defiant Saddam Hussein remains firmly entrenched in Baghdad, many Bible prophecy students await what the future holds for Nebuchadnezzar's self-proclaimed heir.

Whatever Saddam's fate, the Middle East will remain a region of unique importance for biblical prophecy, for it is here where Yahweh of the Old Testament chose to reveal Himself to mankind as the living and true God. But the region also has been called the birthplace of the occult, and many believe that the Bible predicts the ascendance of a nefarious world leader in possession of awesome paranormal powers. This personage, called the antichrist, will turn his attention to this part of the world that has nurtured dark forces throughout the ages. Later in this book we will examine this mysterious individual, and various fascinating speculations about how close we may be to the final confrontation between God and the powers of evil.

Babylon also has great symbolic importance in the Bible, and denotes temporal power in

The Lord and the Tower

"Now the whole earth had one language and the same words. And as they migrated from the east, they came upon a plain in the land of Shinar and settled there. And they said to one another, 'Come, let us make bricks, and burn them thoroughly.' And they had brick for stone, and bitumen for mortar. Then they said, 'Come, let us build ourselves a city, and a tower with its top in the heavens, and let us make a name for ourselves; otherwise we shall be scattered abroad upon the face of the whole earth.' The Lord came down to see the city and the tower, which mortals had built. And the Lord said, Look, they are one people, and they have all one language; and this is only the beginning of what they will do; nothing that they propose to do will now be impossible for them. Come, let us go down, and confuse their language there, so that they will not understand one another's speech. So the Lord scattered them abroad from there over the face of all the earth, and they left off building the city" (Genesis 11:1-8).

active rebellion against God. In the Apocalypse, Babylon symbolizes the spiritual apostasy of the last days in the form of a woman sitting on a fearsome beast:

This title was written on her forehead:

> *"MYSTERY BABYLON THE GREAT, MOTHER OF PROSTITUTES AND OF THE ABOMINATIONS OF THE EARTH"* *(Revelation 17:5; New American Standard Version)*

Mystery Babylon symbolizes the natural alternative to the true worship of God. Because of this, rebellious mankind will not be able to resist Babylon's seductive charm: "With whom the kings of the earth have committed fornication, and with the wine of whose fornication the inhabitants of the earth have become drunk" (Revelation 17:2).

This prophetic passage, apparently yet to be fulfilled, indicates that one day an iniquitous force will exercise its power of enchantment over the whole earth. Without doubt, Babylon remains a city that, like no other, symbolizes the pinnacle of earthly power.

Ezekiel's Vision of Dry Bones: Israel Reborn

A remarkable prophecy found in the book of Ezekiel has proved to be endlessly fascinating to students of biblical prophecy, many of whom see its fulfillment in our day. The prophecy in question leads many to believe that the modern state of Israel is no accident, but part of the divine plan for the end of day.

In 597 B.C. the prophet Ezekiel, along with other captives from Judea, was carried away by the Babylonians to Tel-Abib, where he lived near the river Chebar. While there he was commanded by God to prophesy to his fellow Judeans: "I will take you out of the nations; I will gather you from all the countries and bring you back into your own land" (Ezekiel 36:24).

This "regathering" is foretold to take place at the latter stages of human history, a time of preparation for a great cataclysmic battle between God and the forces of evil:

> *"For then, in those days and at that time, when I restore the fortunes of Judah and Jerusalem, I will gather all the nations and bring them down to the valley of Jehoshaphat, and I will enter into judgment with them there, on account of my people and my heritage Israel, because they have scattered them among the nations"* *(Joel 3:1-2).*

When will the fortunes of Judah and Jerusalem be restored? Biblical scholars can point to only two historical periods that suggest the "restoration" of the Jewish people and the subsequent gathering of the nations against the land of Israel. Let's take a look at each in turn.

The Hasmonean Kingdom

The year was 169 B.C., a time of great messianic expectation. Hundreds of years had elapsed since the prophecies of Joel and Zechariah, and the belief was widespread that the Jewish people were in the "latter days" that would see the restoration of Israel. At that time the Jewish people were being sorely oppressed by the Seleucid ruler Antiochus (Epiphanes) IV. Antiochus set up the "abomination of desolation" in the Temple, which was an altar to Zeus upon which the Jews were commanded to sacrifice.

Scripture contains two distinct references to the "abomination of desolation." The first is in Daniel 11:31, which is generally agreed to be addressing the desecration of the Jewish Temple by Antiochus in 169 B.C. Jesus also speaks of the "abomination of desolation" (Matthew 24:15), which, judging from context, clearly occurs at the end of time.

For pious Jews, the presence of a pagan altar in the Temple, upon which ritually unclean

Outraged by the paganism of Seleucid ruler Antiochus, Jews led by the Maccabean brothers fought for their faith in 169 B.C., defeating a formidable force that included 32 warrior elephants.

swine were sacrificed, was an almost unimaginable outrage. This final indignity proved too much, and the Jews rose up against their foreign oppressors. The Jews were ready to give their lives for the freedom of Zion. There was a growing belief that a period of unprecedented suffering was approaching, which would end with the downfall of the evil kingdom and the inauguration of the messianic age. Jews resolved to fight in order to bring about that downfall. The Maccabean brothers led the battle charge against the Seleucids, whose formidable weaponry included a troop of 32 elephants.

In a series of brilliant victories, the Maccabees triumphed over their Seleucid oppressors, which led to the establishment of the Hasmonean kingdom. This independent Jewish "state," which lasted for nearly a century, was larger and more "religious" than the present State of Israel. Daily animal sacrifices were offered in the restored Temple, and the Sanhedrin, the supreme Jewish religious council, was sitting in Jerusalem. The Jewish people were convinced that all this was the fulfillment of prophecy about the restoration of Israel.

But the messianic expectations of the Jews soon faded. The Hasmonean dynasty was gradually weakened by internal strife and finally overthrown by Roman intervention in 63 B.C. No battle of the Hasmonean period resembles the prophecies of Ezekiel and Joel. The time of the fulfillment of the return of the Jewish people to Israel was, it seemed, still to come.

Israel Reborn

The second historical possibility for fulfilling the prophecy of Ezekiel and Joel exists provocatively close to the present day. In the nineteenth century, after 1,800 years of Diaspora (wandering), the Jewish people once again began immigrating to Palestine. In 1948, after withstanding British mismanagement of Palestine and, later, concerted attacks by combined Arab armies, the State of Israel was reborn. The prophecy of Ezekiel mentions several things that appear to be remarkably similar to the development of the modern-day State of Israel.

"After many days you shall be mustered; in the latter years you shall go against a land restored from war, a land where people were gathered from many nations on the mountains of Israel, which had long lain waste; its people were brought out from the nations and now are living in safety, all of them" (Ezekiel 38:8).

We read here that the restoration will occur in the "latter years" and that the Jewish people will be brought from "many nations." During the Hasmonean kingdom, the Jewish people had returned from one nation: Babylon. But the modern state of Israel is composed of Jews who have returned from over 100 nations.

Furthermore, until the end of the nineteenth century, the land of Palestine was a neglected backwater of the Turkish Ottoman empire. The impoverished population huddled in decaying villages surrounded by barren countryside. A Turkish tax on trees (!) had led to the systematic denuding of the land.

It was to this land of "continual waste" that succeeding waves of Jewish immigration came, clearing fields and establishing new cities, such as Tel Aviv, Israel's largest, which was founded on sand dunes in 1909. Since then, more than 50 million trees have been planted to restore forests to the hills of Judea and Galilee. Today, Israel is considerably greener than is commonly thought by outsiders.

While the indications are that the present age may indeed be the "latter days," many biblical scholars are cautious, suggesting that this prophecy is speaking of a time yet in the future, beyond the current state of events—perhaps even a time that supersedes the modern State of Israel.

After all, these scholars point out, those living in the second century before the time of Jesus were firmly convinced that the Hasmonean Jewish state was the fulfillment of the prophecy. There were a number of good reasons for that conviction, as there are for similar feelings about the modern State of Israel.

The "blooming of the desert," for example, is often cited as proof that the modern State of Israel is the fulfillment of the prophecy of Ezekiel. Yet an even greater level of development occurred during the Hasmonean period, when the Negev desert of southern Israel was more extensively cultivated by the Nabateans than it is under the modern Israelis. The Roman and Byzantine periods also saw widespread settlement in the Negev.

Because Ezekiel mentions several more prophetic signposts related to the return of Israelites to their land, the interpretation of the regathering of Israel continues to be hotly debated by scholars. As always, it is prudent to keep in mind that the divine timetable remains shrouded from human perception.

The general contexts of Ezekiel 36 and 37 present several stages related to the regathering of Israel. The first is that of the divine judgment, which led to the dispersion among the nations: "I scattered them among the nations, and they were dispersed through the countries; in accordance with their conduct and their deeds I judged them" (Ezekiel 36:19).

This Diaspora began with the destruction of Jerusalem in 586 B.C., when the Israelites were exiled to Babylon. From there they found their way to distant lands. Until the modern era there was scarcely a land that did not have some Jewish representation among its peoples. But this worldwide scattering of the Jewish people would one day be reversed:

> *"But you, O mountains of Israel, shall shoot out your branches, and yield your fruit to my people Israel; for they shall soon come home. See now, I am for you; I will turn to you, and you shall be tilled and sown; and I will multiply your population, the whole house of Israel, all of it; the towns shall be inhabited and the waste places rebuilt" (Ezekiel 36:8-10).*

We already have indicated that the Hasmonean kingdom of the second and first centuries B.C. does not fulfill the prophecy of the regathering. That appears to leave the modern State of Israel as the only remaining candidate—to date, at least. In the midst of this return to the land there will be a second stage—the spiritual revival of Israel's people:

> *"A new heart I will give you, and a new spirit I will put within you; and I will remove from your body the heart of stone and give you a heart of flesh. I will put my spirit within you, and make you follow my statutes and be careful to observe my ordinances" (Ezekiel 36:26-27).*

In Israel today, Orthodox Jews are zealous about the observance of the Law, one of the

A revival of Jewish faith in Israel, promised in the book of Ezekiel, continues to this day—as witness this ultra-Orthodox Jew in modern Jerusalem.

primary concerns of which is faithful observation of the Sabbath. With carefully delineated exceptions, it is forbidden to perform work of any kind on the Sabbath. Since almost any physical exertion qualifies as "work," observant Jews follow strict rabbinical laws regarding what is permitted and forbidden. Many elevators in Israel, for example, are programmed to run continuously throughout the entire 24-hour period of the Sabbath, stopping on every floor as they ascend and descend. This makes for unavoidable slowness and tedium, yet also ensures that no one will be guilty of "breaking the Sabbath" by pressing the elevator button.

Similarly, apartments throughout Israel have timers that automatically turn lights and other appliances on and off during Sabbath so that electrical switches do not have to be engaged. Ovens are built with a special Sabbath setting so they do not have to be manually turned on or off. Refrigerators built in Israel are designed so that the interior light bulb does not go on when the door is opened during Sabbath. This is because to turn on the refrigerator light by opening the door is considered work.

Automobiles are not to be driven on the Sabbath because the ignition of the spark plugs constitutes "building a fire" —which qualifies as work, according to the rabbinical authorities. There is only one exception to these stringent rules: In a life-threatening situation on the Sabbath, one may perform what is considered work.

One allegedly true story illustrates the devotion of many Israelis to the Law: A rabbi in Mea Shearim, the Orthodox quarter of Jerusalem, apparently suffered a heart attack during the Sabbath synagogue service. An ambulance was summoned and street barriers were removed so that the vehicle could enter the quarter. To everyone's relief, examination revealed that the rabbi had suffered nothing worse than a severe case of indigestion. The medics packed up their equipment and returned to their vehicle. But before they could start the engine they were surrounded by a

The Valley of Dry Bones

Using the evocative imagery of a valley strewn with bones that come to life, Ezekiel ignited an age-old controversy over the meaning of his cryptic prophecy:

"The hand of the Lord came upon me, and he brought me out by the spirit of the Lord and set me down in the middle of a valley; it was full of bones . . .

"He said to me, 'Mortal, can these bones live?' I answered, 'O Lord God, you know.'

"Then he said to me, 'Prophesy to these bones, and say to them: "O dry bones, hear the word of the Lord.

"Thus says the Lord God to these bones: I will cause breath to enter you, and you shall live . . . .' "

"I prophesied as he commanded me, and

Ezekiel observes the shaping of "sinews" and "flesh" on human skeletons.

the breath came into them, and they lived, and stood on their feet, a vast multitude.

"Then he said to me, 'Mortal, these bones are the whole house of Israel. . . I am going to open your graves, and bring you up from your graves, O my people; and I will bring you back to the land of Israel" (Ezekiel 37:1, 3-5, 7-8, 10-12).

crowd, which forbade them to move. The medics had to abandon their vehicle and walk. Why? Because although it was permissible to drive an automobile to save a life, now, when no life was in danger, the "work" of returning the ambulance to the hospital was forbidden.

Old rabbinical tradition holds that the Messiah will come the moment every Jew in the world observes the Sabbath. This is why Orthodox Jews are so zealous in their attempts to enforce the observation of the Sabbath in modern Israeli society. Those Christians who see Ezekiel referring to a latter-day spiritual revival in Israel would also look for signs of Jewish acceptance of Jesus' status as Messiah, since the New Testament claims that the Messiah has already come.

The third stage related to the "regathering" of Israel predicted in Ezekiel is the reunification of the land. Israel was formerly divided into the Kingdom of Israel in the north and the Kingdom of Judah in the south. However, according to Ezekiel the land will once again be reunited: "I will make them one nation in the land, on the mountains of Israel; and one king shall be king over them all. Never again shall they be two nations, and never again shall they be divided into two kingdoms" (Ezekiel 37:22).

One can readily see parallels between this stage and the most pressing dilemma facing the modern Jewish state: ongoing Arab demands for a separate, non-Jewish Palestinian state in the midst of the Land of Israel. The issue has become increasingly contentious since the Six-Day War of 1967, when, for the first time in 19 centuries, the whole Land of Israel was united under Jewish control.

Despite this return of Jewish dominance of Israel, the nation's heartland, termed the "West Bank" (of the Jordan River), remained populated by an Arab majority that maintained its own nationalistic goals. In the years following the Six-Day War, discontent grew until it erupted in the Palestinian "Intifada," or uprising, of the late 1980s. Prophecy watchers are absorbed by ongoing developments in the Middle East, to see if the land of Israel will remain undivided, in fulfillment of Ezekiel's prophecy.

One ominous stage of the "regathering" is a final attempt to possess the land—not by Jews who have returned to it, but by the armies of a cryptic roster of mysterious personages and nations, whose identification has eluded scholars. Some suggest that the growing demands for a Palestinian state will be a catalyst for the final, end-of-time conflict in the Middle East,

A Nation Is Born

The official *Declaration of the Establishment of the State of Israel* is a poignant description of the age-old aspirations of the Jewish people:

"After being forcibly exiled from their land, the people kept faith with it throughout their Dispersion, and never ceased to pray and hope for their return to it and for the restoration in it of their political freedom. Impelled by this historic and traditional attachment, Jews strove in every successive generation to re-establish themselves in their ancient homeland. In recent decades they returned in their masses. Pioneers, immigrants, and defenders, they made deserts bloom, revived the Hebrew language, built villages and towns, and created a thriving community, controlling its own economy and culture . . . and aspiring towards independent nationhood."

—*Official Gazette* (Tel Aviv, Israel), May 14, 1948

precipitated by the arcane forces addressed by Ezekiel: "After many days you shall be mustered; in the latter years you shall go against a land restored from war, a land where people were gathered from many nations on the mountains of Israel, which had long lain waste; its people were brought out from the nations and now are living in safety, all of them" (Ezekiel 38:8).

Conflict in Israel seems never-ending. Here, a masked Palestinian youth prepares to hurl a stone at Israeli border police in Jerusalem.

This invasion will occur "after many days," at a time when the regathered Jews are "living in safety." Some assume that this means the inhabitants have been lulled by a false sense of "peace." But the prophecy can also refer to a high state of security in the presence of threats. This certainly describes the high level of preparedness maintained by the Israeli Defense Forces, a fighting organization ranked among the world's best.

Visitors to the country quickly learn that Israel is extremely security-conscious. Each passenger passes through an elaborate security check at the airport, and citizens are on constant alert for suspicious objects as they go about their daily lives. Armed soldiers seem to be everywhere. As perhaps nowhere else on earth, Israel lives with the tension of constant threats against its security. The government is forced to expend an inordinate percentage of the national budget to ensure that the population is "living in safety."

The Bible indicates that, despite efforts for peace, one day the Middle East will erupt in a war of a magnitude never before seen. We will now speculate on that future battle and its bizarrely named participants.

Future Fuhrers: Gog and Magog

One of the most enigmatic and ominous prophetic passages in all of holy writ is found in chapters 38 and 39 of the book of Ezekiel. The passage, and some that follow, suggest the activities of an evil army, and a great swath of plunder and destruction that will be cut through village and wasteland alike. Many commentators believe that the mayhem described in Ezekial is no ordinary military campaign, but a great battle at the end of the age, in which a mysterious figure called Gog embarks with his confederate nations on a cruelly unprecedented expedition:

> *"Thus says the Lord GOD: I am against you, O Gog, chief prince of Meshech and Tubal; I will turn you around and put hooks into your jaws, and I will lead you out with all your army, horses and horsemen, all of them clothed in full armor, a great company, all of them with shield and buckler, wielding swords. Persia, Ethiopia, and Put are with them, all of them with buckler and helmet; Gomer and all its troops; Beth-togarmah from the remotest parts of the north with all its troops – many peoples are with you. . . . After many days you shall be mustered; in the latter years you shall go against a land restored from war, a land where people were gathered from many nations on the mountains of Israel, which had long lain waste; its people were brought out from the nations and now are living in safety, all of them"*
>
> *(Ezekiel 38:3-6,8-9).*

Who are these peoples, and what is the land they are invading? Who is their master, and what motivates them? Some students of Bible prophecy are convinced that there is only one viable historical possibility for the fulfillment of this passage: the modern State of Israel. Indeed, some students detect several clues in the text that they believe indicate that modern-day Israel is in view, including the fact that the land invaded by Gog is one which has been "restored from war."

In 1948 the declaration of the establishment of the State of Israel led almost immediately to the War of Independence, in which the surrounding Arab nations attempted to destroy the nascent state. In succeeding decades the Israeli nation would fight several major wars with its Arab neighbors, confirming that the Holy Land is one of the most fought-over regions of the world.

In the midst of continual threats against her very existence, Israel has become one of the most modern and prosperous nations in the Middle East. To achieve this stunning economic miracle the nation relied in large part upon the immigration of Jews from around the world. The citizenship of Israel is currently composed of people from more than 100 countries. Could this be the nation which Ezekiel refers to as being "gathered from many nations"? Ezekiel also describes the nation that will be invaded by Gog as having "long lain waste." Again, this is an apt description of Palestine before the waves of Jewish immigration that began in the nineteenth century. Before the immigrants' arrivals, the land had been a neglected backwater of the Ottoman (Turkish) Empire for centuries; its impoverished population scratched out a meager life in the countryside or languished in disease-ridden, decaying cities. Western travelers to Jerusalem in the last century describe scenes of abject poverty and desolation.

All that changed with the Jewish immigrants, who established agricultural settlements, drained malarial swamps, and cleared fields choked with rocks and boulders. As the immigrants' numbers increased, ancient cities were reinvigorated and modern new towns established. The mountains, denuded by Turks who imposed a harsh tax on trees, once again became lush and green. Trees were eventually planted by the tens of millions, and today whole forests cover the land.

Now one can travel on modern highways the length and breadth of a land that a century ago possessed treacherous roads scarcely fit for oxcarts. The traveler will pass prosperous farming regions and growing industrial cities. Modern Israel is one of the economic miracles of our time, experiencing extraordinary progress since the days when it might appropriately have been described as a land that "had long lain waste."

Finally, the passage from Ezekiel that we have cited describes the inhabitants of the land invaded by Gog and Magog as "living in safety." This may refer to the safety that comes from military security. If so, then it is yet another fitting parallel to modern Israel. Few nations invest as much in their defense as the Jewish nation, which requires all young Jewish men and women to serve in the military—a force that has repeatedly demonstrated its impressive capabilities on the battlefield.

If the prophetic vision of Ezekiel is indeed describing the modern State of Israel, then it appears that one day that war-torn land will face an invasion by the forces of Gog of the land of Magog. According to Ezekiel, Gog stands at the head of a confederation of forces that includes those with the cryptic names of "Meshech" and "Tubal." These are joined by others: "Persia, Ethiopia, and Put are with them, all of them with buckler and helmet; Gomer and all its troops; Beth-togarmah from the remotest parts of the north with all its troops—many peoples are with you" (Ezekiel 38:5-6).

North by Northeast

Throughout much of the twentieth century, as the Cold War raged, many students of Bible prophecy identified Gog of the land of Magog as the former Soviet Union. This identification was in large part due to certain translations of the Bible, which simply transliterated the Hebrew word "rosh," which means "chief" (in the phrase "chief prince"), taking it to be the proper name of a nation.

"Rosh" sounds very much like "Russia," an idea bolstered by Ezekiel's assertion that the invaders would come "from the remotest parts of the north" (Ezekiel 38:6). Indeed, a line drawn on a map north from Israel runs not only through Russia, but almost directly through Moscow, thus seeming to give more weight to the identity of the invaders as Russians.

This would seem to be confirmed by another verse, which identifies Gog as the "chief prince of Meshech and Tubal" (Ezekiel 38:3); some scholars interpret this as a reference to the Russian cities of Moscow and Tobolsk. (However, it should be noted that in this verse, the Hebrew "rosh" is translated as "chief," and not as a place name.)

Assuming that the place-name mindset has credence, the scenario of an invasion of Israel by Rosh, Meshech, and Tubal – in the form of their modern namesakes Russia, Moscow, and Tobolsk – was an all-too-real possibility during the post-World War II era, when the Soviet Union was actively involved in supporting and equipping the Arab armies in their struggle against the Jewish state. But the collapse of the Soviet Union led to the subsequent diminishment of Russia's ability to project military force abroad. The possibility of a Russian invasion of Israel became increasingly implausible. Many Bible students were left scratching their heads, wondering whether they had miscalculated. If they had, a big mistake they made was to attempt to identify place names purely on the basis of superficial phonetic

Jeremiah's prophecies, which were recorded by Baruch (seated), the son of Neriah, encompassed great geopolitical shifts.

similarities, a practice that is linguistically unsound. Moscow and Tobolsk would have been quite unknown to the biblical writers: Tobolsk, for example, was founded only in the seventeenth century.

But surely the text is speaking of an invasion from the area of the extreme north: i.e., Russia—is it not? The answer, surprisingly, is: not necessarily. In what at first glance appears to be a curious anomaly, the Old Testament prophets sometimes referred to invasions that originated in the east as coming from the "north." An example of this is the warning of the prophet Jeremiah: "Raise a standard toward Zion, flee for safety, do not delay, for I am bringing evil from the north, and a great destruction" (Jeremiah 4:6).

Jeremiah is here prophesying the destruction of Jerusalem by the Babylonians, which occurred in several stages leading up to the year 586 B.C. However, a quick check of a map shows that Babylon is not north of Israel but rather directly east.

Similarly, Jeremiah foretells another defeat: "Egypt shall be put to shame; she shall be handed over to a people from the north" (Jeremiah 46:24). This occurred in 605 B.C., when Pharaoh Neco II was defeated at Carchemish—by the neo-Babylonians led by Nebuchadnezzar. However, the Babylonians lived not to the north of Egypt, but to the east.

Were the biblical writers so ignorant of geography that they mistakenly thought that Babylonia was to the north of Israel? The answer to the puzzle lies in a peculiar geological feature of the Middle East. The biblical world is sometimes called "the Fertile Crescent" because of the swath of arable land that curves upward from the Tigris and Euphrates rivers in Mesopotamia to northern Syria and down into the Promised Land.

In the middle of this boomerang-shaped curve of arable land lies the Syrian/Arabian desert, impassable but for the hardy Bedouin and their caravans. In ancient times, people traveling from Mesopotamia to Israel would skirt the inhospitable desert in order to follow the fertile crescent, where they would be assured of water and sources of food. This is the route followed by Abraham when he left Ur, pausing in Haran in northern Mesopotamia until the death of his father, Terah.

Armies requiring considerable supplies of water would attempt a desert crossing at their peril. On one occasion much later, a Roman legion lost its way in the Syrian desert. This led to one of the most ignominious debacles of Roman history, in which the army apparently ran out of food and water and was never heard from again.

In order to avoid such danger on its way to attack Israel, the Babylonian army marched along the fertile crescent and entered the Promised Land from the north. The Hebrew prophets are thus referring to the *direction* of the invasion. Even though the Babylonians' place of origin was to the east, the invaders descended upon the Promised Land from the north.

So: If Russia is not the land of Gog and Magog, what then is known that might help reveal the origins of these strange names? While the historical identity of Gog of the land of Magog is uncertain, many scholars believe he is Gugu, the king of Lydia around 660 B.C.

Lydia was located in Asia Minor, in what is now Turkey. A guess as to the identity of Magog, however, remains more problematic. The name is not mentioned in Assyrian literature, which is our main source of information for the eighth and seventh centuries B.C.

Intriguingly, though, we do have some firm historical clues as to the identity of Rosh. The name has been identified with the Assyrian "Rashu" on the northwest border of Elam, which is in the northern corner of Iran and Iraq. Meshech and Tubal are the people whom the Assyrian inscriptions call "Tabal" and "Musku," and occupied what is now Turkey.

Gog's remaining allies, Persia, Ethiopia, and Put (or Libya) are easily identified by their modern counterparts. The less-accessible Gomer was often incorrectly identified by Rosh/Russia theorists as East Germany, for no other reason than that an Eastern European communist nation would be likely to join Russia's invasion of the Middle East!

Once again the ancient Assyrians provide identification. Gomer was known by them as the Gimmirrai, an eighth-century B.C. people who lived in Asia Minor. The final name, Bet-togarmah, is associated with the Hittite "Tegarama" and the Assyrian "Til Garimmu," a people also from central Asia Minor.

All of this indicates that the participants in the battle involving Gog from the land of Magog were to come from two geographical areas: North Africa and the conjunction of eastern Turkey, northwest Iran and Iraq, and perhaps extending into the southern Central Asian republics.

To be sure, certain nations that now occupy these ancient lands have posed a military threat to Israel since its inception. Prior to the 1978 Camp David Accords, Egypt and Libya (located in North Africa) were enemies of Israel. Iran and Iraq are implacably hostile to the Jewish state. The Central Asian Republics have sizable Muslim populations, which are proving to be hostile toward Israel.

If the battle of Gog from the land of Magog is indeed upcoming on the prophecy calendar, we can be certain that there will one day be no more doubt as to the identification of the now-mysterious participants.

Countdown to the Final Battle

If the great battle of Gog and Magog predicted in Ezekiel is to take place, when will it occur? Context indicates that the invasion of

The triumphant Judean reign of the Maccabean brothers, who rose to power after defeating the pagan Antiochus, ended when Herod the Great ordered the brothers' murders. Here, their mother mourns.

the Middle East will occur after the great worldwide dispersion of the Jews known as the Diaspora. Prior to the description of the battle, Ezekiel's text tells us that the Jews will return to their own land: "But you, O mountains of Israel, shall shoot out your branches, and yield your fruit to my people Israel; for they shall soon come home" (Ezekiel 36:8).

Historically, there have been four periods when the world witnessed a return of Jews to the land of Israel. The first was the return from Babylonian exile, which began in 539 B.C. A second took place in 458 B.C.

The third return was in the second century B.C., when Judea was controlled by the Seleucids, the successors to the Greeks. In 169 B.C. the Jews, horrified when Antiochus IV desecrated their Temple with a pagan altar, revolted against the Seleucid ruler.

The battle charge was led by the Maccabean brothers, who fought the 32 elephants and other weapons fielded by the Seleucids. The Maccabees were convinced they were living in the end of days, when the powers of evil—which they took to be their Seleucid overlords—would be vanquished.

The Jews fought brilliantly, triumphing over their foes and establishing the Hasmonean kingdom.

However, the messianic expectations of the Jewish people eventually faded as the Hasmonean dynasty was torn with internal dissent. Rome finally intervened in 63 B.C., putting an end to the Jewish nation.

In retrospect, it is clear that the historical period of the Hasmonean dynasty could be said to fulfill the apocalypse described in the Hebrew Scriptures. The Hasmonean kingdom was overthrown by Rome, which, after the Second Jewish Revolt in 135 A.D., would systematically blot out virtually all Jewish presence in the land.

The fourth historical return of Jews to the Promised Land occurred in the twentieth century. In 1948, after 1900 years of Diaspora, the Jewish people once again established an independent Jewish state in the land of Israel, despite fierce opposition from their Arab neighbors. As we have seen, many believe the modern State of Israel is the fulfillment of the ancient prophecy of Ezekiel.

However, when all the evidence is mustered it does not add up to absolute certainty. It is entirely possible that the geopolitical map could change into something quite different from what exists today.

It is also a very real possibility that the linking of the modern State of Israel with the return mentioned in Ezekiel is mistaken. More than 2000 years ago, the Hasmoneans thought they had good reason to think *they* were the fulfillment of Ezekiel's prophecy. After all, the Hasmonean kingdom, which lasted more than 100 years, was larger and more religious (that is, with forced conversion of non-Jews) than modern Israel. The supreme Jewish council known as the Sanhedrin was sitting, and daily sacrifices were being offered in the Temple; neither is being undertaken in modern Israel.

Clearly, reasonable interpretation of enigmatic passages of biblical prophecy requires a thorough knowledge of the past and a prudent, cautious view of the future.

Daniel and the Monarch's Enigmatic Dreams

In a prophecy traditionally dated to the sixth century B.C., Nebuchadnezzar, the greatest monarch of his day, had a series of extraordinary dreams that outlined the course of history for centuries to come. So accurate were his visions, which appear in the book of Daniel, that, if they occurred as the Bible says they did, they constitute a powerful argument for the divine inspiration of the Bible.

In ancient times, those who denied the supernatural origin of the Bible took particular pains to deny the authenticity of the dreams and visions of the book of Daniel. In the third century A.D., for example, Porphyry, a pagan neo-Platonist and foe of Christianity, asserted that the prophecy of Daniel was in fact a forgery dating from the second-century B.C. In his 15-volume *Against the Christians* he claimed that instead of foretelling the future the book of Daniel actually relates what were by then well-known *past* events.

Porphyry's basic premise is simple: It is impossible to predict the future; therefore, all claimed attempts to do so must be considered false. Many modern scholars, like Porphyry, consider Daniel to have been written by an unknown Judean some two centuries before Christ. If this view is correct, the book is a creative but rather unremarkable recitation of a series of known historical events.

However, some scholars question the rejection of the possibility of the miraculous that underlies this view. They point out that the language of the text, a mixture of Hebrew and Aramaic, is consistent with extant ancient Near Eastern texts and inscriptions of the fifth and sixth centuries B.C.

It once was thought that the presence of Greek and Persian words in Daniel was evidence that the text was written much later than the sixth century B.C. It is now known, however, that Greek influence in the region began even earlier than Daniel's time. Greek mercenaries, for example, were serving in the Assyrian army as early as 683 B.C. If the visions related in the book of Daniel are indeed genuine, they are a truly remarkable example of the prophetic gift being given not to the Hebrew prophet but to the ruler of the mighty kingdom of Babylonia.

We read that in the second year of his rule—identified by historians as 603 B.C.—Nebuchadnezzar summoned his staff of prognosticators, which included magicians, enchanters, and sorcerers, to interpret a dream that troubled him. But on this occasion the king made a novel demand of his wise men. Instead of relating his dream to the prognosticators and asking them to interpret it, he ordered them to declare to him the content of his dream.

The Babylonian wise men, clearly unprepared to comply with Nebuchadnezzar's demand, strongly protested what they viewed as an unreasonable request:

> *"There is not a man on earth who can do what the king asks! No king, however great and mighty, has ever asked such a thing of any magician or enchanter or astrologer. What the king asks is too difficult. No one can reveal it to the king except the gods, and they do not live among men"*
>
> *(Daniel 2:10-11 NIV).*

An enraged Nebuchadnezzar, realizing he had allowed himself to take the counsel of incompetent charlatans, ordered that all the wise men of Babylon be put to death. The Hebrew prophet Daniel and his companions, who had been exiled to Babylon from Judea three years earlier, fell under the sweeping execution order. Daniel took the bold step of requesting an

Nebuchadnezzar

audience with Nebuchadnezzar. Asked if he is able to relate the content of the dream, Daniel gave his famous reply:

> *"No wise man, enchanter, magician or diviner can explain to the king the mystery he has asked about, but there is a God in heaven who reveals mysteries. He has shown King Nebuchadnezzar what will happen in days to come.... As for me, this mystery has been revealed to me, not because I have greater wisdom than other living men, but so that you, O king, may know the interpretation and that you may understand what went through your mind"* (Daniel 2:27-28,30 NIV).

The wise men of Babylon used their magical arts to discern future events in the stars and other heavenly bodies. Daniel, however, emphasizes that his knowledge about the dream comes not from human wisdom but from the God of heaven. He then continues to describe the awesome vision that had been revealed to Nebuchadnezzar in a dream.

In his dream the king saw an immense statue of a human form that exuded a great brilliance. The image was composed of different metals: The head was made of gold; the breast and arms were silver; the abdomen and thighs were brass (i.e., bronze or copper); and the legs were made of iron. In a curious anomaly, the feet of the statue were composed of an unusual mixture of iron and clay (or pottery).

Statue and Empires

Daniel then proceeds to reveal to Nebuchadnezzar the meaning of the statue. The different metals signify various kingdoms either in existence or destined to one day arise on the world scene. As for the golden head of the statue, Daniel tells Nebuchadnezzar: "You, O king, are the king of kings. The God of heaven has given you dominion and power and might and glory; in your hands he has placed mankind and the beasts of the field and the birds of the air. Wherever they live, he has made you ruler over them all. You are that head of gold" (Daniel 2:37-8 NIV).

Daniel informs Nebuchadnezzar that "after you shall arise another kingdom inferior to yours"—a kingdom symbolized by the silver breast and arms. In the ancient Near East, as today, gold was considered the most precious of metals. Silver was also a coveted metal but did not attain the value of gold.

Yet another world empire is then described; "one of bronze," which will "rule over the whole earth" (Daniel 2:39 NIV). Again, we note the decreasing value of the metals described in the vision, with bronze (brass) having a strictly utilitarian value.

The fourth kingdom is evidently of great importance for future world events; Daniel spends more time describing it than he does the other three combined. We read that this empire will be "as strong as iron," and "just as iron crushes and smashes everything, it shall crush and shatter all these" (Daniel 2:40).

The decreasing value of the components of the statue is again apparent, as iron was a relatively common base metal. But the mention of the strength of the final kingdom introduces another aspect of the relationship between the various metals. Scholars have long noted that along with the decrease in value there is a corresponding *increase* in the hardness, or strength, of each metal.

Perhaps the statue is intended to signify that succeeding empires in the course of human history will become increasingly base while at the same time excelling in certain arts, such as

This image of the worship of the mysterious metal statue of King Nebuchadnezzar dates from about 950 A.D. The lower image depicts the fates of three Hebrews whom the king has ordered thrown into a furnace.

warfare. This is, in fact, the view taken by certain Classical writers, such as Hesiod and Ovid.

Iron, for example, has little beauty and is not particularly prized. However, it has great utilitarian value, especially for the making of tools and weapons. (Implements made of a prized but soft metal, such as gold, would have little practical use.) The technological development of iron tools, arrows, and spears was a qualitative improvement over those made of copper or brass.

The reference to the statue's feet and toes as consisting of the peculiar mixture of iron and clay has puzzled biblical scholars. Daniel offers clues to the meaning, stating that the fourth empire will be "a divided kingdom" that will be "partly strong and partly brittle." The iron/clay mixture supports Daniel's assertion that the people of this kingdom will "mix with one another in marriage, but they will not hold together" (Daniel 2:41-43 NIV).

According to Daniel, a momentous event is destined to occur in the days of that mixed empire: "In the time of those kings, the God of heaven will set up a kingdom that will never be destroyed, nor will it be left to another people. It will crush all those kingdoms and bring them to an end, but it will itself endure forever" (Daniel 2:44 NIV).

When will this earthshaking event take place? To answer that question, students of Bible prophecy have attempted to identify the succession of kingdoms symbolized by the various metals in Nebuchadnezzar's statue. The first is identified by Daniel himself as Nebuchadnezzar's kingdom of Babylon.

It has been suggested that the second kingdom, comprising the silver breast and arms of the statue, is that of Persia, which conquered Babylon in 539 B.C., succeeding Nebuchadnezzar's empire as the primary player on the stage of the ancient Near East. The Persians conquered more territory than the Babylonians ever did; their superior military prowess may be indicated by the harder, more utilitarian value of silver against that of malleable gold.

But a greater empire was still to follow. In 330 B.C. the Persian army suffered a stunning defeat at the hands of a 22-year-old Macedonian Greek, who the world would know as Alexander the Great. In time, the territory conquered by Alexander stretched from India to Egypt, exceeding that of Persia. Many Bible scholars identify the brass abdomen and thighs of Nebuchadnezzar's statue with Greece. Once again we see a qualitative advance in "hardness," or military power.

The most powerful empire of ancient times, however, was yet to come. By the mid-second century B.C. an emergent Rome controlled mainland Greece as well as the western Mediterranean and parts of Asia Minor. The iron legs of Nebuchadnezzar's statue are an apt description of the "iron heel" of Rome, whose disciplined legions crushed all resistance. The breadth of the Roman empire, which stretched from the British Isles to North Africa, and to the Caspian Sea in the east, eclipsed that of the earlier empires.

Some scholars view Daniel's reference to a "divided kingdom" as an allusion to the political separation of the Roman empire. This division occurred in 364 A.D., when the Emperor

Valentinian I recognized that the capital city of Rome was unable to cope with the sheer vastness of the empire. Valentinian established a second administrative capital in Constantinople (modern Istanbul), thereby dividing the empire into East and West. The city was eventually named New Rome, and became the world center of Christendom. It was besieged by a variety of would-be conquerers until the thirteenth century.

If the succession of empires symbolized by Nebuchadnezzar's statue may be identified as Babylon, Persia, Greece, and a divided Rome, what then can be said of the enigmatic feet of the image, composed of iron mixed with clay? A number of solutions have been proposed, none of which are wholly satisfactory. Perhaps all that can be said with certainty is that the mix of iron with clay symbolizes a fundamental weakness in the latter stage of the kingdom of iron.

It has been suggested that the iron-clay mixture indicates the decline and fall of the Roman empire. However, any explanation must take into account the final portion of Nebuchadnezzar's vision, which speaks about a stone cut out, not by human hands, which struck the statue, shattering it. Daniel himself offers an interpretation of this final portion of the vision:

An angel observes the mysterious dream of King Nebuchadnezzar. The dream was subsequently interpreted by Daniel.

> *"In the time of those kings, the God of heaven will set up a kingdom that will never be destroyed, nor will it be left to another people. It will crush all those kingdoms and bring them to an end, but it will itself endure forever. This is the meaning of the vision of the rock cut out of a mountain, but not by human hands – a rock that broke the iron, the bronze, the clay, the silver and the gold to pieces"*
>
> *(Daniel 2:44-45 NIV).*

The meaning of this can scarcely be disputed: Daniel is speaking about the eternal reign of the Messiah, which will supersede all earthly kingdoms. But what is the connection between this future event and the succession of kingdoms presumed in hoary antiquity?

The Ultimate Kingdom

New Testament scholars point out that, with over a hundred references in the Gospels, the kingdom of God—or God's rule—was a central theme in the preaching of Jesus. A recurrent thread is evident in parables in which he instructs his disciples that the kingdom of God is both a present reality and something that grows and develops over time.

In the parable of the sower, for example, Jesus likens the kingdom of God to a farmer planting his field. Inevitably, along with the wheat (the faithful) grow weeds (false believers). When asked whether the impostors should be rooted out, Jesus replies: "No, because while you are pulling the weeds, you may root up the wheat with them. Let both grow together until the harvest. At that time I will tell the harvesters: 'First collect the weeds and tie them in bundles to be burned; then gather the wheat and bring it into my barn'" (Matthew 13:29-30 NIV).

Jesus is here indicating that just as a crop takes time to grow in the field, the kingdom of

Nebuchadnezzar's Vision of the Great Image

With divine assistance the Hebrew prophet Daniel was able to describe an alarming vision in which the Babylonian monarch Nebuchadnezzar saw in a dream:

"You looked, O king, and there before you stood a large statue—an enormous, dazzling statue, awesome in appearance. The head of the statue was made of pure gold, its chest and arms of silver, its belly and thighs of bronze, its legs of iron, its feet partly of iron and partly of baked clay. While you were watching, a rock was cut out, but not by human hands. It struck the statue on its feet of iron and clay and smashed them. Then the iron, the clay, the bronze, the silver and the gold were broken to pieces at the same time and became like chaff on a threshing floor in the summer. The wind swept them away without leaving a trace. But the rock that struck the statue became a huge mountain and filled the whole earth" (Daniel 2:31-35 NIV).

God is developing. At the end of time, at the final judgment, the true believers will be separated from the false.

This concept of God's kingdom as developing through the ages also is suggested in the parable of the mustard seed, where Jesus tells his disciples: "The kingdom of heaven is like a mustard seed, which a man took and planted in his field. Though it is the smallest of all your seeds, yet when it grows, it is the largest of garden plants and becomes a tree, so that the birds of the air come and perch in its branches" (Matthew 13:31-32 NIV).

Then there is Nebuchadnezzar's vision of the stone that strikes and overthrows other, earthly kingdoms. Assuming that the kingdom of iron represents the Roman Empire, the vision would seem to indicate that a decisive new phase of God's eternal kingdom began during that age. According to the New Testament this is precisely what occurred in the first century A.D., when Judea was under Roman occupation. At the beginning of his ministry Jesus announces: "The time has come. The kingdom of God is near. Repent and believe the good news!" (Mark 1:15).

We need look no further than a few chapters later in the book of Daniel for the next major prophetic passage. Beginning in chapter seven, the identification of Nebuchadnezzar's statue with the successive kingdoms of Babylon, Persia, Greece, and Rome finds remarkable confirmation in a series of extraordinary visions experienced by the prophet Daniel himself.

Daniel's Mysterious Visions

The book of Daniel contains the most comprehensive and detailed prophecies found anywhere in the Hebrew Scriptures. We already have discussed the first of these, which in chapter two occurred to Nebuchadnezzar, king of Babylon. Chapter seven opens with Daniel lying upon his bed one night during the first year of the reign of King Belshazzar, identified by historians as 553 B.C. As he lay prone, Daniel experienced a horrifying vision of a series of four beasts—each more fearsome than the one preceding—rising out of the sea. Many commentators have recognized the similarity between these beasts and the kingdoms alluded to by Nebuchadnezzar's statue.

Some take the sea to mean the world, or humanity, out of which the beasts arise. The first creature has the appearance of a lion with eagle's wings. That this is a reference to Babylon is supported by the fact that winged lions were a symbol of the Babylonian empire, and guarded the gates of the empire's royal palaces. The combination of the lion as king of the beasts and the eagle as chief among the birds was chosen to express Babylon's might and grandeur.

Yet as the vision continues, that great empire is shaken to its foundation. An amazed Daniel watches as the eagle's wings are plucked off and the beast is made to stand on two feet. Then it is given a human heart. This part of the prophecy recapitulates Nebuchadnezzar's own experience, described earlier in chapter four, where he was humbled by God by being driven insane. He fled Babylon and for seven years ate grass in the fields like an animal, until he acknowledged that there was a power greater than himself.

Daniel describes a graphic vision, with terrifying implications, of four beasts that rise from the sea.

A second beast, this one with the appearance of a bear, arises from the sea. Curiously, this creature appears raised on one side, or lopsided. Clenched in its teeth are three tusks, or ribs. A voice commands, "Arise, devour many bodies!" Some scholars take the command to be a historical reference to the Median empire, a powerful kingdom based in northern Mesopotamia, which, in 612 B.C., was instrumental in defeating the Assyrian empire.

However, by 550 B.C. Media had been absorbed into the growing Persian empire, leading other scholars to interpret the bear as representing the Medio-Persian empire. After Persia itself, Media was the second-most important portion of the empire. It is thought by some that the bear's lopsided appearance symbolizes the unequal union of Media and Persia, with the greater power and authority belonging to the Persians.

Numerous suggestions have been offered as to the meaning of the three tusks in the mouth of the bear. One of the most plausible was proposed by Father Jerome of the early Church, who identified the three tusks as the three major nations comprising the Persian empire: Media, Persia, and Babylon. The command to "eat much flesh" may refer to the tremendous expansion of the Persian empire, which greatly exceeded that of Babylon.

The third beast to emerge from the sea is the most bizarre. Daniel sees a four-headed leopard with four wings on its back, to which dominion was given. A comparison with Alexander the Great can scarcely be avoided.

With the swiftness of a leopard Alexander conquered in one decade most of the known world, from Macedonia to Egypt, and India in the east. Never had so much territory fallen to an army marching with such lightning speed. The four heads of the leopard have been taken to refer to the four principal successors of Alexander, who after his death divided the greatly expanded empire of Greece.

Mighty Rome

The fourth beast is the most horrific of all. Daniel describes it as "terrifying and dreadful and exceedingly strong." Unlike the other creatures, this one defies comparison with any known beast. In a parallel with the iron legs of Nebuchadnezzar's statue, the fourth beast possesses "great iron teeth," leading many to conclude that the Roman Empire is also being alluded to here. The reference to this beast "devouring" and "breaking in pieces" everything it encounters is taken by some to refer to the crushing military power of Rome. While Rome's legions rarely moved as far or as quickly as Alexander's, the empire's expansion, nevertheless, was inexorable.

A variety of beasts do the bidding of the antichrist. This engraving by eighteenth-century artist B. Picart depicts two particularly fearsome creatures.

Rome also was known for its ruthlessness toward any perceived opposition, as typified by the destruction of Carthage in 146 B.C., a half century after that North African empire had ceased to be a credible threat to Rome's interests. Similarly, in its fanatical zeal to protect its border against the Parthians, Rome ordered its legions to brutally suppress uprisings in Judea in the years 66 A.D. and 132 A.D., leaving the country devastated and much of its surviving population enslaved or exiled.

As Daniel continues to gaze at this vision, something amazing happens: Another horn, "a little one," arises from the among the other horns. In the process three of the other horns are "plucked out by the roots." This horn possesses "eyes like human eyes" and a "mouth speaking arrogantly." Many commentators believe this little horn refers to a despotic ruler. In a similar vision in chapter eight, Daniel refers to another "little horn"; this individual is apparently related to the Seleucid (Greek) empire.

The Four Great Beasts

Lying upon his bed while in exile in Babylon, Daniel saw a vision of the four winds of heaven churning up the great sea. As he continued to gaze, he saw four great beasts arising out of the sea:

"The first was like a lion, and it had the wings of an eagle. I watched until its wings were torn off and it was lifted from the ground so that it stood on two feet like a man, and the heart of a man was given to it.

"And there before me was a second beast, which looked like a bear. It was raised up on one of its sides, and it had three ribs in its mouth between its teeth. It was told, 'Get up and eat your fill of flesh!'"

"After that, I looked, and there before me was another beast, one that looked like a leopard. And on its back it had four wings like those of a bird. This beast had four heads, and it was given authority to rule.

"After that, in my vision at night I looked, and there before me was a fourth beast—terrifying and frightening and very powerful. It had large iron teeth; it crushed and devoured its victims and

Whatever its identity, the little horn will not prevail. What follows is a vision of the Last Judgment, presided over by an "Ancient One" described as having clothing "white as snow" and hair as "pure wool." The "books" are opened, the court sits in judgment, and the

trampled underfoot whatever was left. It was different from all the former beasts, and it had ten horns.

"While I was thinking about the horns, there before me was another horn, a little one, which came up among them; and three of the first horns were uprooted before it. This horn had eyes like the eyes of a man and a mouth that spoke boastfully.

"As I looked, thrones were set in place, and the Ancient of Days took his seat. His clothing was as white as snow; the hair of his head was white like wool. His throne was flaming with fire, and its wheels were all ablaze.

"A river of fire was flowing, coming out from before him. Thousands upon thousands attended him; ten thousand times ten thousand stood before him. The court was seated, and the books were opened.

"Then I continued to watch because of the boastful words the horn was speaking. I kept looking until the beast was slain and its body destroyed and thrown into the blazing fire. (The other beasts had been stripped of their authority, but were allowed to live for a period of time.)" (Daniel 7:4-11 NIV).

boastful, arrogant little horn receives the expected verdict: He is killed and his body burned with fire.

Even though Daniel sees that the appalling little horn has met his end, the prophet desires to understand more about this enigmatic personage: "I, Daniel, was troubled in spirit, and the visions that passed through my mind disturbed me. I approached one of those standing there and asked him the true meaning of all this" (Daniel 7:15 NIV). We find many parallels to Daniel's request in the book of Revelation, where on numerous occasions the Apostle John asks and is given the interpretation (by an angel) of a vision he has witnessed.

Daniel is told that the beasts are four kings who arise out of the earth. And additional information concerning the nefarious deeds of the little horn is provided: "He will speak against the Most High and oppress his saints and try to change the set times and the laws. The saints will be handed over to him for a time, two times and half a time" (Daniel 7:25).

The Ultimate Evil

Many scholars believe these verses are the first indication in the Bible of a particular individual, known later as the antichrist, who will lead a rebellion against the forces of good at the end of time. Many believe that the antichrist—like the little horn spoken of here—will "oppress" all who desire to serve God. The duration of the power of the little horn, given as "a time, times and half a time," likely refers to three and one-half years.

Once again Daniel is assured that the fate of the little horn is certain, as well as the ultimate triumph of God: "Then the sovereignty, power and greatness of the kingdoms under the whole heaven will be handed over to the saints, the people of the Most High. His kingdom will be an everlasting kingdom, and all rulers will worship and obey him" (Daniel 7:27 NIV).

While the outcome of human history is assured, many prophetic details in the pages of Scripture were revealed to Daniel only later, as he experienced further visions to complement the general outline recorded in chapter seven.

The Vision at Susa

Two years would pass before Daniel would experience his next recorded vision. We read that as the vision begins he sees himself by the river Ulai in Susa, later known as the winter capital of the Persian empire. (The famous Code of Hammurabi was found during excavations at Susa in 1901.)

It is, in fact, not known whether Babylon controlled Susa during the time of Daniel's vision. Interestingly, Daniel is wide awake and does not appear to be experiencing a dream vision, as in chapter seven. Scholars disagree as to whether he is presented as actually being in Susa or transported there only in vision.

In any event, while there Daniel sees a two-horned ram standing beside the river. The ram's horns are of unequal lengths—a curious anomaly with symbolic importance. The ram begins thrusting toward the west, the north, and south, and none was able to stand against him.

Later in the chapter the two-horned ram is identified as Media and Persia. Historically, the Persians and their Median subjects were a formidable military alliance that withstood all attacks for nearly two centuries, until the time of Alexander the Great. The detail of the differing lengths of the horns is significant here, as it is thought by some to refer to the relative strength of the two allies. Intriguingly, the guardian spirit of Persia was a ram with sharp-pointed horns; the Persian king, instead of wearing the standard diadem (royal headband), put on the head of a ram.

As Daniel is observing this scene another goat appears from the west. This goat has a horn between its eyes, and proceeds to attack the ram, who is unable to defend itself against the powerful onslaught. Most commentators agree with the identification of the ram with Greece. Further, Daniel's vision seems to match the historical details of Alexander's conquests.

The Legacy of Alexander

It was from the west that Alexander's forces attacked and defeated the Persian army. After initially defeating the Persians in Asia Minor (modern Turkey) in 330 B.C., Alexander's army proceeded to drive them from the eastern Mediterranean. Two years later, after fighting his way down the Syrian coastline, the Greek army occupied Judea.

The Jews offered no resistance as the Greek army entered Judea, with Jerusalem surrendering voluntarily. There is no record of Alexander himself entering the hill country of Judea, a region of little consequence in his grand plan of conquest.

The Jewish historian Josephus, however, records a curious incident in which the High Priest journeyed to Alexander dressed in finery befitting his office. The emperor was shocked by the priest's appearance, and when asked why replied that while still in Macedonia he had had a vision of this very same priest appearing before him. In the dream the High Priest implored him to seize control of the Persian Empire in the name of the God of Israel.

Alexander was only too happy to oblige, and his armies continued their eastward trek. In an unprecedented 14,000-mile march, his forces destroyed the Persian army. He entered the Persian capitals at Babylon, Susa, and Persepolis, capturing intact the immense Persian treasury. Inflamed by his successes, Alexander pressed eastward until, in 326, he engaged and defeated his most formidable opponent, the Indian king Porus. The plain of the Ganges lay before him... but was destined to escape his grasp. Alexander's war-weary army refused to continue, and he was forced to forego further conquests.

Alexander's campaign in the east appears to agree with further, surprising details of Daniel's vision. We read that at the height of the ram's power it is cut down: "The goat

This fifteenth-century miniature by Jean Vauquelin shows the supremely ambitious Alexander the Great, astride his barely tamed horse, Bucephalus.

became very great, but at the height of his power his large horn was broken off, and in its place four prominent horns grew up toward the four winds of heaven" (Daniel 8:8).

On the return trip from India along the desolate Makran coast, the elements accomplished what the enemies of Greece failed to do on the battlefield. Scourged by a pitiless sun and lacking food and water, great numbers of Alexander's troops perished.

Alexander and what remained of his army entered Babylon, where he became entranced with the mythical proportions of the primeval city with links to mythical antiquity. He drew up grandiose plans for rebuilding Babylon, and began to restore its imposing buildings.

But alas, it was not to be. A minor wound sustained—as Greek historians are careful to add—in battle festered, and Alexander died from fever on June 13, 323 B.C. He was 33 years old.

After Alexander's death his generals rushed to divide his vast empire among themselves. The lands of the eastern Mediterranean—or Levant—was of strategic importance as a buffer against Greece's ancient enemy Persia. It was vital that the harbors along the Syrian coast down to Egypt remained firmly under Greek control.

In the years after Alexander's death the Levant changed hands repeatedly as his generals vied for dominance of the eastern Mediterranean. By the year 301 B.C., the spoils had been bloodily divided, with Ptolemy taking control of Egypt, and Seleucus, another of Alexander's generals, acquiring Syria. The remainder of Alexander's empire was divided between two more of his generals, Lysimachus and Cassander.

This partition of the Greek empire by four generals is thought to fulfill Daniel's vision of "four kingdoms arising from the horned ram, but not with his power" (Daniel 8:22). None of Alexander's successors attained his stature: However, Daniel mentions "a little horn" who, like his counterpart in the previous chapter, rose to great heights of power and arrogance. This little horn has been identified as Antiochus IV, a descendent of Seleucus, Alexander's general who had gained control of Syria after his master's death.

The Tyranny of Antiochus

In 168 B.C., after a failed military expedition against his rival Ptolomies of Egypt, Antiochus determined to ensure the loyalty of his client state of Judea, which served as a buffer between Syria and Egypt. To accomplish this he decided, rather unwisely, to rigidly enforce the cult of Olympian Zeus, which required his subjects to worship him as a personification of Zeus. Antiochus assumed the surname Epiphenes – meaning "to be manifested (as a god)."

When it became clear that Antiochus would settle for nothing less than the full implementation of Greek religion and emperor worship, the stage was set for a religious war that would have far-ranging historical consequences.

In 167 B.C. Antiochus made his first move.

The wickedness perpetrated by Antiochus against the Jews was divinely punished when he fell from his chariot: His body was infested by worms and his flesh fell from his bones.

He planned a military parade in Jerusalem during the Sabbath—a brazen violation of the Jewish holy day. On cue, while ostensibly marching outside the city walls, Antiochus's army suddenly burst into and forcibly occupied the city. For the next 25 years, through the wars to come, the Syrian garrison in Jerusalem would remain a source of vexation for the Jews.

Worse outrages were still to come. Antiochus put into effect a prohibition—on pain of death—of all observance of the Jewish law and Temple sacrifice. The Jewish books of the Law, or Torah, were destroyed and in its place were instituted the ceremonies of a Hellenistic cult. Some have argued that Antiochus's actions were intended to be pro-Syrian and anti-

Egyptian, rather than anti-Semitic.

Whatever the intention, the indignation of the Jews could scarcely have been greater, especially as they observed to their horror what has come to be known as the "Abomination of Desolation," the physical desecration of the Temple by a pagan altar to Zeus Olympus set upon the Jewish Altar of Sacrifice. In his vision Daniel states that the little horn "set itself up to be as great as the Prince of the host; it took away the daily sacrifice from him, and the place of his sanctuary was brought low" (Daniel 8:11 NIV).

Sacrifices, which included the ritually unclean pig, were commanded to be made on the twenty-fifth of every month. Since Antiochus's own birthday was celebrated on the twenty-fifth, the sacrifices were clearly meant to be offered to him. Jews were forced to offer the sacrifices and to eat the forbidden swine flesh. Similar sacrifices were offered at other Jewish worship sites around the land; for instance, an altar to Zeus was set up at the Samaritan temple at Gerizim.

While some Jews meekly submitted to Antiochus, many others refused to comply, while still others escaped to the hills or died for their beliefs. The rising popular revolt against Antiochus's outlawing of Judaism and imposition of pagan practices found zealous leadership in an elderly village priest named Mattathias, and in his five sons.

The book of II Maccabees records how Mattathias fled his priestly duties in Jerusalem, horrified at having witnessed the desecration of the Temple. Returning to the town of Mod-

The Goat and the Ram

Daniel's second vision, like his first, involved strange, fantastic creatures that manifest aggressive and malignant behavior. Interpretation of these beasts remains a matter of controversy for biblical scholars:

"I looked up, and there before me was a ram with two horns, standing beside the canal, and the horns were long. One of the horns was longer than the other but grew up later.

"I watched the ram as he charged toward the west and the north and the south. No animal could stand against him, and none could rescue from his power. He did as he pleased and became great.

"As I was thinking about this, suddenly a goat with a prominent horn between his eyes came from the west, crossing the whole earth without touching the ground.

"He came toward the two-horned ram I had seen standing beside the canal and charged at him in great rage.

"I saw him attack

ein, located between Jerusalem and the sea, Mattathias soon discovered that the persecution had reached his village. His family, along with the other townspeople, were collected together by a Seleucid officer and ordered to take part in a pagan sacrifice to Zeus.

The indignant Mattathias drew his sword

the ram furiously, striking the ram and shattering his two horns. The ram was powerless to stand against him; the goat knocked him to the ground and trampled on him, and none could rescue the ram from his power.

"The goat became very great, but at the height of his power his large horn was broken off, and in its place four prominent horns grew up toward the four winds of heaven.

"Out of one of them came another horn, which started small but grew in power to the south and to the east and toward the Beautiful Land.

"It grew until it reached the host of the heavens, and it threw some of the starry host down to the earth and trampled on them.

"It set itself up to be as great as the Prince of the host; it took away the daily sacrifice from him, and the place of his sanctuary was brought low.

"Because of rebellion, the host of the saints and the daily sacrifice were given over to it. It prospered in everything it did, and truth was thrown to the ground" (Daniel 8:3-12 NIV).

and slew not only the Jewish collaborator but the emissary sent by Antiochus to enforce the sacrificial offering. The elderly priest and his sons fled to the desert, where they were joined by others, including the Hasidim—"the Pious Ones"—who were devoted to Jewish Law. From their ranks guerrilla bands were formed to fight the Seleucid army and their Hellenist collaborators, a struggle that would continue until December 164 B.C., when the Jews finally gained control over the Temple, ritually cleansed it, and reinstituted the Levitical sacrifices.

Many scholars believe that Daniel's vision of the little horn denotes Antiochus's campaign against the Jews and their religion. When the distressed prophet asks how long the "sanctuary and host" will be "trampled," he receives the reply: "It will take 2,300 evenings and mornings; then the sanctuary will be reconsecrated" (Daniel 8:14 NIV).

Numerous suggestions have been offered regarding the meaning of "2,300 evenings and mornings." As we have noted, the sanctuary was reconsecrated in December 164 B.C., which may be taken as the terminus date of the 2,300-day time period. Subtracting 2,300 days from December 164 B.C. would fix the beginning of the time period in 171 B.C. In that year the legitimate High Priest was murdered by agents of Antiochus, who installed a puppet priest in his place. According to Daniel's prediction, this provocative act set in motion the events that would culminate 2,300 days later with the cleansing of the Temple.

This vision of Daniel closes with the fate of the little horn: "He will cause deceit to prosper, and he will consider himself superior. When they feel secure, he will destroy many and take his stand against the Prince of princes. Yet he will be destroyed, but not by human power" (Daniel 8:25). In 164 B.C., the same year as the rededication of the Jewish Temple (an event celebrated by Jews everywhere as the holiday of Hanukkah), Antiochus IV died while conducting a military campaign in Media.

The Seventy Weeks of Daniel

Even the casual reader of the Bible will notice the diverse means by which the visions of the book of Daniel are revealed. It is this variety that suggests the visions' authenticity for, as some scholars point out, if the book were the second-century forgery that some critics allege, it would likely have a carefully composed regularity instead of its distinguishing feature: sheer disregard for uniformity and convention. Daniel's prophecies are presented vividly, but without the sense of order that would have appealed to a forger.

In Daniel chapter two, for example, the vehicle for the prophetic vision concerning the future is Nebuchadnezzar, the pagan ruler who conquered the Jews. This would scarcely have been expected if the book were simply a second-century B.C. literary invention designed to impress pious Jews, who would expect the divine revelation to come through a Hebrew prophet.

In chapter seven, Daniel himself, while dreaming, receives the vision of the beasts arising out of the sea. In the next chapter, the way in which the prophecy is revealed changes yet again: While awake Daniel is transported to Susa in the neighboring kingdom of Elam.

It is the ninth chapter of Daniel that contains one of the most cryptic and detailed prophecies in the book, including an amazingly precise chronological timetable for events past and yet to come. On this occasion Daniel receives the vision through another novel conduit: the angel Gabriel.

There are only four mentions of this high-ranking divine messenger in the Bible. Daniel has already encountered Gabriel in chapter eight, in which Gabriel helps him interpret the vision of the goat and the ram.

In the New Testament Gabriel appears at two critical junctures. The first is to announce to the elderly priest Zechariah that his wife, Elizabeth, will bear John the Baptist. Gabriel's exalted position is apparent in his reply to Zechariah, who registers a not-unreasonable disbelief that his aged wife Elizabeth could yet bear children: "The angel replied, 'I am Gabriel. I stand in the presence of God, and I have been sent to speak to you and to bring you this good news. But now, because you did not believe my words, which will be fulfilled in their time, you will become mute, unable to speak, until the day these things occur'" (Luke 1:19-20). In another reflection of his status as a trusted messenger of God, six months later Gabriel is sent to tell Mary that she has been chosen to bear the Christ child.

Counting the Weeks

In chapter nine of Daniel we find the prophet engaged in a prolonged session of praying, confessing his sins and those of his people in Israel. He implores God's deliverance for the exiled Jews. Suddenly he sees Gabriel coming to him "in swift flight at the time of the evening sacrifice" (Daniel 9:21). The angel has been sent with a divine message in response to Daniel's prayers.

The message reveals momentous events in the future of Israel, which are described as taking place within a time frame of "seventy weeks." While scholars disagree as to the meaning of Daniel's 70 weeks, all agree that literal weeks are not at issue here. One reason is the sheer magnitude of the events described, which include those that can be seen to have occurred as early as the fifth century B.C. and others reserved for an unspecified time in the future. These events occur, then, during a span of time considerably greater than our present-day conception of 70 weeks.

Some have interpreted the 70 weeks as symbolic of an indefinite period of time, pointing out that 70 is a multiple of seven, which in Scripture is sometimes used to signify completion or perfection. On the seventh day, for example, God rested after completing the work of creation; the Jewish festivals of Passover and Tabernacles last seven days; and Jesus commanded that his followers be willing to forgive others "seventy times seven" times.

Others point out that the Hebrew word

When Daniel pleads with God for the deliverance of the Jews, he is visited by the angel Gabriel, who brings a message of great importance to the future of Israel. Fourteenth-century painting by Guariento di Arpo.

commonly translated into English as "weeks" actually means "sevens," and that the 70 weeks ("sevens") actually refers to *seventy groups of seven years*—a total of 490 years. Those who hold to this view see literal, historical fulfillment in the admittedly cryptic text of Daniel, which further subdivides the 70 weeks ("sevens") into two periods.

According to this view, the first division includes the first 69 "weeks," or 69 groups of seven years, totaling 483 years. This period begins with the decree "to restore and rebuild Jerusalem," and lasts until an "anointed one shall be cut off." The reference to an "anointed one " is taken to refer to the Messiah, whose name means "Anointed One"; in fact, some translations of the Bible use the word "Messiah" here, instead of "anointed one."

Can the restoration of Jerusalem and the cutting off of an anointed one within 69 of the prophesied 70 weeks be concretely linked to historical dates? Many students of the Bible believe that they can. It is thought that the decree to rebuild Jerusalem is described in the book of Nehemiah, where the Persian king Artaxerxes commissioned his Hebrew court official Nehemiah to go to Jerusalem for the express purpose of rebuilding the city. The date of Artaxerxes's decree is given by historians as 445 B.C.

Even though the first exiles had returned to Jerusalem in 538 B.C., almost a century before, the walls of the city remained in a state of disrepair. Because of the hostility of the neighboring nations it was imperative that the city be defensible. Nehemiah, sensing impending danger, organized the Herculean task of rebuilding the walls in just 52 days.

The period of 69 "weeks" concludes with the anointed being "cut off." Many believe that this is a reference to the death of Jesus. A combination of astronomical observations and information taken from the New Testament yield an approximate time period for that event. Astronomical data related to the first century A.D. suggest that the Passover at the time of Jesus' trial and crucifixion occurred in A.D. 30 or 33. And we learn from Luke that John the Baptist began his ministry, "In the fifteenth year of the reign of Emperor Tiberius, when Pontius Pilate was governor of Judea, and Herod was ruler of Galilee" (Luke 3:1). The "Herod" mentioned here is not Herod the Great but his son, Antipas, who ruled in Galilee and who inherited the title "Herod." Since Pontius Pilate was prefect of Judea between 26-36 A.D., it is thereby certain that Jesus' crucifixion occurred during that span.

The fifteenth year of the Emperor Tiberius was 28-29 A.D. John baptized Jesus in that year, marking the beginning of Jesus' ministry. As already noted, the Gospels mention at least three Passovers, which fit chronologically with a date of 31-32 A.D. for Jesus' crucifixion.

The matter, however, remains unsettled, with some scholars maintaining that the period of Jesus' ministry was actually one year rather than three; these scholars support a crucifixion date of 30 A.D.

In summary then, the beginning of Daniel's 69 weeks may be dated to Artaxerxes's decree in 445 B.C. The end of that period may also be said to occur at the death of Jesus, somewhere between A.D. 30-32.

The Numbers Match

Here things become particularly intriguing: The difference between 445 B.C. and 30-32 A.D. is 478 years—quite close to the magic number of 483 years mentioned above. But that is not the whole story, for the Jewish calendar, by which these years would have been calculated, is only 360 days long. When the 69 weeks —or 483 years— are calculated according to the Jewish calendar, they are actually the equivalent of 478 years as reckoned by modern calendars. In other words, the 478-year span of the modern calendar is the same as 483 years in the Jewish calendar! Thus, in an apparent feat of astounding accuracy, the biblical text appears to have predicted the exact length of time separating the decree to rebuild Jerusalem, and the death of the Messiah Jesus.

The Seventieth Week

Daniel's vision continues, stating that following the events of the 69 weeks: "The people of the ruler who will come will destroy the city and the sanctuary" (Daniel 9:26, NIV). Jerusalem and the Temple were destroyed by Roman legions under Titus in 70 A.D.

There has been considerable speculation about the identity of *the ruler who is to come,* whose people are responsible for the destruction of Jerusalem. Since, as we have noted, those people are the Romans, the ruler spoken of here is also Roman.

Yet what follows seems to refer to events that came after the first century. Attention is now focused on this ruler, who will confirm a covenant with many for one "seven." In the midst of that period of time, however, he will put an end to sacrifice and offering. The most ominous of this ruler's actions follows: "And on a wing of the temple he will set up an abomination that causes desolation, until the end that is decreed is poured out on him" (Daniel 9:27).

None of these events can be ascribed to the Roman commander Titus. There is no historical evidence that he entered into any covenant or other agreement with the Jewish people. Similarly, as we have previously noted, the abomination that causes desolation first occurred in 169 B.C., when Antiochus (Epiphanes) IV set up the "abomination of desolation" in the Temple. This blasphemous act consisted of erecting an altar to Zeus upon which the Jews were commanded to sacrifice.

The prophet Daniel, depicted here as part of the enormous Sistine Chapel painting by Michelangelo, is closely tied to biblical prophecies related to Nebuchadnezzar.

No record exists to suggest that such a thing occurred during the First Revolt against Rome in A.D. 66-70. Titus did not erect anything resembling an abomination of desolation in the Temple; nor would he have been able to do so, because the Temple remained in Jewish hands until the very end of the revolt. It was only when Jerusalem finally fell that overzealous soldiers torched and destroyed the edifice.

So who then is this ruler—a man connected with the Romans and who destroyed Jerusalem? Many believe he is the coming antichrist described in the book of Revelation, who will wage war against the Jews.

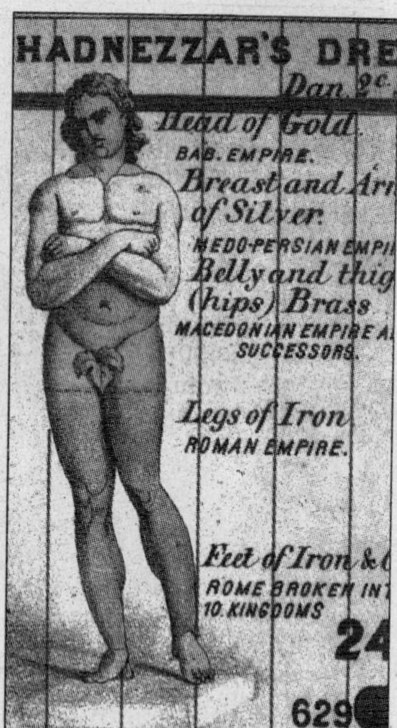

Schematic-type image of the provocative statue of Nebuchadnezzar, as seen in a vision and described by Daniel. The various materials symbolized different empires.

The second chapter of Daniel notes that the feet of the statue of Nebuchadnezzar were iron mixed with clay. Some commentators believe that this refers to a revived Roman (European) empire that will exist at the final stages of human history. Similarly, the fourth beast who appears in Daniel's vision of chapter seven, out of which springs a "little horn" who "wages war against the saints," has been identified by many as the antichrist arising out of a revived Roman empire.

Seventy Weeks to Eternity

Commentators have been intrigued by a cryptic prophecy concerning "seventy weeks" recorded in the ninth chapter of Daniel. The 70 weeks embrace a far-ranging prophetic timetable, from the rebuilding of the city of Jerusalem by returning exiles in the fifth century B.C., to the ushering in of an age of "everlasting righteousness" yet to come.

Gabriel tells Daniel:

"'Seventy weeks are decreed for your people and your holy city: to finish the transgression, to put an end to sin, and to atone for iniquity, to bring in everlasting righteousness, to seal both vision and prophet, and to anoint a most holy place.

'Know therefore and understand: from the time that the word went out to restore and rebuild Jerusalem until the time of an anointed prince, there shall be seven weeks; and for sixty-two weeks it shall be built again with streets and moat, but in a troubled time.

'After the sixty-two weeks, an anointed one shall be cut off and shall have nothing, and the troops of the prince who is to come shall destroy the city and the sanctuary. Its end shall come with a flood, and to the end there shall be war. Desolations are decreed.

'He shall make a strong covenant with many for one week, and for half of the week he shall make sacrifice and offering cease; and in their place shall be an abomination that desolates, until the decreed end is poured out upon the desolator'"

(Daniel 9:21-27).

Curiously, Jesus refers to the vision of Daniel in chapter nine, as he instructs his disciples regarding the time of the end:

> *"So when you see standing in the holy place 'the abomination that causes desolation,' spoken of through the prophet Daniel – let the reader understand – then let those who are in Judea flee to the mountains. Let no one on the roof of his house go down to take anything out of the house. Let no one in the field go back to get his cloak. How dreadful it will be in those days for pregnant women and nursing mothers! Pray that your flight will not take place in winter or on the Sabbath"*
>
> *(Matthew 24:15-20, NIV).*

Whatever the identity of this sinister ruler, his end is swift and certain: Daniel simply but conclusively states that he will heedlessly pursue destruction "until the decreed end is poured out upon the desolator" (Daniel 9:27).

Apocalypse Now: The Day of the Lord

Through the ages, a variety of ideas has been advanced regarding the future. Some people believe that billions of years from now the world will become a cold, lifeless rock as our sun expands mightily, then burns itself out. Others have grand hopes for the progressive evolution of the human species as it overcomes all obstacles to its survival, perhaps by migrating to another part of the universe.

According to the Bible, however, the earth and all that is in it will not die gradually; neither will the onward march of human progress continue unabated. In a theme that first appears in the writings of the Hebrew prophets, and one that can be traced throughout Scripture, the world is destined to one day come to a *cataclysmic* end. This terminus point of human history is called the day of the Lord.

The eighth-century B.C. prophet Amos was an unlikely messenger for an ominous prophecy concerning the end of the world. Though his message would be brought before kings, Amos never forgot his humble origins: "I am no prophet, nor a prophet's son; but I am a herdsman, and a dresser of sycamore trees, and the Lord took me from following the flock, and the Lord said to me, 'Go, prophesy to my people Israel'" (Amos 7:14-15).

The nature of Amos's prophecies stands in sharp contrast to the circumstances of the period in which he lived, which was a time of relative peace on the international political scene. With the major powers of Egypt and Assyria in decline and thus not in a position to threaten the northern and southern Jewish kingdoms of Israel and Judah, both of the latter experienced an interlude of prosperity.

But even as Israel and Judah enjoyed material affluence they suffered from spiritual poverty. Amos, a lonely voice who prophesied against both kingdoms from the desert and remote villages, condemned his fellow Jews for their wickedness, false worship, and oppression of the poor. As Amos foretold it, the sins of Israel and Judah would eventually result in destruction and exile.

The time when these things will come to pass is called the day of God's judgment: "The end has come upon my people Israel; I will never again pass them by. The songs of the temple shall become wailings in that day," says the Lord God; "the dead bodies shall be many, cast out in every place" (Amos 8:2-3).

The day of God's judgment fell upon Israel in 722 B.C., when the Assyrians crushed the northern kingdom. The southern kingdom of Judah lasted another century, until the new Mesopotamian superpower of Babylon set its gaze upon Jerusalem. Amos's prophecy was finally fulfilled in 586 B.C., when Nebuchadnezzar's army breached the walls and inflicted terrible destruction upon the city. Most citizens who were not slaughtered were led into captivity.

Blood and Chaos

But even as Amos describes this future day of judgment upon the people of Israel and Judah, it is clear that a far more catastrophic "day" is also in view. Apparently, some people in Amos's time mistakenly believed that a future day of reward and blessing was imminent. The prophet, however, makes it clear that while the future holds a great "day of the Lord," it will be one of darkness and gloom, and will fall upon men as an unexpected disaster:

> *"Alas for you who desire the day of the Lord! Why do you want the day of the Lord? It is darkness, not light; as if someone fled from a lion, and was met by a bear; or went into the house and rested a hand against the wall, and was bitten by a snake. Is not the day of the Lord darkness, not light, and gloom with no brightness in it?"* (Amos 5:18-20).

It will be a day like no other, marked by dramatic and terrifying cosmic aberrations. Amos later expands upon the idea that the day of the Lord will be one of darkness: "On that

The prophet Amos, depicted here by Gustav Doré, prophesied that the day of the Lord will be one of startling cosmic upset.

day, says the Lord God, I will make the sun go down at noon, and darken the earth in broad daylight" (Amos 8:9). Some Bible scholars have compared Amos's description to that of a full eclipse of the sun. However, the scope of the day of the Lord seems to far exceed a temporary—and geographically isolated—solar phenomenon.

Interestingly, the prophet Joel also makes reference to the moon in his description of the same inexplicable event: "I will show portents in the heavens and on the earth, blood and fire and columns of smoke. The sun shall be turned to darkness, and the moon to blood, before the great and terrible day of the Lord comes" (Joel 2:30-31).

It has been suggested that the "blood and fire" spoken of here refers to violence and subsequent bloodshed, an idea that fits well with the overall picture of the end of the age as a time of cataclysmic wars.

The reference to the moon being turned to blood has resisted attempts at a literal explanation—with the exception of one frighteningly plausible possibility. Could Joel be referring to the atmosphere of earth being dangerously polluted by airborne particulate matter? This sort of pollution gives the moon the appearance of being red. The phenomenon could be caused, for example, by natural disasters such as volcanoes spewing unprecedented levels of dust and ash into the atmosphere. As we shall later see, Jesus predicted that at the end of time disturbances would strike the earth's crust.

While the volcano theory remains a possibility, dust and ash from earthquakes would normally only dim and obscure the moon rather than seem to redden it. But consider this: There is an even more ominous explanation of Joel's reference to the moon being turned to blood. Some have suggested that the atmospheric disturbances will result from a disaster created by man—the result of a worldwide nuclear holocaust, an unimaginable possibility which, fortunately, has never been experienced.

Dark Terrors

Terrible, frightening darkness is a key element of the promised day of the Lord, when evil shall be punished. Recall the strangeness of a total eclipse, when suddenly the bright sunlight is replaced by eerie murkiness. Deprived of the expected appearance of the sun—perhaps the one great natural constant of life—many people become disoriented and frightened. In ancient times an eclipse was an awe-inspiring, unexplained phenomenon that was regarded as an evil omen.

Similarly, virtually all of us know what it is like to be at least temporarily deprived of illumination, as when the electricity unexpectedly fails in the night. A sense of panic can quickly set in if we are unable to locate a flashlight or matches, or if we happen to be in unfamiliar surroundings. When taken to an extreme, a person's fear of darkness can indicate a specific psychological disorder called achluophobia.

In the Bible, as well as in writings from other religions of the ancient Near East, darkness is associated with chaos, destruction, death, and the underworld. The earth that existed prior to the creative acts of God is described in the Bible as "a formless void [where] darkness covered the face of the deep," a marked contrast to the divine order of creation (Genesis 1:2).

The Psalmist laments the apparent triumph of evil, which threatens to thrust him into the darkness of death: "For the enemy has pursued me, crushing my life to the ground, making me sit in darkness like those long dead" (Psalms 143:3). Job also conceives of death as the netherworld of dark shadows inhabited by those without hope: "If I look for Sheol as my house, if I spread my couch in darkness. . . where then is my hope?"(Job 17:13,15).

Supernatural events in the Bible are sometimes accompanied by darkness. In the story of the Exodus a series of ten plagues, each more dreadful than the last, is unleashed against the land of Egypt. After the Pharaoh refuses yet again to let the Israelites go, his land suffers a ninth plague. "Then the Lord said to Moses, 'Stretch out your hand toward heaven so that there may be darkness over the land of Egypt, a darkness that can be felt'" (Exodus 10:21). For three days darkness covered the land, with the ensuing terror among the Egyptians prompting events that led to the Passover and the subsequent Exodus from Egypt.

In the New Testament, the Gospels mention that during Christ's crucifixion darkness came over the whole land until three in the afternoon (Luke 23:44). Jesus himself describes a future time of great tribulation, which will be followed by the world being cast into darkness at his Second Coming:

> *"Immediately after the suffering of those days the sun will be darkened, and the moon will not give its light; the stars will fall from heaven, and the powers of heaven will be shaken. Then the sign of the Son of Man will appear in heaven, and then all the tribes of the earth will mourn, and they will see the Son of Man coming on the clouds of heaven with power and great glory"* *(Matthew 24:29-30).*

According to Jesus, evildoers attempt to use darkness to conceal their actions: "For all who do evil hate the light and do not come to the light, so that their deeds may not be exposed" (John 3:20). This is demonstrated with horrifying vividness in the book of Revelation, where those who are opposed to God make a desperate attempt to conceal themselves in dark places during the tribulation that precedes the day of judgment.

We read that during that time rebellious people from all walks of life—from the "rich and powerful" to "slaves"—will hide "in the caves and among the rocks of the mountains, calling to the mountains and rocks, 'Fall on us and hide us from the face of the one seated on the throne and from the wrath of the Lamb'" (Revelation 6:15-16).

The attempts at concealment will ultimately prove futile, as the world is visited with another plague of darkness reminiscent of that suffered by the ancient Egyptians: "The fifth angel poured his bowl on the throne of the beast, and its kingdom was plunged into darkness; people gnawed their tongues in agony, and cursed the God of heaven because of their pains and sores, and they did not repent of their deeds" (Revelation 16:10-11).

Ironically, like the Pharaoh of old, Revelation indicates that those who rebel against God will willingly choose to suffer the pain of divine wrath rather than submit to the call to repentance. For the irredeemably wicked there remains but one fitting judgment that befits their disdain for the truth: "They are waterless clouds carried along by the winds; autumn trees without fruit, twice dead, uprooted; wild waves of the sea, casting up the foam of their own shame; wandering stars, for whom the deepest darkness has been reserved forever" (Jude 1:12-13).

The Return of Elijah

The litany of calamity promised by the Bible to occur on the day of the Lord continues. In the book of Malachi, the last of the Hebrew prophets, the divine prophecy states: "Lo, I will send you the prophet Elijah before the great and terrible day of the Lord comes. He will turn the hearts of parents to their children and the hearts of children to their parents, so that I will not come and strike the land with a curse" (Malachi 4:5-6).

As we have already mentioned, the prophet Elijah lived in the ninth century B.C., and was one of the greatest and most complex of the Hebrew prophets. The mention of Elijah returning before the day of the Lord has generated considerable discussion among students of biblical prophecy, both ancient and modern.

The mystery of Elijah's reappearance is deepened by the fact that the prophet was one of only two mortals who never experienced death. The other is Enoch of the book of Genesis, of whom it was said, "Enoch walked with

God; then he was no more, because God took him" (Genesis 5:24).

In the book of Kings we have an explicit description of Elijah's dramatic departure from earth. After crossing the river Jordan with his successor, Elisha has a profound experience: "As they continued walking and talking, a chariot of fire and horses of fire separated the two of them, and Elijah ascended in a whirlwind into heaven" (2 Kings 2:11).

Some interpret this passage to mean that another prophet resembling Elijah will appear before the day of the Lord. This new prophet may be John the Baptist, for in the New Testament John is spoken of as possessing "the spirit and power of Elijah" (Luke 1:17).

Others believe that, having never died, Elijah was uniquely qualified to be sent back to earth at the end of the age. This seems to have been a common belief in first-century Judea. When the Jews asked Elijah to confirm his identity, he did not simply refuse, but issued a denial. Later, after John's death, some considered Jesus to be Elijah.

Curiously, the fact that Elijah actually appears during the ministry of Jesus is often overlooked in the discussion. We read that Jesus took his closest disciples with him atop an unknown mountain—identified henceforth as the Mount of Transfiguration—to pray: "And while he was praying, the appearance of his face changed, and his clothes became dazzling white. Suddenly they saw two men, Moses and Elijah, talking to him. They appeared in glory and were speaking of his departure, which he was about to accomplish at Jerusalem" (Luke 9:29-31).

Peter, John, and James were enveloped in a dense cloud, from which issued the voice of God, instructing that Jesus is "my Son, my Chosen" (Luke 9:35). When the cloud lifts, Moses and Elijah are gone.

On this occasion, Elijah apparently did not fulfill the prophecy of Malachi, which holds that upon his return he will "turn the hearts of parents to their children and the hearts of children to their parents."

Shut the Sky

In an extraordinary passage in the book of Revelation, which many believe refers to the return of Elijah, we read about the astonishing exploits of two "witnesses" who appear in the midst of the unspeakable events at the end of time. Wearing sackcloth, these two witnesses proceed to prophesy for 1260 days. They also demonstrate supernatural powers:

> *"And if anyone wants to harm them, fire pours from their mouth and consumes their foes; anyone who wants to harm them must be killed in this manner. They have authority to shut the sky, so that no rain may fall during the days of their prophesying, and they have authority over the waters to turn them into blood, and to strike the earth with every kind of plague, as often as they desire"*
>
> (*Revelation 11:5-6*).

This is interpreted by some as a fulfillment of Malachi's prophecy that Elijah would preach upon his return to earth during the final days of human history. While the identity of the second witness remains unclear, some see a clear reference to

The prophet Elijah was thought to have special powers, and may be one of the "two witnesses" to the end of time.

Elijah in the mention of the witnesses having "authority to shut the sky so that no rain may fall," a power demonstrated by Elijah.

However, the story takes a bizarre twist as the two witnesses are confronted by a "beast" identified by many scholars as the antichrist:

> *"When they have finished their testimony, the beast that comes up from the bottomless pit will make war on them and conquer them and kill them, and their dead bodies will lie in the street of the great city that is prophetically called Sodom and Egypt, where also their Lord was crucified. For three and a half days members of the peoples and tribes and languages and nations will gaze at their dead bodies and refuse to let them be placed in a tomb"*
>
> *(Revelation 11:7-9).*

Popular hostility to the message of the two witnesses will lead to a time of rejoicing where "the inhabitants of the earth will gloat over them and celebrate and exchange presents, because these two prophets had been a torment to the inhabitants of the earth" (Revelation 11:10).

The celebrations prove to be premature, for in the midst of their reveling the two witnesses are miraculously revived: "But after the three and a half days, the breath of life from God entered them, and they stood on their feet, and those who saw them were terrified. Then they heard a loud voice from heaven saying to them, 'Come up here!' And they went up to heaven in a cloud while their enemies watched them'" (Revelation 11:11-12).

The shock and dismay experienced by those observing the revival of the two prophetic witnesses fits well with the depiction of the day of the Lord as a time of unexpected disaster that will fall upon the wicked. As we shall later see, the book of Revelation promises that the Second Coming of Christ and final judgment will follow on the heels of this dramatic event.

The Eye of the Storm

We see also that the two witnesses of the Revelation prophecy are in "the great city that is prophetically called Sodom and Egypt, where also their Lord was crucified" (Revelation 7:8). This indicates that the events of the day of the Lord will be centered in the city of Jerusalem. The prophet Zechariah, writing in the late sixth century B.C., after the Judeans returned from the Babylonian exile, spoke of a great tribulation that will fall upon the city:

> *"See, I am about to make Jerusalem a cup of reeling for all the surrounding peoples; it will be against Judah also in the siege against Jerusalem. On that day I will make Jerusalem a heavy stone for all the peoples; all who lift it shall grievously hurt themselves. And all the nations of the earth shall come together against it"*
> *(Zechariah 12:2-3).*

Situated at the crossroads of the continents of Africa, Asia, and Europe, few regions on earth have been invaded and conquered as frequently as the land of Israel throughout its long and turbulent history. The Egyptians, Assyrians, Babylonians, Persians, Greeks, Romans, Arab nations, Crusaders, and the British have left their marks on this tiny land. Because Israel possesses few natural resources, the primary interest of most of these invaders has been strategic. Indeed, Israel has been characterized as that land whose people "who live at the center of the earth" (Ezekiel 38:12). (The Hebrew translation literally reads "navel of the earth.")

For much of the preceding two millennia, however, few would have considered the land

Zechariah, by Michelangelo. The prophet had an ominous warning for Jerusalem.

of Israel the center of anything. Jerusalem was largely destroyed in 70 A.D. and razed by the Roman emperor Hadrian after the Second Revolt of the Jews against Rome in A.D. 132-135. With many of the inhabitants of Judea either killed or exiled, the remaining Jews fled to villages in the countryside and in Galilee.

Palestine took on renewed importance in the fourth century, when Christianity became the official religion of the Roman Empire, with churches and monasteries soon sprouting up around the land. This period of renaissance, however, abruptly ended in 636 A.D., when the armies of the new religion of Islam swept into Palestine. But the soldiers of the Muslim crescent considered Mecca and Medina in Arabia—not Jerusalem—to be their holy places.

For the next 12 centuries—excepting the Crusader interlude of almost two centuries, in

A.D. 1096-1270—the land remained an impoverished backwater of a succession of Muslim dynasties. The real currents of power ran elsewhere, and those in power had little interest in Palestine beyond the maintenance of Muslim holy sites in Jerusalem.

The Impact of Zionism

All of that changed in the nineteenth century with the rise of the Jewish Zionist movement. For the first time since the Second Revolt in the second century A.D., here was an organized, concerted attempt by Jews to resettle their Holy Land. The energy and vigor brought by the Zionists to their task soon yielded tangible results. Agricultural settlements, called Kibbutzim, were established, drawing enthusiastic, idealistic Jews from Europe and America. Rock-strewn fields were cleared and malarial swamps drained by backbreaking labor and often at considerable cost in human suffering and disease.

As the decades passed, tensions grew between the Jews and the indigenous Arab population, which cast a wary eye upon the non-Muslim immigrants and their claim upon what Islam considered inviolable Muslim territory. A small minority of non-Muslim Arabs and others—including Jews—had always lived in Jerusalem and other places, but these people were considered "protected minorities"; in effect, second-class citizens.

But the brash new Jewish settlers, with their determination and Western ways, were threatening to upset a delicate political balance that was decidedly tilted in the favor of Muslim Arabs. What remained of that balance was thrown into disarray in 1917 with the collapse of the Turkish Ottoman Empire at the close of the First World War. The Muslim nation had sided with Germany, and when the Axis powers lost the war Turkey lost her empire.

The Western powers scrambled to fill the void left by the Ottomans, with Great Britain being granted its ill-fated "Palestinian Mandate." By now, the Jewish presence in Palestine was considerable. Kibbutzim and other agricultural settlements occupied a growing percentage of the countryside, and wholly Jewish-founded cities such as Tel Aviv were beginning to thrive. Modern Jewish suburbs sprang up outside the walls of the ancient city of Jerusalem; these new settlements soon overshadowed the Old City in size and importance, radically altering the city's traditional character.

The level of fighting between Jews and Arabs increased until the British, unable to control the escalating violence or arrive at a political solution, finally abandoned their Mandate. When the last British High Commissioner for Palestine set sail from Jaffa in 1947, the Jewish population declared the establishment of the State of Israel, an act that plunged the newborn nation immediately into war. The Arab armies of Egypt, Jordan, and Syria attacked in what Israelis call their War of Independence, the first of several major conflicts between Israel and her Arab neighbors.

More than a half century later, the struggle between Arabs and Jews for control of the land of Israel still defies a political solution. The fundamental issue revolves around who—Arab or Jew—has the right of sovereignty over a land claimed by both. Israelis point to the ancient promise given to Abraham and his sons, that the land of Israel would belong to their descendants. The archaeological remains of thousands of years of Jewish history can be found in the land, evidence of a continuous Jewish presence dating from the time Joshua crossed the Jordan River and conquered the region.

Muslim Arabs consider Palestine a sacred trust that, like all Muslim lands, can never return to its pre-Islamic condition. It is forbidden for Muslims to live under non-Islamic control; it is unthinkable that they should remain subjects of a Jewish state. And then there is another, non-religious issue: Arabs controlled Palestine until the nineteenth century, and bitterly resent seeing their lands come under the control of others.

Meaning for the Modern Age

Nineteen centuries after the writing of the Bible was completed, biblical passages indicating the centrality of Israel in the events of the day of the Lord are stunningly relevant. Nowhere is this more explicit than in the book of Zechariah, where the divine prophecy speaks of a coming invasion of the Holy Land: "See, I am about to make Jerusalem a cup of reeling for all the surrounding peoples. . . . On that day I will make Jerusalem a heavy stone for all the peoples; all who lift it shall grievously hurt themselves. And all the nations of the earth shall come together against it" (Zechariah 12:2-3).

Since the Gulf War of 1991 it is no longer an unthinkable proposition that a major military

Zechariah's vision of four chariots likely heralded the day of the Lord.

force composed of many nations may descend upon the Middle East—it has happened. The Middle East conflict continues to preoccupy nations and organizations around the globe. From the Israeli perspective, much of the pressure from the world community is hostile, and fails to take into account their legitimate security needs and concerns. Israeli diplomats joke that even nations with no involvement in the Middle East, who field diplomats who could scarcely locate Israel on a map, maintain an anti-Israeli foreign policy.

During the Gulf War, many openly wondered whether the unfolding events were related to the biblical prophecies about the day of the Lord. Others cautioned that because the war's focus was on Iraq and not Israel, the prophecy was not coming together.

Still, Israel suffered physical assault during the war. This reminds one that Zechariah makes it clear that the events of the day of the Lord will include a brutal conquest of Jerusalem: "See, a day is coming for the Lord. . . . For I will gather all the nations against Jerusalem to battle, and the city shall be taken and the houses looted and the women raped; half the city shall go into exile, but the rest of the people shall not be cut off from the city" (Zechariah 14:1-2).

At no time in Israel's history since the time of Zechariah's writing could this prophecy be said to have been fulfilled literally. Although Jerusalem was conquered and destroyed numerous times, the passage in Zechariah continues to describe a unique event that, to date, has not taken place:

> *"Then the Lord will go forth and fight against those nations as when he fights on a day of battle. On that day his feet shall stand on the Mount of Olives, which lies before Jerusalem on the east; and the Mount of Olives shall be split in two from east to west by a very wide valley"*
>
> *(Zechariah 14:3-4).*

Many Christians believe this refers to the Second Coming of Christ, who, at the time of the day of the Lord, will return to execute judgment against evildoers.

Unlike Amos and Joel before him, Zechariah does not mention the darkness associated with the onset of the day of the Lord. However, the prophet does note that the coming of the Lord will bring unusual changes. "On that day," he writes, "there shall not be either cold or frost. And there shall be continuous day (it is known to the Lord), not day and not night, for at evening time there shall be light" (Zechariah 14:6-7).

Harmony and Glory

And finally, the day of the Lord will usher in a new era of peace in which the Kingdom of God will be established on earth. According to the prophecy of Zechariah, "all who survive of the nations that have come against Jerusalem shall go up year after year to worship the King, the Lord of hosts" (Zechariah 14:16).

As spoken by the prophet Isaiah, this Messianic age will be a time of harmony among all creatures, human and animal alike: "The wolf shall live with the lamb, the leopard shall lie down with the kid, the calf and the lion and the fatling together, and a little child shall lead

Blood on the Moon

According to the prophet Joel, a future prophetic event called the day of the Lord will be accompanied by mysterious signs in the heavens, followed by the final climactic battle of human history:

"I will show portents in the heavens and on the earth, blood and fire and columns of smoke. The sun shall be turned to darkness, and the moon to blood, before the great and terrible day of the Lord comes. Then everyone who calls on the name of the Lord shall be saved; for in Mount Zion and in Jerusalem there shall be those who escape, as the Lord has said, and among the survivors shall be those whom the Lord calls. For then, in those days and at that time, when I restore the fortunes of Judah and Jerusalem, I will gather all the nations and bring them down to the valley of Jehoshaphat, and I will enter into judgment with them there, on account of my people and my heritage Israel, because they have scattered them among the nations" (Joel 2:30-3:2).

them" (Isaiah 11:6). Other passages indicate that the curse God placed upon the ground after the Fall will be removed.

Though involving travail, the day of the Lord will be, as the Apostle Paul puts it, a glorious event which "the creation itself awaits with eager longing" (Romans 8:19).

Is America Mentioned in Biblical Prophecy?

Since the founding of the earliest American colonies, pious Americans have searched in Holy Writ for references to what they believed to be a divinely ordained republic. After all: Had not Christopher Columbus sailed to the New World with the conviction that God had providentially guided him to the "new heaven and the new earth" spoken of in the book of Revelation?

It's not surprising, then, that we find abundant historical references to glorious futures in store for the New World. Jonathan Edwards, the greatest theologian of eighteenth-century America, confidently proclaimed that the founding of the nation paved the way for the overthrow of Satan and the establishment of the kingdom of God. John Adams, second president of the United States, wrote of America's sacred destiny, which, he felt, was destined to open the way for the spiritual "illumination" of the planet. Other Founding Fathers, in the Declaration of Independence and the Constitution, attached a cosmic significance to the founding of the Republic.

The conviction that America was destined to play a unique role in the Divine Plan has persisted throughout American history. Works such as Harriet Beecher Stowe's novel *Uncle Tom's Cabin,* Julia Ward Howe's anthem "Battle Hymn of the Republic," and the addresses of Abraham Lincoln are permeated with scriptural references and assertions of America's sacred purpose. Shortly before his death in 1919, President Woodrow Wilson spoke movingly of America's moral obligation to bring about the "liberation and salvation of the world."

Crisis of Confidence

These attitudes were radically altered by the social upheavals that followed World War I, a conflict that had been confidently proclaimed as "the war to end all wars." Pious Americans were concerned that the moral laxness of the hedonistic Roaring Twenties jeopardized America's special divinely anointed role. The optimism that attended the 1919 founding of the League of Nations dissipated ten years later as America—followed by the rest of the world—was plunged into the Great Depression. In the early thirties, many watched unbelievingly as the despot Adolf Hitler rose to power in Germany, a nation long considered to be one of

Was the American Depression foretold by the Bible?

Europe's most culturally advanced and civilized.

The social and moral changes in the post-World War I era led many prophecy teachers and preachers to believe that the world was entering a calamitous period at the end of time foretold by the Bible. America, some claimed, was in particular danger, and passages like the following warning of St. Paul were interpreted to apply to conditions in that nation:

> *"You must understand this, that in the last days distressing times will come. For people will be lovers of themselves, lovers of money, boasters, arrogant, abusive, disobedient to their parents, ungrateful, unholy, inhuman, implacable, slanderers, profligates, brutes, haters of good, treacherous, reckless, swollen with conceit, lovers of pleasure rather than lovers of God, holding to the outward form of godliness but denying its power. Avoid them! For among them are those who make their way into households and captivate silly women, overwhelmed by their sins and swayed by all kinds of desires, who are always being instructed and can never arrive at a knowledge of the truth" (2 Timothy 3:1-7).*

Students of biblical prophecy began to locate other scriptural texts that they believed referred to the spiritual decline of the United States. And what more apt comparison could be found to a now-corrupt America than the tale of the infamous Sodom and Gomorrah? Thus, Jesus' ominous warning about the time of the End was taken by some to refer to the moral climate in the United States:

> *"Just as it was in the days of Noah, so too it will be in the days of the Son of Man. They were eating and drinking, and marrying and being given in marriage, until the day Noah entered the ark, and the flood came and destroyed all of them. Likewise, just as it was in the days of Lot: they were eating and drinking, buying and selling, planting and building, but on the day that Lot left Sodom, it rained fire and sulfur from heaven and destroyed all of them – it will be like that on the day that the Son of Man is revealed"*
>
> *(Luke 17:26-30).*

For many, conditions in America were distressingly similar to those of ancient Sodom and Gomorrah prior to the cities' destruction. Indeed, America would endure the Depression, wage a titanic war, and finally embark upon a period of unprecedented economic prosperity marked, like Sodom and Gomorrah, with eating and drinking, buying and selling, planting and building. In the years following World War II, many felt that America was abandoning its moral foundation in the face of growing materialism, sexual license, and impiety.

In the Cold War period of atomic proliferation that marked the fifties and sixties, many openly wondered if America would meet a fate similar to that of Sodom and Gomorrah. The description of fire and sulfur raining from heaven to destroy the cities seemed frighteningly similar to the disastrous effects of an atomic holocaust. Could a comparable judgment against a spiritually decadent America, a nation once favored by God, be long in coming?

To such pessimists, there was no lack of biblical passages that seemed to apply in general ways to the United States. But does biblical prophecy contain any specific references to the role of America? In the nineteenth century some commentators found what they believed to be a distinct mention—albeit obscured in symbolism—of the United States. This is in chapter 38 of the book of Ezekiel.

We already have seen how this passage is thought by some Bible students to describe an invasion of Israel at the end of time by "Gog of the land of Magog." The text describes the intentions of Gog and his confederates:

> *"You will say, 'I will go up against the land of unwalled villages; I will fall upon the quiet people who live in safety, all of them living without walls, and having no bars or gates'; to seize spoil and carry off plunder; to assail the waste places that are now inhabited, and the people who were gathered from the nations, who are acquiring cattle and goods, who live at the center of the earth" (Ezekiel 38:11-12).*

As previously suggested, a number of indicators in these verses have been taken by some to apply to the modern nation of Israel, whose inhabitants come from more than 100 countries and may truly be said to have been "gathered from the nations." Over the past century these immigrants have transformed the "waste places" of the land into productive farmlands and cities. Israel also can be said to "live in safety" because of its powerful military.

However, while there is apparently little resistance to Gog's planned invasion among the nations, Ezekiel briefly mentions a curious exception to the apathy among the world community: "Sheba and Dedan and the merchants of Tarshish and all its young warriors will say to you, 'Have you come to seize spoil? Have you assembled your horde to carry off plunder, to carry away silver and gold, to take away cattle and goods, to seize a great amount of booty?'" (Ezekiel 38:13).

Mystery City: Tarshish

Interest has focused on the meaning of "Tarshish and all its young warriors." In his attempt to avoid the Divine command to go to Nineveh, Jonah sailed in the opposite direction, toward Tarshish. While the location of Tarshish is uncertain, the few references to the place in the Hebrew Bible indicate that it was an important maritime city. Some commentators have identified the biblical Tarshish with the city of Tarsus, located on the Mediterranean along the southern coast of Asia Minor (modern Turkey). Others have suggested Tartessus, a city located at the southern tip of Spain. Others have located it on the island of Sardinia, on the basis of a Phoenician inscription found there, in which the word "Tarshish" may occur.

There is another, more intriguing interpretation. At the close of the nineteenth century Great Britain ruled the high seas and freely exercised its will over its vast empire. This led some to suggest that Tarshish was a reference to England, a theory bolstered by the older King James Version of the Bible, in common use at the time, which reads: "Tarshish with all its *young lions.*" [emphasis added] The lion was a symbol of the British Empire. What else then, could the young lions —or cubs—refer to but the colonies of England, and specifically the former British colony that became the United States?

In fact, the Hebrew word that translates as "young warriors" or "young lions" does mean "villages," or "colonies." However, the identification of Tarshish with England has been rejected by almost every commentator as lacking foundation. The implications of the verse are also unclear: The colonies of Tarshish are apparently impotent, and do little more than question the intentions of Gog. It is thought that even a decadent United States would possess sufficient military might to exert itself more forcefully.

Some scholars, while admitting that the alleged connection between Tarshish and England is inadmissible, nevertheless claim that America was colonized in ancient times by Mediterranean seafaring powers. They point to archaeological evidence indicating the existence of colonies of ancient Judeans in the New World.

Still other students of biblical prophecy, exercising considerable ingenuity, point to a passage in Isaiah as foretelling America's doom:

> *"At evening time, lo, terror! Before morning, they are no more. This is the fate of those who despoil us, and the lot of those who plunder us. Ah, land of whirring wings beyond the rivers of Ethiopia, sending ambassadors by the Nile in vessels of papyrus on the waters! Go, you swift messengers, to a nation tall and smooth, to a people feared near and far, a nation mighty and conquering, whose land the rivers divide"* (*Isaiah 17:14; 18:1-2*).

The reference to a "land of whirring wings" is taken by some to mean the national symbol of America, the bald eagle, as well as the United States aircraft industry, which dominates the world market. The description of a nation tall and smooth is said to refer to the relative height of well-fed, clean-shaven Americans in contrast to the appearances of inhabitants of much of the rest of the world. And surely, these interpreters note, no republic is feared near and far, a nation mighty and conquering like the United States. Finally, the continental United States, with its great river systems, can be described as a land whose rivers divide.

As is common with the popularizers of such theories, however, the less-applicable portions of the prophecy are often glossed over. The United States, for example, has not been known for sending ambassadors by the Nile in vessels of papyrus on the waters. And, it must be admitted, the other aspects of the prophecy could with little ingenuity be applied to numerous nations, both past and present. Indeed, any world power—economically sound, well-armed, and secure within and without its borders—could be cited.

The Scarlet Woman

Undeterred, some claim to find a reference to the United States in one of the most vile and fearsome entities described in Holy Writ: Babylon the Great Whore, described by John in the book of Revelation:

> *"I saw a woman sitting on a scarlet beast that was full of blasphemous names, and it had seven heads and ten horns. The woman was clothed in purple and scarlet, and adorned with gold and jewels and pearls, holding in her hand a golden cup full of abominations and the impurities of her fornication; and on her forehead was written a name, a mystery: 'Babylon the great, mother of whores and of earth's abominations'."* *(Revelation 17:3-5).*

The Great Whore of Babylon is adorned with finery and the trappings of wealth, the result of her worldwide political and economic power. We read that "the kings of the earth have committed fornication with her, and the merchants of the earth have grown rich from the power of her luxury" (Revelation 18:3). It is agreed that the United States is unmatched in its exertion of political and economic influence on a worldwide scale. And, like the Great Whore, despite its great material affluence the United States is considered by many observers to be filled with wickedness and immorality.

In the text John is further told that the Great Whore of Babylon "is seated on many waters," and that "the waters that you saw, where the whore is seated, are peoples and multitudes and nations and languages" (Revelation 17:1,15). What other nation, it is asked, is—like the United States—bordered on both coasts by great oceans? Also, America, like few other nations, is a land of immigrants speaking a variety of languages.

While the similarities between the Great Whore of Babylon and the United States seem obvious, overzealous commentators avoid confronting other aspects of the prophecy. The discussion of the Great Whore of Babylon comprises a full two chapters in the book of Revelation, with much of this material seemingly disproving any association with the United States. In one of the most glaring contradictions, for instance, the Great Whore is said to be responsible for the persecution of Christians: "And I saw that the woman was drunk with the blood of the saints and the blood of the witnesses to Jesus. When I saw her, I was greatly amazed" (Revelation 17:6). While a number of modern nations condone or actively perpetrate religious persecution, the United States can scarcely be said to be among them.

Also, the location of the Great Whore is described cryptically: "This calls for a mind that has wisdom: the seven heads are seven

The Final Decline?

Preachers of Bible prophecy and teachers in twentieth-century America have not been the first to hold the conviction that they were living during the decadent period at the end of human history known as the "time of the end." Writing about 250 A.D., the Early Church Father Cyprian, bishop of Carthage, expressed a similar conviction regarding his age: "Who cannot see that the world is already in its decline, and no longer has the strength and vigor of former times? There is no need to invoke Scripture authority to prove it. The world tells its own tale and in its general decadence bears adequate witness that it is approaching its end.... There is less innocence in the courts, less justice in the judges, less concord between friends, less artistic sincerity, less moral strictness."

mountains on which the woman is seated; also, they are seven kings" (Revelation 17:9). The only historical identification of a location with seven mountains is Rome, which was said to have been founded upon seven hills. By no stretch of the imagination can a connection be made between the United States (or its capital, Washington, D.C.) and seven mountains.

However intriguing Revelation's Great Whore of Babylon, the entity's clear link to the modern world remains illusive. Similarly, all efforts to clearly identify the United States in Scripture have to date proved fruitless.

Ancient Judean Colonies in America?

Archaeological discoveries that may lend support to an interpretation of Tarshish as the far-flung colonies of a Mediterranean seafaring power have been made in relatively recent times. The story begins in 1889, when the Smithsonian Institution was surveying ancient mounds near the Little Tennessee River some 40 miles south of Knoxville, Tennessee. In one mound the researchers discovered nine skeletons, eight of which faced north and one that faced south. Beneath the skeleton facing south were found several curious objects, including a small inscribed stone and a pair of brass bracelets.

The stone, which came to be known as the Bat Creek Inscription, had eight characters scratched across its surface. Since the stone was found in Cherokee Indian territory, the archaeologists at first assumed that the letters were from a Cherokee alphabet that dated from the 1820s.

The Bat Creek Inscription elicited little attention at the time and was consigned to the bowels of the National Museum of Natural History in Washington, D.C. In the late 1960s, some 80 years later, the inscription was reexamined and found to resemble the ancient script of Phoenicia, which is related to both the Canaanite and Hebrew scripts. Subsequent evaluation revealed close similarities between the inscription and a form of ancient Hebrew called paleo-Hebrew.

The noted Semitic languages scholar Cyrus Gordon translated several of the letters of the inscription to read: "...for the Judeans." Gordon's translation, which possibly indicated the presence of Judeans in the New World, was deemed so improbable that it was ignored by other scholars for two decades. (Indeed, the inscription does not prove that Judeans were present at the site. Phoenician sailors could easily have made inscriptions mentioning the Judeans.) However, recent evidence regarding the other artifacts found at Bat Creek supports Gordon's conclusions.

The pair of bracelets found there appeared to be made of copper, a metal often found in such burial mounds. But after conducting a scientific analysis the metal was found to be heavily leaded yellow brass. Of special interest were the proportions of the metals used: copper with approximately 27 percent zinc and 3.3 percent lead.

Initially, the percentage of lead appeared to contradict Gordon's theory, for ancient Roman brass was thought never to contain more than 1 percent lead. However, recently discovered ancient brass artifacts from the first and second centuries A.D. contain up to 3 percent lead—the same as the Bat Creek bracelets.

Analysis of these recent finds indicates that the Bat Creek bracelets date from before 200 A.D. This is confirmed by a new method of radio-carbon dating that has been used to test the fragments of wood found at Bat Creek. The fragments were dated to from between 32 A.D. to 769 A.D., a range that at least partially agrees with the suggested date of sometime earlier than 200 A.D. Granted, these facts do not prove an ancient Judean presence in what is now Tennessee; nevertheless, they are at the very least quite provocative.

If the ancient Judeans did end up in Tennessee, how did they travel there? While there is no evidence that Judea possessed boats capable of negotiating oceans, the Hebrew

Bible states that King Solomon employed such ships: "For the king had a fleet of ships of Tarshish at sea with the fleet of Hiram. Once every three years the fleet of ships of Tarshish used to come bringing gold, silver, ivory, apes, and peacocks" (1 Kings 10:22). Other texts indicate this fleet sailed to the coasts of Arabia and Africa, and as far as India.

References in the Hebrew Bible indicate Tarshish was an important seafaring city. Jonah likely sailed on a ship of Tarshish in his flight away from Nineveh; elsewhere we read that ships of Tarshish were utilized when Judah traded precious metals with Tyre.

Other passages suggest that the seafaring nation had settlements in distant places: "From them I will send survivors to the nations, to Tarshish, Put, and Lud—which draw the bow—to Tubal and Javan, to the coastlands *far away* [emphasis added] that have not heard of my fame or seen my glory; and they shall declare my glory among the nations" (Isaiah 66:19).

Some have raised an intriguing question: Could these "far away" coastlands include America? Evidence suggests that the colonists at Bat Creek possessed a sophisticated knowledge of metallurgy, which would have required locating and mining various mineral ores. Once a colony had been established, it is reasonable to assume that the settlers explored the territory for minerals and other wealth.

Coincidentally, it is known that other early explorers of the American interior took a route that brought them near to Bat Creek. In the mid-sixteenth century the Spanish explorer Hernando De Soto crossed the Appalachians and traveled down the Tennessee River to within 12 miles of Bat Creek.

It should be noted that the scholar Cyrus Gordon also believes that Phoenicians sailed to Brazil. He is virtually the only scholar to hold that Phoenicians reached the Americas, and his take on the Bat Creek site remains extremely controversial.

Still, if the mound at Bat Creek can indeed be linked to ancient Judeans who traveled to the New World on ships of Tarshish and resided in Tarshish settlements, it will have provided the most convincing evidence to date of a biblical reference to America.

Foretold: The Destruction of the Temple

The Temple in Jerusalem was justifiably a source of great pride for first-century

Judeans. Begun by Herod the Great before the birth of Jesus, work on the magnificent edifice continued throughout Jesus' life, until A.D. 64, when the Temple was officially dedicated. While visiting Jerusalem one of Jesus' disciples, eager to impress upon his Master the grandeur of the colossal structure, received a startling reply: "As he came out of the temple, one of his disciples said to him, 'Look, Teacher, what large stones and what large buildings!' Then Jesus asked him, 'Do you see these great buildings? Not one stone will be left here upon another; all will be thrown down'" (Mark 13:1-2).

The destruction of the Temple was destined to take place in the midst of a terrible onslaught in the city. To Judeans of the day, the temple's destruction seemed as awful as the destruction of America's places of worship would seem to Americans today. In the Gospel of Luke fur-

A Roman soldier carries a menorah from the Jewish Temple in 70 A.D.

ther details concerning this ominous event are provided:

> *"When you see Jerusalem surrounded by armies, then know that its desolation has come near. Woe to those who are pregnant and to those who are nursing infants in those days! For there will be great distress on the earth and wrath against this people; they will fall by the edge of the sword and be taken away as captives among all nations; and Jerusalem will be trampled on by the Gentiles, until the times of the Gentiles are fulfilled" (Luke 21:20,23,24).*

Jesus spoke these words during the administration of Pontius Pilate, who was the Roman procurator of Judea from 26-36 A.D. While no major uprisings of the Jews against their hated Roman occupiers are recorded during this period, a number of incidents that occurred during Pilate's tenure indicate the simmering tension beneath the surface of a fragile peace enforced by Roman soldiers.

Still, few would have imagined a conflagration of the devastating magnitude mentioned by Jesus. One revolutionary Jewish movement, few in numbers but with strong popular appeal, was preparing for just such a confrontation with Rome. For the Zealots, death and destruction were preferable to continued subservience to a foreign power.

In A.D. 66 the uprising the Zealots longed for was finally precipitated by a series of events culminating in a massacre of Jews at the Mediterranean port city of Caesarea. The land erupted with violence against the Romans, who responded decisively by sending Vespasian and his legions to quell the revolt.

The story of Vespasian's campaign comes to us first-hand from the Jewish historian Josephus, who was the military commander of Galilee until his forces were overrun by the Romans. Choosing life over valor, he declined at the last moment to commit suicide with the rest of his trapped men and instead surrendered. Through a remarkable chain of circumstances, Josephus joined Vespasian's entourage and chronicled the progress of the revolt for all history.

The bloody conflict between the Jews and Rome raged for four years, during which Vespasian, having been proclaimed Emperor, returned to Rome and left command of the campaign to his son Titus. Finally, in A.D. 70 Jerusalem fell after a year-long siege during which, as Jesus prophesied, the entrapped inhabitants of the city endured the unimaginable horrors of famine and disease.

Oddly, as Josephus tells it, it was never Titus's intention that the Temple be destroyed. Roman commanders were known to spare some grandiose building or structure as a witness to the greatness of the people which they, the Romans, had conquered. However, in the fanatical tumult of the moment, and contrary to Titus's orders, the Temple Mount was set ablaze.

The fierceness of the conflagration contributed to the fulfillment of Jesus' prophecy that not one stone will be left upon another. Limestone, the material used to construct the Temple, has the capacity to absorb moisture. When the large limestone blocks used in the construction of the Temple were quickly heated by the raging fire, the moisture inside the ashlars (squared stone) was turned to steam, causing the buildup of enormous pressure.

Josephus claimed that the sound of the exploding ashlars could be heard at the Dead Sea some 30 miles distant. In any event, the destruction was total. Today, visitors to the site still can view some of the large ashlars of Herod's Temple. The wall in which they are found, however, is the retaining wall of the Temple. True to the prophecy of Jesus, not a single stone of the superstructure remains.

Have the "Times of the Gentiles" Ended?

The Jewish people are no strangers to suffering and misfortune. By the time of Jesus they already had endured much abuse at the hands of foreign oppressors. A long list of major empires from the ancient Near East and beyond, including Egypt, Assyria, Babylonia, Persia, Greece, and Rome, as well as a host of lesser powers, had invaded the land of Israel. Each of these regional powers was determined to impose its rule over the fiercely independent Jews, with some leaving murderous slaughter in their wake.

But even the tragic history of the Jewish people could scarcely prepare them for the dire prediction uttered by Jesus while in Jerusalem in the week prior to his crucifixion: "When you see Jerusalem surrounded by armies, then know that its desolation has come near" (Luke 21:20).

This prophecy of doom, very likely spoken within eyesight of the imposing city Temple, must have sent shock waves through those listening to the Galilean prophet. Could it really be that the glorious Temple, the magnificent center of Jewish life and worship, was destined for destruction?

At the time, Judea was firmly under the control of the greatest power of the ancient world, Rome, and it was Rome's designated ruler, Herod the Great, who built the Temple, utilizing the finest Roman technology of the day. Unrest, to be sure, was endemic to the independent-minded Jews, who chafed under any foreign domination. Jesus understood the potential for awful conflict, and continued to describe a future cataclysm almost beyond comprehension, so much so that he warned,

"Then those in Judea must flee to the mountains, and those inside the city must leave it, and those out in the country must not enter it" (Luke 21:21). It will be a time of "great distress on the earth and wrath against this people" (Luke 21:23). Jerusalem would fall "by the edge of the sword," followed by the surviving inhabitants being driven into captivity "among all nations."

In a curious reference that occurs nowhere else in the New Testament, Jesus states that the city will be "trampled on" by foreign powers "until the times of the Gentiles are fulfilled" (Luke 21:24).

In the Bible "Gentiles" (sometimes translated as "nations") is a general term for all the peoples of the world other than the Jews. As the chosen people of God, the Israelites saw themselves as standing apart from all other nations. In their obedience and service to Yahweh, they were to be a testimony to those who persisted in the worship of pagan gods. Indeed, the prophet Isaiah long before had given the divine prophecy regarding the Jews: "You are my servant, Israel, in whom I will be glorified . . . . I will give you as a light to the nations, that my salvation may reach to the end of the earth" (Isaiah 49:3,6).

The divine blessings upon Israel included a national homeland, for Yahweh had promised the patriarch Abraham that the land of Canaan would be an everlasting inheritance for his descendants: "[F]or all the land that you see I will give to you and to your offspring forever" (Genesis 13:15).

But according to the prophecy of Jesus, the land of Judea was to be taken from them, and their unique status as the "light to the gentiles" replaced by captivity and slavery. This period of national humiliation, called "the times of the Gentiles" (Luke 21-24), will last until a time when "the powers of the heaven will be shaken" (Luke 21:26), an event to occur at some point preceding the return of Jesus Christ.

Israel Under Siege

The last nineteen centuries have seen the often dramatic fulfillment of the words of Jesus, as the land of Israel has been continually

Roman legions savaged Jerusalem in 70 A.D. Here, the doomed city burns.

"trampled on" by foreign powers. First came the catastrophic siege and destruction of Jerusalem by the Roman army in 70 A.D. at the close of the First Jewish Revolt.

Any who were familiar with Jesus' words would have been wise to heed his advice and abandon the city while they had the opportunity: "Then those in Judea must flee to the mountains, and those inside the city must leave it, and those out in the country must not enter it" (Luke 21:21).

The Jewish historian Josephus, an eyewitness to the fall of Jerusalem, described with textbook thoroughness the way in which the Romans encircled the city with siege walls. Citizens caught attempting to enter or leave the city were summarily crucified in full view of their horrified countrymen, who observed the executions from the city walls. According to Josephus, more than a million Jews, many of whom had fled to the city from around the land, perished "from famine or the sword" when the city fell. A large number of others were carried off into captivity.

Interestingly, Christians living in Jerusalem did obey their Master's warning to flee "to the mountains." The Early Church Father and historian Eusebius records that at the onset of hostilities the members of the Jerusalem church escaped to the city of Pella in Trans-Jordan. From the safety of that remote vantage point the Christians observed as the Romans lay waste to the land.

Any semblance of Jewish sovereignty ended after the fall of Jerusalem in 70 A.D. But the fires of nationalist independence would be rekindled yet again. In 132 A.D. the Emperor Hadrian, determined that the seditious Jews would be deprived of any further opportunity to rebel, ordered that Jerusalem be razed.

Led by Bar Kokhba, whom many believed was the Messiah, the Jews reacted by once again revolting against their hated occupiers with a fierceness that surpassed even that of the First Revolt. An entire Roman legion, the twenty-fifth stationed in Egypt, disappears from history at this point, and is thought to have been decimated in the Judean campaign. When the revolt was finally suppressed three years later, in 135 A.D., the commander of the legions returned to Rome, where he made the traditional appearance before the Senate. But instead of the customary greeting "the emperor and the legions are well" he is recorded as saying merely, "The emperor is well." Clearly, the Roman forces had absorbed fierce punishment.

The Spread of Christianity

The costly Roman victory enabled Hadrian to level Jerusalem and build a new city, called Aelia Capitolina, on the site. Jews were barred from entering the city of their forefathers but were permitted to live in Galilee and the Golan. When the Roman empire became Christianized under Constantine in 324 A.D., dreams for Jewish national independence dwindled as Palestine became a center for Christian pilgrimage. Churches and monasteries were built across the land.

Emperor Hadrian

A brief moment of hope occurred under the abortive reign of the Emperor Flavius Claudius Julianus (361-363), better known as Julian the

Apostate for his attempts to restore pagan religion to the empire. Julian granted the Jews permission to rebuild their temple, but his plans came to an end with his premature death while campaigning in Persia.

Interestingly, excavators at the temple mount would later find an inscription from Isaiah carved into one of the huge Herodian ashlars (squared stones): "Then you shall see this, and your heart shall be glad . . . ." The location of the epitaph indicates that may have been written during the time of Julian by Jews elated over their short-lived anticipation of regaining their land.

Any hopes for the end of the "times of the Gentiles" would only grow dimmer as the centuries passed. True to the words of the prophecy, Palestine was "trampled on" by a succession of powers and empires. Muslim dynasties that began in the sixth century would control the Holy Land for the next thirteen centuries, except for an interlude of Crusader dominance lasting from A.D. 1096 to 1270.

The Ottoman Turks were the last of the Muslim dynasties to control Palestine. They ruled for almost exactly 400 years, from 1517 until the end of World War I in 1918. During much of this period of outside control, Palestine was a neglected backwater of impoverished villages, swamps, and untilled land.

This changed in the late nineteenth century with the rise of a new movement called Zionism—the rekindling of the Jewish aspirations for their ancient land. Inspired by the fervent appeals of Theodore Hertzl and other Jewish thinkers, Jews began to immigrate to Palestine. Agricultural settlements were established, fields were cleared, and new Jewish cities and towns founded.

Despite growing Arab opposition, the Jewish presence in Palestine continued to grow. With the downfall of the Ottoman Turks (who had made the mistake of taking up with Germany and her allies in World War I), Palestine came under British control. The final gentile power to control Palestine quickly found itself embroiled in the increasing tensions between the Arabs and Jews. After decades of mismanagement and violence, the British withdrew on May 14, 1948.

A New Nation—and a Note of Caution

The world was electrified when, upon the departure of the last British representatives to Palestine, the Jewish state of Israel was immediately proclaimed, thus ending over 1,900 years of Gentile dominance of Palestine. War broke out at once between the nascent state and its hostile Arab neighbors, and armed conflict would continue to erupt in the succeeding decades. Arab-Israeli friction would capture world attention as the superpowers of America and the Soviet Union dueled by proxy in the Middle East—the United States firmly supporting Israel, and the USSR lending military assistance to its Arab clients.

Curiously, with the millennium drawing to a close many perceived a new threat to the security of the State of Israel. Having failed in their attempts to militarily defeat the Jewish state, some of the surrounding Arab countries have embraced the idea of a negotiated settlement of the "Palestinian question"; that is, the issue of Arabs and their land displaced by Israelis during the 1948 and 1967 wars, or confiscated in the intervening years.

The unified Arab position during the negotiations is that all confiscated Palestinian land—including Jerusalem—must be returned to Palestinian control. However, many Israelis believe they have historic and legal rights to these lands, which were, after all, lost in wars of aggression waged against the Jewish state.

Furthermore, the return to Palestinians of significant territories within the borders of Israel poses, to Israeli minds, an unacceptable security threat. Under the proposed withdrawal of Israeli troops from the occupied territories, Israel's heavily populated coastal region would be left largely defenseless

Ancient Hopes Rekindled as a Nation is Reborn

After 1,900 years of Diaspora (scattering of settlements), the Jewish people once again are in the land of Israel. In 1948 their ancient aspirations were expressed in the *Declaration of the Establishment of the State of Israel*:

"After being forcibly exiled from their land, the people kept faith with it throughout their Dispersion and never ceased to pray and hope for their return to it and for the restoration in it of their political freedom. Impelled by this historic and traditional attachment, Jews strove in every successive generation to re-establish themselves in their ancient homeland. In recent decades they returned in their masses. Pioneers, immigrants, and defenders, they made deserts bloom, revived the Hebrew language, built villages and towns, and created a thriving community, controlling its own economy and culture...and aspiring towards independent nationhood."

against terrorist attacks from the heights overlooking the coast.

Underlying the political debate is a fascinating question asked by those attempting to interpret biblical prophecy: Does the establishment of the State of Israel mean that we are no longer in the "times of the Gentiles"? If so, many believe it would mean the first definite fulfillment of the prophecies related to the end of time.

However, the Hasmonean period in the second-century B.C., which was marked by a powerful, independent Jewish state (its borders, in fact, surpassed those of modern-day Israel), was a time when many Jews considered themselves to be fulfilling the ancient biblical prophecies about returning to their land from exile.

But the Hasmonean kingdom was not the fulfillment of the biblical prophecies regarding a restored Jewish kingdom. In 63 B.C., after a long period of internal conflict, the Hasmonean kingdom eventually came under the control of the expanding Roman republic. Likewise, it remains a possibility that the present state of Israel may fail to live up to the expectations of students of biblical prophecy. Only time will tell whether we have seen the last of the age known as the "times of the Gentiles."

A Nineteen-Century Historical Interlude

In 70 A.D., 40 years after Jesus issued his ominous prophecy regarding the destruction of Jerusalem, the city was destroyed by the Romans, thus ushering in a period of non-Jewish domination of the Holy Land. Jesus called this period "the times of the Gentiles" Many believe that that "historical interlude" came to an end with the establishment of the modern State of Israel, an event that will precede the end of the age: "When you see Jerusalem surrounded by armies, then know that its desolation has come near. Then those in Judea must flee to the mountains, and those inside the city must leave it, and those out in the country must not enter it; for these are days of vengeance, as a fulfillment of all that is written. Woe to those who are pregnant and to those who are nursing infants in those days! For there will be great distress on the earth and wrath against this people; they will fall by the edge of the sword and be taken away as captives among all nations; and Jerusalem will be trampled on by the Gentiles, until the times of the Gentiles are fulfilled. There will be signs in the sun, the moon, and the stars, and on the earth distress among nations confused by the roaring of the sea and the waves. People will faint from fear and foreboding of what is coming upon the world, for the powers of the heavens will be shaken" (Luke 21:20-26).

Will the Jewish Temple Be Rebuilt?

To many Jews, Christians, and Muslims the Temple Mount is more than a fascinating archaeological and historical site: It is sacred ground, a symbol of the aspirations of the three great monotheistic religions—and a flashpoint for convictions that are passionately held. The passage of millennia has not dimmed the hopes of many students of biblical prophecy that the Jewish Temple will one day rise again on its ancient site: a massive raised platform that still dominates the Old City of Jerusalem.

It is here, in 1010 B.C., that King David established his capital and the compelling drama of the Israelite nation was played out on the pages of the Old Testament. Many visitors to the City of Peace are unaware that the original Jerusalem – the Jebusite city that King David conquered to make his capital – lies outside the "modern" Turkish walls.

The first Jerusalem, called the "City of David," is located on a finger of land extending southward from the Temple Mount. Because the City of David comprised a mere 15 acres, no room was available on which to build the Temple. It was left to David's son and successor, Solomon, who ruled between B.C. 971-931, to enlarge Jerusalem, enclosing Mount Moriah and making room for the Temple and his palace complex.

A Growing Power

Those were days of unparalleled glory, for the United Monarchy under David and Solomon was the period of the greatest expansion in Israel's history. As a result of David's military prowess, nearly all of Israel's age-old enemies were defeated and subdued. The borders of the Jewish nation were extended

Solomon, the son of David, brought his considerable wisdom to bear as ruler of Israel.

northward to include much of what is today Lebanon and Syria. David established trading outposts as far away as the Euphrates River.

Israel's expansion during the eleventh century B.C. coincided with a period of stagnation in the great river civilizations of the Nile and the Euphrates. The relative weakness of Egypt and the Mesopotamian powers, Assyria and Babylon, during this time enabled the nation of Israel to become the most powerful kingdom in the eastern Mediterranean.

Solomon consolidated the gains of his father David, while developing an efficient system of government. He abolished the old tribal boundaries and divided the land into administrative districts. Solomon also expanded his role in the international arena, establishing trading links throughout much of the known world. His ships sailed from his port at Ezion-geber to as far away as Africa, Asia, Arabia, and Asia Minor. Ezion-geber was located near modern Eilat, Israel's southernmost city situated at the head of the Gulf of Aqaba at the Red Sea.

Solomon's crowning achievement, the building of the Temple, was meant to symbolize the unique covenantal relationship between the Lord and His people, and as a testament, a message to the known world that God was with Israel.

The ornate furnishings and lavish use of gold and other precious metals in the Temple served as a reminder that God was the source of all blessings. And indeed, the building of the Temple coincided with an unmatched era of peace and prosperity for Israel.

Destruction and Rebuilding

Solomon's Temple stood until 586 B.C., when the armies of the Babylonian King Nebuchadnezzar conquered Jerusalem and destroyed the structure, according to the Jewish calendar, on the ninth day of the month of

Aviv. Many of the surviving Israelites were taken into captivity to Babylon. After 70 years in Babylon, Cyrus the Great, monarch of Persia, allowed groups of Jewish exiles to return to Judea. (The decision was Cyrus's because Persia had deposed Babylon as the superpower in the ancient Near East.) Under the direction of Joshua, the High Priest, and Zerubbabel, a descendant of King David, a modestly scaled rebuilding of the Temple was begun in about 536 B.C., and ultimately completed early in 515 B.C.

Zerubabbel's Temple stood through the Persian period and the Greek empire that followed it. At the end of the first century B.C., the empire of Rome held firm control of the Eastern Mediterranean, and had installed a puppet ruler, the self-proclaimed Herod the Great, in Judea.

The remnants of Herod's grandiose building projects can still be seen throughout the Holy Land. None, however, exceeded the magnificent Temple he built both as a favor for the Jews and as a lasting tribute to himself.

Beginning in 20 B.C. Herod razed Zerubabbel's Temple and greatly enlarged the supporting platform to accommodate the imposing new structure. Because, according to the Torah, only priests were allowed inside the

Temple, 1,000 Levites were trained as stonemasons to build the Temple proper.

Work on Herod's Temple continued throughout Jesus' lifetime. It finally was completed and dedicated in 64 A.D. To the inconsolable dismay of the Jewish people, the Temple would stand for but a few short years, for it was destroyed in 70 A.D. at the conclusion of the First Jewish Revolt against Rome. Even the Roman armies, however, could not demolish the massive rectangular platform Herod had constructed as the Temple's base. That platform, almost 1,600 feet long and 1,050 feet wide, occupies fully a quarter of the area of Jerusalem's Old City. To stand next to the gigantic limestone blocks of the retaining wall is to be overwhelmed by the genius of Roman engineering. (This same period produced two other marvels of Roman architecture: the Pont du Gard viaduct in France, and the Colosseum in Rome.) Some of the Temple ashlars (squared stones) weigh hundreds of tons and were laid so skillfully—without cement or mortar—that after 2,000 years a piece of paper cannot be slid into many of the joints between the immense blocks. It remains a mystery to this day as to how the Roman engineers, under Herod's direction, built the Temple.

Noble Shrine

Centuries came and went. Nearly 600 years later Muslim armies marched into Palestine and the Caliph Omar claimed the ruined Temple Mount for Islam. The Muslims named it the *Haram esh-Sharif,* or noble sanctuary, and the Temple Mount would become the site of two of the most important shrines of Islam: the al-Aksa Mosque and the shrine of the Dome of the Rock. For the past 1,300 years these Muslim structures have stood on what is sacred ground for the Jewish people.

After regaining control over the Old City in 1967, the Israeli government decided, out of respect to the various religious traditions, to preserve the status quo over the holy sites of the city. This means that to the present day the Muslim *Wakf* (religious administration) retains control over the Temple Mount. This authority is guarded zealously. But while Israeli archaeologists are not permitted to conduct excavations of any kind on the Temple Mount, pious Jews continue to pray and hope for its eventual return to Jewish hands.

Many Christians as well as Jews believe that the current state of affairs on the Temple

Mount will one day change. Though opinion is divided, a number of biblical passages are thought to indicate that the Muslim edifices will somehow be removed in order to make way for the Temple to be rebuilt.

Recipe for Disaster

But will the al-Aksa and the Dome of the Rock actually cease to occupy their present locations? The consequences of such an event are almost unthinkable, as the destruction of the third-most-holy of Islamic places would immediately galvanize the Muslim world. The result, at the very least, would be a ferocious regional war. At worst, according to some observers, it could ignite a conflagration with the potential to metamorphose into world war. As we will note throughout this publication, the Book of Revelation calls this sort of final battle *Armageddon*.

Those who believe that the Jewish Temple is destined to be rebuilt point to the last eight chapters of the book of Ezekiel, which describe in great detail the measurements of a Temple without historic parallel. Will this future third Temple one day appear—or are these chapters intended to be taken symbolically?

Artist Gustav Doré captured the rebuilding of the Temple after the Babylonian captivity of the Jews.

Another cryptic passage is found in the prophetic book of Daniel, where a future "prince" is described; this figure, some biblical scholars believe, is the evil antichrist. Other biblical passages describe this satanically inspired, charismatic leader as a master of deception who will lead the armies of the world to battle in the land of Israel. The book of Daniel indicates that in the midst of the antichrist's brief yet incalculably destructive reign, he will conclude a peace treaty that he will himself later discard:

> "*He shall make a strong covenant with many for one week, and for half of the week* he shall make sacrifice and offering cease; *and in their place shall be an abomination that desolates, until the decreed end is poured out upon the desolator*"
>
> (*Daniel 9:27; emphasis added*).

Because the Hebrew word for "week" is "seven," many scholars hold that the "week" mentioned in Daniel refers to *seven years*. If so, this passage could refer to a seven-year period known as the Tribulation, when the earth will undergo unheard-of upheaval that culminates in the battle of Armageddon.

It is interesting to note that the "prince"—or ruler—will cause all "sacrifice and offering" to cease. Historically for the Jews, there is only one place where sacrifices and offerings are permitted to take place: at the Temple.

If this interpretation is correct, it indicates that in some form the Jewish Temple will be standing when the future antichrist is pursuing his evil designs. When discussing the period known as the Tribulation, Jesus warned his followers about the same ill omen: "So when you see the desolating sacrilege standing in the holy place, as was spoken of by the prophet Daniel (let the reader understand), then those in Judea must flee to the mountains (Matthew 24:15-16).

Again, to the Jewish mind the "Holy Place" could only mean the Temple. Many would argue that the events spoken of in Matthew 24 and Daniel 9 have not occurred at any time in history. The first revolt against Rome, ending with the destruction of Herod's Temple, indeed devastated the Jewish nation. The Jewish historian Josephus describes in ghastly detail this Roman siege of Jerusalem, which he reports as costing the lives of more than one million Jews. Yet even the horrific destruction levied against the Temple and Jerusalem in A.D. 70 did not fulfill Jesus' "holy place" prophecy recorded in Matthew 24. The same passage indicates that the desecration of the holy place, or Temple, will take place immediately preceding Christ's return to earth: "Then the sign of the Son of Man will appear in heaven, and then all the tribes of the earth will mourn, and they will see 'the Son of Man coming on the clouds of heaven' with power and great glory" (Matthew 24:30).

The apostle Paul, in his Letter to the Thessalonians, also mentions a Temple that will exist during the reign of the future antichrist:

> *"Let no one deceive you in any way; for that day will not come unless the rebellion comes first and the lawless one is revealed, the one destined for destruction. He opposes and exalts himself above every so-called god or object of worship, so* that he takes his seat in the temple of God, *declaring himself to be God"*
>
> *(2 Thessalonians 2:3-4, emphasis added).*

Once again we see the antichrist at a site called the "Temple," a structure that at the present time does not exist. Students of the Bible differ as to the exact nature of that future Temple, but much speculation, unsurprisingly, has focused on the Temple Mount in Jerusalem.

Violence of the Zealots

Unfortunately, the desire to see biblical prophecy fulfilled has sometimes taken a misguided and violent turn as individuals and extremist groups have attempted to take matters into their own hands. In 1969 a mentally disturbed Christian tourist set fire to the al-Aksa Mosque, believing that the Messiah would not come until all "abominations" had been cleared from the Temple Mount. That arson attempt severely damaged the interior of the mosque, destroying a priceless 1,000-year-old wood and ivory pulpit (minbar) that had been sent from Aleppo by the great Muslim general Saladin. The outraged Arab world angrily protested the senseless vandalism, which shortly became an international incident.

In 1982 a demented Israeli soldier went on a rampage in the al-Aksa Mosque, killing one

Lament and Plea

"Because of our sins we were exiled from our country and banished from our land. We cannot go up as pilgrims to worship Thee, to perform our duties in Thy chosen house, the great and Holy Temple which was called by Thy name, on account of the hand that was let loose on Thy sanctuary. May it be Thy will, Lord our God and God of our fathers, merciful King, in Thy abundant love again to have mercy on us and on Thy sanctuary; rebuild it speedily and magnify its glory" (from *The Jewish Prayer Book*).

Arab and wounding several others. At his trial he claimed he had expected to become "King of the Jews" by liberating the Temple Mount.

Since that date Israeli police have foiled numerous attempts by Jewish extremists to destroy the Muslim buildings on the Temple Mount. The most serious of these occurred in 1984, when a heavily armed band of men carrying explosives was narrowly prevented from blowing up the Dome of the Rock.

Although a dangerously touchy subject, the desire of fervent Israelis to see a restoration of the Temple Mount to Jewish control and worship continues to intensify. The most deadly incident occurred in 1990, when an attempt by radical Jews to flout the Muslim Wakf and lay the "cornerstone" of the rebuilt Temple led to a riot on the Temple Mount. Twenty-two Muslim Arabs died in the ensuing clash with police, and hundreds were injured.

The medieval Jewish sage Maimonedes, in his *Code of Jewish Law,* argued that every generation of Jews was obliged to maintain the Temple in Jerusalem if it is in existence—and to rebuild it speedily if it is not. Mindful of his words, growing numbers of Orthodox Jews are making preparations in anticipation of a rebuilt Temple. In the Jewish Quarter of the Old City, priests are being trained in yeshivas (rabbinical schools) for Temple service. Orthodox Jewish scholars are attempting to meticulously replicate the ritual implements used in Temple worship.

The Talmud states that the Temple is one of the "Seven Secrets" hidden in the blueprints of Creation, and that it was part of the Divine plan from the very foundation of the world. If so, then we may not have heard the last of this remarkable and mysterious hallowed ground, which elicits passionate and conflicting sentiments from so many.

WHAT IS THE RAPTURE?

The date is sometime in the future. The world has reached a state of crisis as the result of hitherto unimaginable natural disasters, economic collapse, and social disintegration. The peace and prosperity of the civilized nations have evaporated, replaced everywhere by a dark, ominous foreboding. In the midst of the unparalleled turmoil a controversial political leader arises who promises to establish a New World Order that will deliver the nations from the anarchy threatening the planet.

But there is a price, which many cannot understand and that offends their sensibilities. As a visible sign of the new trans-ethnic, multicultural unity he intends to establish, this new leader demands that the peoples of the world set aside their separate religious views and collectively participate in an act of worship, bowing before an enormous statue symbolizing the Human Spirit.

Frantic for the restoration of peace and order, the vast majority set aside their uneasiness and agree to participate. Faithful Jews and Christians, however, recognize such a demand as idolatrous and refuse to bow before the image. This earns them the wrath of the political leader, who orders their executions.

Suddenly the planet is thrown into chaos as millions around the world abruptly disappear. Terror spreads when it is realized that the vanished people were those who had refused to worship the image. To resist, then, is to invite the ultimate punishment. Enraged, the political leader embarks upon systematic programs of oppression and military campaigns against any who would stand in his way. Obviously, the leader is a fiend who will not allow himself to be defied. It becomes horrifyingly clear to increasing numbers that, desperate for a solution to their appalling predicament, they have made a pact with the Devil himself.

Interpreting the Rapture

This hypothetical scenario is anything but imaginary to millions of Christians, who believe that a period of great tribulation will one day descend upon the earth. There is, to be sure, a wide range of opinion among biblical scholars as to the nature and precise order of the prophetic events described in the Bible. Many prefer to interpret such dire passages symbolically, and find their specific referents as already past, relegated to the end of time, or never to be taken literally.

Others, however, remain convinced that the Bible consistently foretells a brief but unavoidable Dark Age yet ahead, followed by the return of Jesus Christ and the establishment of the Kingdom of God. And key to the beliefs of many is a teaching unknown through much of the history of Church: that before the onset of this period of tribulation believers will be removed from the planet in a secret "rapture."

The roots of this widespread teaching have been traced to Port Glasgow Scotland in 1830, where a young Scottish woman named Margaret MacDonald experienced a startling revelation while dangerously sick and confined to her bed. In her vision, Margaret claimed to have learned that prior to the period of tribulation a select group of Christians would be mysteriously caught up in the air—or "raptured"— to meet Christ, thus escaping the evil devices of the antichrist.

Rev. Edward Irving

News of MacDonald's novel teaching about a rapture gradually spread, and caught the interest of a Scottish Presbyterian pastor named Edward Irving. Irving had already won notoriety for his deviant theological ideas, such as his teaching that Jesus' earthly nature was sinful—an opinion that eventually earned him the charge of apostasy and subsequent excommunication. Despite the controversies surrounding him, the charismatic preacher attracted crowds so large that a new church was built in central London at Regent Square to accommodate the throngs who came to hear him.

Irving taught that the Return of Jesus Christ to earth was to be expected momentarily, and that the Second Coming would be preceded by miraculous signs and gifts. In what was an unusual departure from the staid worship of those days, Irving encouraged the practice of glossolia ("speaking in tongues") and other "spiritual gifts," such as prophecy and healing. Irving embraced Margaret MacDonald's allegedly divinely revealed new teaching about the rapture, and began to promote it.

Edward Irving and his followers would soon fade from the scene, but the commotion stirred up by the new teaching attracted the third and most-influential figure in the propagation of the rapture teaching. John Nelson Darby was the ordained son of a naval commander who fought with Admiral Horatio Nelson. The younger Darby left the Church of Ireland in 1825 to join a sect called the Brethren, which rejected the hierarchical structure of the Church of Ireland in favor of locally controlled congregations.

Hearing about the new teaching popularized by Irving, Darby decided to investigate for himself. Traveling to the Glasgow home of Margaret MacDonald, he was introduced to the purported biblical basis for this teaching. Although Darby rejected the manifestations of "spiritual gifts" that he witnessed in meetings at MacDonald's home, he nevertheless accepted the teaching about the secret rapture of the church. Darby was to become an influential proponent of the rapture doctrine via preaching and extensive travel that occupied him for the rest of his life. In later years he toured the United States, where his rapture teaching found a wide audience among the privileged and dispossessed alike.

The belief in a rapture, as taught by Darby and later advocates, is based upon passages in chapter 24 of the book of Matthew, in which Jesus gives a discourse concerning future events to his disciples, comparing the end of the age with the days of Noah:

> *"For as the days of Noah were, so will be the coming of the Son of Man. For as in those days before the flood they were eating and drinking, marrying and giving in marriage, until the day Noah entered the ark, and they knew nothing until the flood came and swept them all away, so too will be the coming of the Son of Man. Then two will be in the field; one will be taken and one will be left. Two women will be grinding meal together; one will be taken and one will be left. Keep awake therefore, for you do not know on what day your Lord is coming" (Matthew 24:37-42).*

Darby and others saw the rapture portrayed in the description of one laborer suddenly and unexpectedly being taken away while the other is left behind. Later commentators, however, held that this passage refers not to a secret rapture but to the judgment following the Second Coming of Christ. In other words, the passage speaks of those who will be "taken away," not to meet the Lord in the sky but for judgment.

Sinners and Believers

For many Bible students, a key element of the rapture is that the coming tribulation is meant for the wicked, not for true believers, who will evade it with divine assistance. One verse said to support this belief is found in the parallel account of Jesus' discourse in the Gospel of Luke, where we read: "Be alert at all times, praying that you may have the strength to escape all these things that will take place, and to stand before the Son of Man" (Luke 21:36).

This verse, however, highlights two opposing views regarding the destiny of true believers during the coming tribulation. The "pretribulational" rapture view holds that

Caught Up in the Clouds

A biblical reference most commonly used to support the idea of true believers being suddenly taken to heaven, or "raptured," is found in St. Paul's First Letter to the Thessalonians. The passage is, well, *rapturous,* promising generous rewards for Christian souls of the dead and the living. Others, however, claim that this passage describes not a secret rapture but an event associated with the Second Coming of Christ, which, far from being hidden, will be visible to all the peoples of the earth:

"But we do not want you to be uninformed, brothers and sisters, about those who have died, so that you may not grieve as others do who have no hope. For since we believe that Jesus died and rose again, even so, through Jesus, God will bring with him those who have died. For this we declare to you by the word of the Lord, that we who are alive, who are left until the coming of the Lord, will by no means precede those who have died. For the Lord himself, with a cry of command, with the archangel's call and with the sound of God's trumpet, will descend from heaven, and the dead in Christ will rise first. Then we who are alive, who are left, will be caught up in the clouds together with them to meet the Lord in the air; and so we will be with the Lord forever. Therefore encourage one another with these words"

(1 Thessalonians 4:13-18).

"escape" means to be literally and physically transported to heaven. Those who do not accept this view of the rapture claim that this verse could just as easily refer to the divine protection of believers in the midst of the terrible events unfolding on planet earth.

A passage, which at first glance appears to teach a rapture, is found in 1 Thessalonians, where St. Paul encourages the Thessalonian believers not to despair at the death of their loved ones, for they will one day be reunited. First, according to Paul, will come the resurrection of the departed faithful. Then those who remain alive will be "caught up in the clouds together with them to meet the Lord in the air; and so we will be with the Lord forever" (1 Thessalonians 4:17).

As with the other supposed "rapture" passages, this verse has been contested by those who deny that it refers to a secret or hidden event. In the previous verse, for example, we see that this event is preceded by the "archangel's call" and "the sound of God's trumpet," followed by Christ's descent from the heavens. In other passages the sound of a trumpet is clearly associated with the Second Coming of Christ in the clouds. As described in the book of Revelation, the return of Christ, far from being a veiled event, will be viewed by people everywhere: "Look! He is coming with the clouds; every eye will see him, even those who pierced him; and on his account all the tribes of the earth will wail. So it is to be. Amen" (Revelation 1:7).

The passage in Thessalonians and the other texts said to refer to a secret rapture continue to be debated among students of Bible prophecy. As with so many biblical passages—prophecies in particular—multiple interpretations are not merely possible, but likely and, given the evidence, often reasonable. Whatever their view about the rapture, however, virtually all Christians look forward to this return of Christ, which will put an end to the final rebellion led by the antichrist and usher in an everlasting kingdom of peace.

The Seven Churches of Revelation

It was on the barren island of Patmos in the Aegean Sea where, according to early Christian tradition, the Apostle John experienced his stunning revelations about the end of the world. These insights are related in the biblical book of Revelation. John had been banished to the island, a common punishment used by the Romans for a variety of offenses, including the practice of magic and astrology. Prophecy, whether pagan, Jewish, or Christian, was included in the same category. It is thought that John was imprisoned on Patmos during the time of the persecution of Christians instituted by the Emperor Domitian (81-96 A.D.).

The mind-boggling visions of the end of the world that are related in Revelation came to John on the island of Patmos.

The meaning of the esoteric visions given to John has long captivated the imaginations of scholars and Bible students: Does the book of Revelation pertain to events in the Apostle's day; to various eras throughout history since the first century; to the cataclysmic end of time yet in the future—or perhaps to a cryptic amalgam of all of these?

In the first chapter of the book John states that he was in the spirit on the Lord's day when he heard "a loud voice like a trumpet" commanding him: "Write in a book what you see and send it to the seven churches, to Ephesus, to Smyrna, to Pergamum, to Thyatira, to Sardis, to Philadelphia, and to Laodicea'" (Revelation 1:11).

When John turned to see who was speaking to him, he experienced an awe-inspiring vision of the Son of Man, who offered this by way of introduction: "I am the first and the last, and the living one. I was dead, and see, I am alive forever and ever; and I have the keys of Death and of Hades. Now write what you have seen . . . ." (Revelation 1:17-19).

So far there can be little doubt that John experienced a vision of the resurrected Christ. But the divergence of opinion regarding the interpretation of Revelation has been inspired by chapters two and three, when a series of specific prophecies is directed toward each of the seven churches. Are these churches to be interpreted literally or symbolically?

Route to Revelation

One approach considered the seven churches, with their individual strengths and weaknesses, to be symbolic of different types of churches throughout the ages. The strength of this view is that Christians of every historical period can apply at least one of the seven churches to their own situation. A weakness of this approach is that the natural tendency is to identify one's own church with those that are more positively commended.

In a variant of this symbolic approach, others see a historical progression of seven distinct ages throughout Church history, with each of the churches representing one age. Unfortunately, few proponents of this interpretation have agreed on the identification of each of the supposed seven ages. As the centuries passed, the "ages" would either be elongated or others added and subtracted from the list. Furthermore, it is difficult to see the practical application of this approach, for each letter would be relevant only to those living in a particular historical period.

Other interpret chapters two and three of Revelation literally, while allowing that the exhortations given to each of the seven churches apply generally to churches throughout all ages. The seven churches—Ephesus, Smyrna, Pergamum, Thyatira, Sardis, Philadelphia, and Laodicea—are prominent cities located in Asia Minor (modern Turkey).

The remains of each of these cities may be seen in the order corresponding to that found in Revelation, along an ancient, circuitous route in southwest Asia Minor. It is thought that the early evangelists traveled along this route, preaching the Gospel and establishing churches.

The first church mentioned is that residing in Ephesus, known to us through the writings of Paul, who spent more than two years ministering in this large and prosperous city. At the time of Paul, Ephesus was thought to be the fourth-largest city in the world, with an estimated population of 250,000. The city was also a center for the Roman Imperial cult and must have presented considerable temptations to Christians to compromise their faith for social or economic advancement. It may be that their earlier fervor that marked the time of Paul had begun to wane. Thus we read the admonishment:

> *"But I have this against you, that you have abandoned the love you had at first. Remember then from what you have fallen; repent, and do the works you did at first. If not, I will come to you and remove your lampstand from its place, unless you repent"* *(Revelation 2:4-5).*

The next city along the route, and the next to be mentioned in Revelation, is Smyrna, located on the coast north of Ephesus. Smyrna, one of only two of the seven churches that received

Ruins of Pergamum, the third city on the route described in Revelation.

no negative admonition, was warned nevertheless about the "synagogue of Satan," an apparent reference to Jews who were opposed to the Church of the city. In 160 A.D. the city's hostility toward the resident Christians erupted into open persecution. The elderly Polycarp, Bishop of Smyrna, became an early martyr of the church. Given one last chance to recant and save his life, the venerable bishop uttered his famous testimony: "For eighty-six years I have been his servant, and he has never done me wrong: how can I blaspheme my King who saved me?"

Pergamum, lying some 50 miles northeast of Smyrna along the ancient Asia Minor route, is the third city mentioned in Revelation. Pergamum was a center of Greek culture and boasted a library of more than 200,000 volumes. It is in the letter to the church at Pergamum that we find the mysterious reference to Satan's throne, the meaning of which is unclear. It may refer to the spectacular great altar

Let Everyone Who Has an Ear Listen!

This exhortation is repeated in the revelation given to John concerning seven churches of Asia. The following letter to the church at Ephesus exhibits the mixture of commendation and admonishment found in each of the seven letters:

"To the angel of the church in Ephesus write: These are the words of him who holds the seven stars in his right hand, who walks among the seven golden lampstands:

"I know your works, your toil and your patient endurance. I know that you cannot tolerate evildoers; you have tested those who claim to be apostles but are not, and have found them to be false.

"I also know that you are enduring patiently and bearing up for the sake of my name, and that you have not grown weary.

"But I have this against you, that you have abandoned the love you had at first.

"Remember then from what you have fallen; repent, and do the works you did at first. If not, I will come to you and remove your lampstand from its place, unless you repent.

"Yet this is to your credit: you hate the works of the Nicolaitans, which I also hate.

"Let anyone who has an ear listen to what the Spirit is saying to the churches. To everyone who conquers, I will give permission to eat from the tree of life that is in the paradise of God" (Revelation 2:1-7).

of Zeus situated prominently on a mountain overlooking the city.

It is interesting that the longest of the seven letters is addressed to the least important of the cities, Thyatira, a center of manufacturing with active trade guilds. It is likely that the temptation to participate in the pagan rites practiced by these guilds lies behind the admonition to avoid "the deep things of Satan." Here also we meet the seductive prophetess Jezebel, who had apparently infiltrated the church of Thyatira with her idolatrous teachings.

The fifth city, wealthy Sardis, was located 45 miles east of Thyatira along the route. The warning to be watchful was especially appropriate for the people of Sardis: "Remember then what you received and heard; obey it, and repent. If you do not wake up, I will come like a thief, and you will not know at what hour I will come to you" (Revelation 3:3).

In 549 B.C. the Persian conqueror Cyrus captured Sardis by sending one of his soldiers up a crevice to the mountain fortress. Two centuries later the city was stealthily conquered by soldiers loyal to Alexander the Great.

Thirty miles beyond Sardis lies Philadelphia, the sixth city along the circuitous route across southwest Asia Minor. A prosperous agricultural and industrial city, Philadelphia suffered a series of devastating earthquakes earlier in the first century. Thus, the promise that the Philadelphians would become like an unshakable pillar in the new Jerusalem was suspect, especially given the city's history.

The final city along the route, Laodicea, was the wealthiest city in the Roman province of Phrygia. Yet Revelation criticizes the Laodiceans for their spiritual poverty: "Therefore I counsel you to buy from me gold refined by fire so that you may be rich; and white robes to clothe you and to keep the shame of your nakedness from being seen; and salve to anoint your eyes so that you may see" (Revelation 3:18). (The city was famous for its medical school, and produced an eye-salve made from a mixture of a substance called "Phrygian powder" and olive oil.) The reference to eye salve is a clear metaphoric allusion to the spiritual blindness of the Laodiceans.

The nature of the prophecies is so remarkable that their relevance probably is not restricted to a particular time and place. Both the commendations and admonitions can easily be directed to churches existing at other times and places.

SIGNS OF THE TIMES

As we have seen, the Hebrew prophets foresaw an ominous period at the end of human history known as the Day of the Lord, a time of unprecedented natural disasters and other frightening signs preceding divine judgment upon the world. For these sages the future did not hold a period of uninterrupted peace and prosperity, but rather stark terrors directed against those who had rebelled against God. Yet, as the night is darkest before the dawn, the Day of the Lord would usher in the everlasting Kingdom of God.

In the week preceding his crucifixion, as he gathered with his disciples on the Mount of Olives overlooking the city of Jerusalem, Jesus spoke about the end of the age. He had just given his dire prediction of the destruction of the Jewish temple, prompting his followers to ask: "Tell us, when will this be, and what will be the sign of your coming and of the end of the age?" (Matthew 24:3).

Jesus responds to this question by giving a list of apocalyptic "signs" that will precede a time of "great suffering" and "tribulation." In recent years, many students of Bible prophecy have perceived the beginning of the fulfillment of Jesus prophecy in our time. Such speculation has been found throughout Christian church history, but many Bible students today believe that the Bible's signs about the future point to our own day.

The parallels between Jesus' words and events in the modern world appear uncanny to many. The first sign concerns false Messiahs who would claim to be Jesus Christ, and who would "lead many astray." Recently, a number of eastern mystics with followings in the West have claimed to be Jesus Christ returned to earth. In the 1970s, for instance, Guru Maharaji, the teenaged "enlightened master" from India, claimed to be the "Christ." The follow-

Maharaji

ers of Maharaji pointed to the words of Jesus concerning his Second Coming to earth: "Then the sign of the Son of Man will appear in heaven, and then all the tribes of the earth will mourn, and they will see the Son of Man coming on the clouds of heaven with power and great glory" (Matthew 24:30). This prophecy was fulfilled, it was claimed, when Maharaji descended from the sky (in a 747 jetliner) to London's Heathrow airport. But subsequent verses, which describe the blast of an angelic trumpet call heard throughout the earth, as well as other mysterious phenomena, were conveniently ignored by Maharaji's followers.

In April 1982, newspaper readers across the United States and Canada were startled to see a full-page advertisement announcing: "THE CHRIST IS NOW HERE." This time the would-be Christ was a shadowy personage called Lord Maitreya, said to be connected with a militant Pakistani Islamic sect. Followers claimed that their Messiah would announce himself via television. However, Lord Maitreya remained in seclusion in East London and made no public appearances. If he was the Messiah, he was a shy and retiring one.

Jesus Warns Us

Ironically, Jesus himself warned against those who hide from public view while claiming to be the Messiah:

> *"Then if anyone says to you, 'Look! Here is the Messiah!' or 'There he is!' – do not believe it.... So, if they say to you, 'Look! He is in the wilderness,' do not go out. If they say, 'Look! He is in the inner rooms,' do not believe it. For as the lightning comes from the east and flashes as far as the west, so will be the coming of the Son of Man"* (Matthew 24:23,26,27).

Jesus' words indicate that the Second Coming will be an unmistakable event that will be recognized immediately throughout the world.

The Endless Threat of War

A second sign of the end of the age given by Jesus is that of "wars and rumors of wars." Despite great advances in industrialization, technology, and the quality of life in many countries, the twentieth century has been marked by almost ceaseless warfare. At least 15 million soldiers were casualties and untold numbers of civilians perished on the European continent when, for the first time in history, great nations participated in what came to be called World War I.

The war ended in 1918. A year later President Woodrow Wilson's ill-fated League of Nations was formed with the noble aim of ensuring that the worldwide conflict just concluded would be recalled as "the war to end all wars." The League was a dismal failure, and a mere 20 years later the world erupted in another war, and one that would become the costliest war in history. World War II destroyed an estimated 50 million lives—a horrendous loss exceeding that of any combination of wars that occurred before the twentieth century.

Events of the postwar years have not brought every nation the elusive goal of peace. Despite the peace efforts of the United Nations, other organizations, and individuals, the world remains a violent place. Dozens of major conflicts have erupted around the globe since 1945. And although the Cold War cooled with the collapse of the Soviet Union, the United States and Russia—joined by a growing number of other nations—continue to maintain huge stockpiles of nuclear weapons, many of which are a thousand times more powerful than the American bomb dropped on Hiroshima, Japan, in 1945. We see in our day the potential for a worldwide conflagration that many think would be similar to that described in the prophecies of the Bible.

Another sign mentioned by Jesus indicative of the time of the end is that of "famines and earthquakes in diverse places." Those who live in the technologically advanced West tend to assume that poverty and disease around the world are steadily yielding to modern medicine and science. In reality, the decade of the 1980s actually saw a sharp increase in poverty levels as per capita income in many Third World countries plummeted.

Recent studies by the United Nations have pointed to one major reason why the battle against starvation is being lost: rampant, uncontrolled arms spending. The governments of an alarming number of Third World countries select to slash spending on health and education in order to divert scarce resources to arms purchases. Billions of dollars in Western loans have been squandered.

Some countries in Africa, for example, spend from 30 percent to an astounding 70 percent of revenues on their respective military forces and debt repayment, leaving little for health, agriculture, and education. The situation becomes all the more appalling when one considers how many illnesses, particularly those that affect children, are easily treatable. Despite these facts, Third World countries are anxious to purchase arms—and the West is only too eager to sell.

A direct link of famine to military conflict is clear. Governments of nations filled with hungry, ill people are often willing to fight in order to survive. Eastern Europe and Africa are just two regions dotted with bloody conflicts that victimize hundreds of thousands. It is no surprise that Jesus mentions wars and famine together, or that the second of the "Four Horsemen of the Apocalypse" described in the book of Revelation is followed by the third horseman, War.

Natural Disaster

Lack of water is another factor that contributes to famine. Without rainfall or other sources of fresh water, there can be no crops. The lack of water and the specter of starvation threaten nations just as surely as foolish leaders or outside aggression. It is almost inevitable that worldwide water shortages and the accompanying famines will drive nations into armed conflict with each other. Nowhere is the danger more apparent than in today's Middle East, where water usage by Israel and her Arab neighbors exceeds the available supply.

Water played a role in one of the major (and most dramatic) Arab-Israeli wars, the 1967 "Six-Day War" that was handily won by Israel. Syria's president,

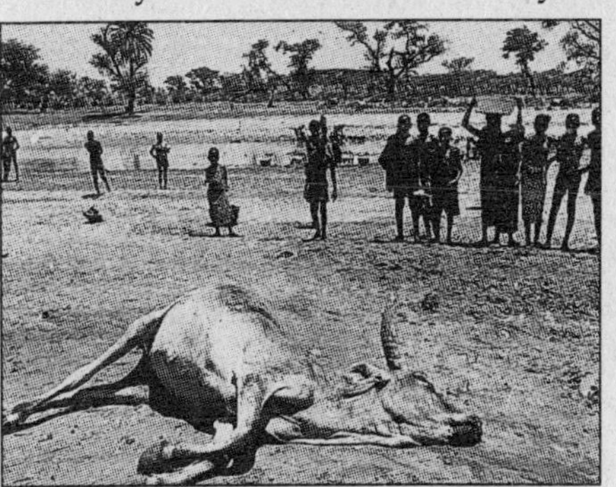

Drought is a specter across the globe, and contributes to famine and war.

Hafez al-Assad, had been pressing forward with a plan to divert to areas throughout Syria water that originated on Syria's Golan Heights. Because these springs fed into the Sea of Galilee, Israel's primary source of water, Israel viewed this development with great alarm. When war broke out in June of that year, the Israeli Army secured the Golan Heights and another primary source of Israel's water, the heights of Mount Hermon.

With Israel understandably reluctant to yield control of its major water sources—the lifeblood of its agricultural economy—the likelihood of a peaceful resolution between that nation and her Arab neighbors appears dim. Some Bible students wonder whether the acute lack of water in the lands of the Bible will lead to the final confrontation referred to in the Bible as Armageddon.

Existing quite apart from water, and one of the most foreboding of all natural phenomena, is earthquakes, which have increased frighteningly in recent years. In northern Iran in 1990, for instance, more than 35,000 people were killed and 400,000 injured by a quake measuring 7.7 on the Richter scale. And in Tangshan, China, in 1976 more than 250,000 perished in two massive quakes that rocked the Richter scale to a reading of 7.8. This incident was one

Earthquakes, such as one that struck China in 1976, have proliferated in the last two decades.

of the worst natural disasters in human history.

Seismologists compare earthquake activity to the breakup of ice on a frozen lake during spring thaw, with each crack signaling more to follow. No more apt metaphoric description of this process can be found than in the epistle of Paul to the Romans: "We know that the whole creation has been groaning in labor pains until now" (Romans 8:22).

Just as the increase of labor pains means that birth is near, some regard the breaking up of the earth's crust as a signal that the end of the age is approaching. True to the prophecy of Jesus, earthquakes are happening in "diverse places," including regions with no previous record of seismic activity.

Until 1960, for example, there had not been one single measurable earthquake in the state of Colorado. However, since that time seismic equipment has detected several thousand earthquakes where none had been measured before. The astounding increase in seismic activity worldwide is a startling phenomena—and for many an indication that human history is writing its final chapter.

Persecution and Tribulation

Jesus gave yet another sign of the end of the age: the persecution of his followers, who will be "handed over to be tortured and will be put to death" (Matthew 24:9). Such oppression usually is associated with the early period of the Church, until the Roman empire became Christianized. The stark fact, though, is that more people have been put to death for their religious faith in the twentieth century than ever before. Although much of the formerly Communist world is now democratized, China, North Korea, and other nations continue to restrict religious expression. In some Muslim countries, conversion to another faith is a punishable offense. Persecution also is increasing in nations that have traditions of religious tolerance. In India, for example, the rise of Hindu nationalism has brought with it a growing hostility toward the Muslim and Christian minorities. Fringe groups in the

And Then the End Will Come

In the week prior to his crucifixion, Jesus took his disciples to a hillside overlooking the imposing Jewish temple. He had just prophesied the destruction of that great edifice, and his followers queried him regarding this and other events to come:

"Jesus answered them, 'Beware that no one leads you astray. For many will come in my name, saying, 'I am the Messiah!' and they will lead many astray. And you will hear of wars and rumors of wars; see that you are not alarmed; for this must take place, but the end is not yet. For nation will rise against nation, and kingdom against kingdom, and there will be famines and earthquakes in various places: all this is but the beginning of

the birth pangs. Then they will hand you over to be tortured and will put you to death, and you will be hated by all nations because of my name. Then many will fall away, and they will betray one another and hate one another. And many false prophets will arise and lead many astray. And because of the increase of lawlessness, the love of many will grow cold. But the one who endures to the end will be saved.'" (Matthew 24:4-13).

United States and western Europe are responsible for hateful attacks upon Jews and other religious minorities. But although the battle rages, Jesus predicts that in the midst of the persecution "the good news of the kingdom will be proclaimed throughout the world, as a testimony to the nations" (Matthew 24:14).

Following a description of the general signs of war, famine, earthquake, and persecution, Jesus then gives a specific portent of the impending time of danger: "So when you see the desolating sacrilege standing in the holy place, as was spoken of by the prophet Daniel (let the reader understand)" (Matthew 24:15).

The caveat "let the reader understand" is well-taken, for one of the mysterious aspects of prophecy is that the texts often have dual references. That is, a prophecy may apply to a historical event that will occur in the near future, but may also have a greater fulfillment in the *far* future. Many believe that Jesus is referring to the destruction of the temple, an event that occurred in 70 A.D., while at the same time looking ahead to the end of time when yet another "desolating sacrilege" (or "Abomination of Desolation") will take place. As previously discussed, the book of Daniel describes an earlier Abomination of Desolation perpetrated by Antiochus (Epiphanes) IV, who constructed a pagan altar on the Temple Mount, an outrage that led to the Maccabean revolt.

Scholars have puzzled over the reference to another Abomination of Desolation. Since the defilement supposedly takes place in the Jewish temple, this prophecy appears to indicate that the edifice will one day be rebuilt. In recent years there has been a flurry of speculation that the temple will be rebuilt soon; however, many of the rumors proved to be ill-founded. Other scholars point out that the Israeli government has ceded control of the Temple Mount to the Muslim religious authorities. The attempt to build a Jewish structure would likely prod the surrounding Arab nations to war in order to defend the honor of what they consider to be their holy site.

One can readily visualize how the various signs mentioned by Jesus could lead to a worldwide crisis and cataclysm of unprecedented proportions. This period, known as the Tribulation, is in itself a prelude to the final days of human history.

Future Shock: The Great Tribulation

The fearful signs in the heavens and upon the earth sound like the apocalypse itself but are, however, only the prelude. According to Jesus, these apocalyptic signs will usher in a time of "great suffering" (or "tribulation"), "such as has not been from the beginning of the world until now, no, and never will be" (Matthew 24:21).

As with other cryptic prophetic texts, biblical scholars disagree as to what is meant by the tribulation. Some see it as a historical reference to the end of the first century—the time of the writing of the book of Revelation— when Christians faced persecution under the Roman emperor Diocletian. Others take such references to be symbolic of the tribulation that believers have faced throughout history.

Still others perceive passages such as these as references to a unique period of brief but intense and horrific oppression at the very end of human history. Indeed, these words of Jesus, some scholars believe, signify an unprecedented series of events that will be unmatched either before or afterwards.

The Time of Anguish

The Hebrew seers gave indications of such a time. At the conclusion of his prophecy Daniel warned: "There shall be a time of anguish, such as has never occurred since nations first came into existence" (Daniel 12:1). Malachi called this frightful stage of human history "the great and terrible day of the Lord" (Malachi 4:5).

In the third chapter of Revelation the church at Philadelphia is promised deliverance: "Because you have kept my word of patient endurance, I will keep you from the hour of trial that is coming on the whole world to test the inhabitants of the earth" (Revelation 3:10).

Some take this as an indication that believers will escape the tribulation through the rapture; others note that this promise is given to only one of the seven churches (Philadelphia) and thus should not be taken to refer to all Christians.

While interpretation of Revelation 3:10 remains a matter of considerable dispute, the passage nonetheless sets forth the ultimate purpose of the tribulation as an "hour of trial" and "test" for the "inhabitants of the earth." During this period many will repent of their sins and gain eternal life, often at the cost of their mortal lives. Many others, however, will continue in their defiance, despite suffering the torment of divine judgment, as borne out by references in the text to the "inhabitants of the earth."

Four Riders

In the book of Revelation the visions of the judgments inflicted upon the earth are often couched in cryptic symbolism. One such description takes the form of four ominous horses and their riders, the identities of which have been the subject of much discussion among biblical scholars. John describes his vision of the first horse: "Then I saw the Lamb

The opening of the sixth seal provokes a violent and ominous reaction from the heavens.

open one of the seven seals, and I heard one of the four living creatures call out, as with a voice of thunder, 'Come!' I looked, and there was a white horse! Its rider had a bow; a crown was given to him, and he came out conquering and to conquer" (Revelation 6:1-2).

Because of a later appearance in Revelation 19 of Jesus Christ astride a white horse, some believe that Christ is also in view here. However, a number of differences between the two visions and the fact that the rider holds a bow have led other scholars to propose that the white horse and rider signify conquest.

At the time of the writing of Revelation, the most feared enemies of Rome were the Parthians, the successors to the Persian empire (modern Iran). The Parthians were the most famous archers of antiquity, and in 62 A.D. used their martial arts to afflict an unprecedented defeat upon a Roman army.

It was not until 117 A.D., under the Emperor Hadrian, that Rome was able to subdue its formidable enemy in the East. For John, likely writing around 90-95 A.D., the symbol of a mounted archer would have been a fitting symbol for military aggression, thus echoing the prediction of Jesus concerning "wars and rumors of wars."

John then sees a second horse and rider: "When he opened the second seal, I heard the second living creature call out, 'Come!' And out came another horse, bright red; its rider was permitted to take peace from the earth, so that people would slaughter one another; and he was given a great sword" (Revelation 6:3-4).

There is little dispute that the color of this horse corresponds to its bloody mission. Some believe that the first horse symbolizes external invasion and the red horse refers to civil disorder and a general increase of the level of violence within society. The Hebrew prophet Zechariah refers to such a time: "On that day a great panic from the Lord shall fall on them, so that each will seize the hand of a neighbor, and the hand of the one will be raised against the hand of the other" (Zechariah 14:13).

Close on the heels of the red horse comes another: "When he opened the third seal, I heard the third living creature call out, 'Come!'

I looked, and there was a black horse! Its rider held a pair of scales in his hand, and I heard what seemed to be a voice in the midst of the four living creatures saying, 'A quart of wheat for a day's pay, and three quarts of barley for a day's pay, but do not damage the olive oil and the wine!'" (Revelation 6:5-6).

The black horse and rider are commonly taken to symbolize famine and the accompanying escalation of the cost of food. The interpretation of the command to not damage the olive oil and the wine has often been colored by modern Western thinking, where olive oil and wine are comparative luxuries. Accordingly, some have interpreted this verse as referring to social inequity during the time of tribulation, in which the poor starve while the rich are not deprived of their "dainties."

In the ancient world, however, olive oil and wine were not luxuries but among the basic commodities of life. Understood this way, the phrase "do not damage the olive oil and the wine" may mean that by divine decree the famine will be limited, and will not lead to a lack of the basic necessities of life. Another historical reference is of interest here: At the time of the writing of Revelation the emperor Domitian had taken strong measures to stabilize the price of wine. These included a decree issued in 92 A.D. calling for the destruction of half of the vineyards in the provinces. In a land and time in which wine was a staple element of daily life, the order was hugely unpopular, and was ultimately rescinded.

The Horseman, Death

Finally, John describes the fourth, and last, horse and rider:

> *"When he opened the fourth seal, I heard the voice of the fourth living creature call out, 'Come!' I looked and there was a pale green horse! Its rider's name was Death, and Hades followed with him; they were given authority over a fourth of the earth, to kill with sword, famine, and pestilence, and by the wild animals of the earth"*
>
> *(Revelation 6:1-8).*

The color of the horse indicates the pallor of death or the blanched look of one seized with terror. Here we see the culmination of the previous three horse-and-rider judgments, as well as a foreboding prophecy: One quarter of the population of the world is destined to perish either by the sword, famine, pestilence, or from attack by wild animals.

The Lost Generation

Throughout the terrible ordeals described in the book of Revelation we find scattered references to a class of people described as "the inhabitants of the earth." These are the majority of humankind who are deceived by the antichrist into joining the final rebellion against God. Inherently weak and gullible, and lacking in essential good judgment, they are, in a word, *human,* and easy prey for the temptations of evil. Their foolishness has put them in an absurdly dangerous position.

As inconceivable as it may sound, Revelation indicates that such people will take an active part in the persecution of the faithful. John, the author of the book, describes in his vision of heaven, "I saw under the altar the souls of those who had been slaughtered for the word of God and for the testimony they had given; they cried out with a loud voice, 'Sovereign Lord, holy and true, how long will it be before you judge and avenge our blood on the inhabitants of the earth?'" (Revelation 6:9-10).

The disobedience on the part of many brings a fearful divine retribution, which causes the inhabitants of the earth to recoil in terror:

> *"Then the kings of the earth and the magnates and the generals and the rich and the powerful, and everyone, slave and free, hid in the caves and among the rocks of the mountains, calling to the mountains and rocks, 'Fall on us and hide us from the face of the one seated on the throne and from the wrath of the Lamb'"*
>
> *(Revelation 6:15-16).*

All attempts at concealment from the Divine presence are futile. Yet as the scale of the horrific judgments increases, we find inexplicable defiance from those living on the earth:

> *"The fourth angel poured his bowl on the sun, and it was allowed to scorch them with fire; they were scorched by the fierce heat, but they cursed the name of God, who had authority over these plagues, and they did not repent and give him glory. The fifth angel poured his bowl on the throne of the beast, and its kingdom was plunged into darkness; people gnawed their tongues in agony, and cursed the God of heaven because of their pains and sores, and they did not repent of their deeds"*
>
> *(Revelation 16:8-11).*

Still later, the inhabitants of the earth are pummeled with "huge hailstones, each weighing about a hundred pounds, dropped from heaven on people." Once again, instead of repenting, people "cursed God for the plague of the hail, so fearful was that plague" (Revelation 16:21).

The reason for the people's expression of contempt becomes clear at the end of the book of Revelation, where these individuals are identified as "the inhabitants of the earth, whose names have not been written in the book of life from the foundation of the world" (Revelation 17:8). The "book of life" contains the names of all the saved. According to Revelation, those who are not inscribed in it are without hope, for "anyone whose name was not found written in the book of life was thrown into the lake of fire" (Revelation 20:15).

Disease and Catastrophe

In this age of sophisticated science it is easy to consider "pestilence" and unnatural science as things of the past. Nothing could be further from the truth. The World Health Organization and the Centers for Disease Control, among other organizations, have collected alarming

Disease and starvation are profound problems, and have been since the dawn of human history.

statistics regarding threats to public health around the globe.

Throughout the technologically advanced twentieth century, tens—perhaps hundreds—of millions have perished worldwide from tuberculosis, malaria, and malnutrition. Hundreds of thousands of others continue to die from curable diseases such as cholera, diphtheria, and typhus. The dreaded bubonic plague, which killed an estimated one-fourth of the population of Europe in the Middle Ages, has reappeared in various regions—including the United States.

Even more threatening are public health dangers for which medical science has no cure. Doctors are increasingly concerned about the growing incidence of bacterial resistance to presently available antibiotics. Exotic strains of deadly Eboli virus and so-called "flesh-eating" bacteria have surfaced in recent years. And most alarming of all, cases of HIV infection number in the tens of millions worldwide. Campaigns to educate people about HIV have helped in developed nations, but the Third World still suffers terribly. The best available treatments are extremely expensive, and are designed to control; they do not cure.

As the century draws to a close many who listen to the pulse of world events hear the approaching hoofbeats of the four horses and their riders. John heard sounds, too. Later in Revelation he witnesses yet other dramatic threats to humankind:

> *"When he opened the sixth seal, I looked, and there came a great earthquake; the sun became black as sackcloth, the full moon became like blood, and the stars of the sky fell to the earth as the fig tree drops its winter fruit when shaken by a gale. The sky vanished like a scroll rolling itself up, and every mountain and island was removed from its place"*
>
> *(Revelation 6:12-14).*

The Hebrew prophet Joel described a similar phenomenon in connection with the day of the Lord:

"I will show portents in the heavens and on the earth, blood and fire and columns of smoke. The sun shall be turned to darkness, and the moon to blood, before the great and terrible day of the Lord comes" (Joel 2:30-31).

Once again scholars disagree as to how to interpret this passage. Some hold for a literal interpretation and others see a mainly symbolic meaning. Whichever point of view one subscribes to, the events described are sufficient to strike terror in the hearts of those dwelling in the earth:

"Then the kings of the earth and the magnates and the generals and the rich and the powerful, and everyone, slave and free, hid in the caves and among the rocks of the mountains, calling to the mountains and rocks, Fall on us and hide us from the face of the one seated on the throne and from the wrath of the Lamb; for the great day of their wrath has come, and who is able to stand?" (Revelation 6:15-17).

Jesus also mentioned earthquakes as a sign of the end, and earthquakes, as noted earlier in this book, are all-too-common occurrences.

The frequency of earthquakes worldwide has been increasing throughout this century.

References to seismic phenomena are found throughout the book of Revelation, as in another vision in chapter eight, which is thought to describe a volcano:

> *"The first angel blew his trumpet, and there came hail and fire, mixed with blood, and they were hurled to the earth; and a third of the earth was burned up, and a third of the trees were burned up, and all green grass was burned up. The second angel blew his trumpet, and something like a great mountain, burning with fire, was thrown into the sea"*
>
> *(Revelation 8:7-8).*

John would have known about the widely reported earthquakes that occurred in the ancient Mediterranean. In 196 B.C., for instance, the Aegean island of Thera experienced a devastating earthquake that resulted in the formation of a new island. In A.D. 79, less than 20 years prior to John's writing of Revelation, Mount Vesuvius erupted with massive force, burying the cities of Pompeii and Herculaneum, which were located in the bay of Naples.

All historical natural disasters, however, pale in comparison with those described in the book of Revelation. The text promises an astonishing wealth of decidedly unnatural plagues and catastrophes, the products of bizarre and gruesome spiritual phenomena.

Wormwood

On April 26, 1986, the world was riveted by reports of an unprecedented nuclear accident at the Chernobyl reactor located in the Ukraine 80 miles north of Kiev. The disaster, which permanently contaminated a region the size of Rhode Island and spread radioactive fallout throughout much of the European continent, bore a remarkable similarity to a prediction found in the book of Revelation: "The third angel blew his trumpet, and a great star fell from heaven, blazing like a torch, and it fell on a third of the rivers and on the springs of water. The name of the star is Wormwood. A third of the waters became wormwood, and many died from the water, because it was made bitter" (Revelation 8:10-11).

The fiery conflagration and poisoning of water caused by the star, Wormwood, is strik-

The 1986 Soviet reactor disaster at Chernobyl frightened the world.

ingly similar to what occurred at Chernobyl. Astoundingly, "Chernobyl" is the Russian equivalent of "Chornobyl," the Ukrainian word for wormwood, a medicinal herb endowed with "magical" powers.

The Chernobyl accident itself was very nearly, if not in fact, a disaster of biblical proportions. In the early hours of April 26 the operators of reactor number 4 at the Chernobyl facility realized that a catastrophe was imminent, and attempted unsuccessfully to shut down the reactor. At 1:30 in the morning two massive explosions occurred, igniting fires and causing serious structural damage to the facility. Sparks, flames, and burning lumps of deadly radioactive material were disgorged into the atmosphere. So great was the explosion's force that a 1,000-ton concrete slab inside the building was overturned like a domino.

A cataclysm as disastrous as that of the biblical Wormwood was narrowly averted at Chernobyl. Because the biblical prophecy was not fulfilled completely, people who are unconvinced of the prophecy's similarity to the Chernobyl incident have a legitimate basis from which to argue their case. But it is a fact that in the days following the reactor accident, as the Soviet government took desperate steps to contain the damage, winds scattered enormous radioactive clouds westward across Europe. The Polissia region surrounding Chernobyl was evacuated and the government decreed that several towns and cities be forcibly and permanently abandoned.

The radioactive strontium and cesium that contaminate the "Zone of Alienation" will require more than two centuries to decay. The deadly plutonium will, practically speaking, retain its potency forever. If the biblical Armageddon and end of human history is delayed for thousands of years, the culture and language of the Ukraine will be forgotten by all but scholars. But some means still will be needed to warn generations as yet unborn about the radioactivity that roils within the 20-story concrete and steel tomb encasing the still "hot" reactor. The "Wormwood" threat will continue.

A Revived Roman Empire?

For many tourists, the modern city of Rome is a thriving capital whose impressive skyline is interspersed with ancient architectural achievements that suggest the power of a once-great empire. For many students of biblical prophecy, however, Rome is more than a monument to the past. Like the beast of the Apocalypse that comes up out of the sea, the "eternal city" is destined to once again become the locus of the final rebellion against God.

For 27 centuries, since its legendary founding by Romulus and Remus, as kingdoms have risen and fallen, Rome has endured. For much of that time the city played a dominant role in the history of Western civilization. Long after the empire founded on the Tiber River ceased to exist, Roman influence continues in the political and legal systems found throughout Europe. For centuries Latin was the *lingua franca* of the West, and Classicist architecture harkens back to the greatness of Rome.

The apostle John did his writing when Rome was nearing the height of its power. The Emperor Domitian had made the unprecedented demand to be worshiped as *Dominus et Deus* (Lord and God), an ultimatum that brought persecution upon Jews as well as the growing numbers of those calling themselves Christians. Most scholars believe that a cryptic reference to Rome is found in the seventeenth chapter of Revelation, which describes a "great whore" who, like Domitian, oppresses the faithful: "And I saw that the woman was drunk with the blood of the saints and the blood of the witnesses to Jesus. When I saw her, I was greatly amazed" (Revelation 17:6).

In his vision, John sees that the woman has an identifier, "Babylon the great, mother of whores and of earth's abominations," written across her forehead (Revelation 17:5). In this mention, Babylon represents Rome, based on an earlier reference in the New Testament in which the Apostle Peter calls Rome "Babylon."

The location of the "great whore" is further clarified by an angel who speaks to John: "This calls for a mind that has wisdom: the seven heads are seven mountains on which the woman is seated" (Revelation 17:9). According to legend, Rome was founded by Romulus and Remus, twin brothers who were abandoned at birth and suckled by a wolf. The brothers founded a town on the Palatine, one of the seven hills upon which the city was eventually founded.

Some believe that John is speaking of a restoration of the Roman Empire at the time of the end.

One such passage in the book of Daniel—Nebuchadnezzar's dream of a towering metallic statue—has been noted earlier in this book. The series of metals used in the statue are thought to depict successive empires, including Babylon, Media-Persia, and Greece. The last empire, represented by the legs of iron, is believed to refer to Rome.

Feet of Clay

However, there is apparently another, final stage to the series of empires, for the toes of the statue are composed of a curious mixture of iron mixed with clay. That this empire is related to Rome is evident from the presence of iron, which represents Rome. But the events prophesied to take place in the time of the empire of "iron mixed with clay" did not take place in the time of the Roman empire, or at any time since:

> *"As the toes of the feet were part iron and part clay, so the kingdom shall be partly strong and partly brittle. As you saw the iron mixed with clay, so will they mix with one another in marriage, but they will not hold together, just as iron does not mix with clay. And in the days of those kings the God of heaven will set up a kingdom that shall never be destroyed, nor shall this kingdom be left to another people. It shall crush all these kingdoms and bring them to an end, and it shall stand forever"*
>
> *(Daniel 2:42-44).*

Daniel is speaking of the establishment of God's eternal Kingdom, an event that, although inaugurated by Jesus, is still to come. This has led some scholars to conclude that the empire described as "iron mixed with clay" will arise at the end of time, and will be somehow related to Rome.

Another passage in Daniel—also previously discussed—indicates that a "revival" of the Roman Empire is the "seventy weeks" prophecy of Daniel's chapter nine. In this vision Daniel is told: "Seventy weeks are decreed for your people and your holy city: to finish the transgression, to put an end to sin, and to atone for iniquity, to bring in everlasting righteousness, to seal both vision and prophet, and to anoint a most holy place" (Daniel 9:24).

The "seventy weeks" prophecy describes events over a long period of human history, including the time of Jesus, who here is called the "anointed one." The destruction of Jerusalem also is foretold: " . . . an anointed one shall be cut off and shall have nothing, and *the troops of the prince who is to come* [emphasis added] shall destroy the city and the sanctuary. Its end shall come with a flood, and to the end there shall be war. Desolations are decreed" (Daniel 9:26).

Note that the destruction of Jerusalem will be accomplished by "the troops of the prince who is to come" (in the future). Who is this "prince?" It is commonly held that it is none other than the evil personage known as the antichrist.

Who, then, are the "troops" who did in fact destroy Jerusalem? Of this there can be no doubt: It was the Roman armies that surrounded and destroyed the city in 70 A.D. Since the "troops of the [future] prince" are Roman, this passage may be interpreted to indicate that the coming "prince" (or antichrist) will also be related to Rome.

The Empire Reborn

Since the fall of Rome in A.D. 476, the revival of the Roman Empire has been a persistent dream of many, with numerous efforts made through the centuries to reestablish it: Charlemagne, Napoleon, even

Rome's power was unmatched. This mosaic depicts a hare hunt, a common Roman activity.

Hitler and his Third Reich, attempted to unify Europe under their own banner as the "protector of Western Christendom," with each invoking the lost grandeur of Rome. None succeeded. But then came the events of the latter half of the 20th century.

Shattered Europe

During the tumultuous early decades of the century, as Europe was devastated by two world wars, few could have imagined that the continent would one day be united. Yet in 1957, a dozen years after the conclusion of World War II, the Treaty of Rome was signed by former enemies Germany and France. Signing with them were Italy, Belgium, the Netherlands, and Luxembourg. The treaty established the European Economic Community (EEC), which in 1967 became the European Community (EC).

Students of biblical prophecy observed developments in the EC with intense interest. Could this finally be the long-foretold revival of the Roman Empire? If so, many expected that one further condition would be met: that the revived Roman empire would consist of ten distinct, but united, European nations.

The magic number of ten countries—often called the "ten-nation confederacy"—is drawn from both Daniel and Revelation. Daniel describes in his seventh chapter his vision of four beasts rising from the sea; the creatures are said to represent four kingdoms. The fourth beast is the most ferocious of all:

> *"After this I saw in the visions by night a fourth beast, terrifying and dreadful and exceedingly strong. It had great iron teeth and was devouring, breaking in pieces, and stamping what was left with its feet. It was different from all the beasts that preceded it, and it had ten horns"*
>
> *(Daniel 7:7).*

By comparing this vision with others in the book of Daniel, including the statue of Nebuchadnezzar, many have concluded that the fourth beast represents Rome. In the interpretation that follows the vision, Daniel is told: "As for the ten horns, out of this kingdom ten kings shall arise, and another shall arise after them" (Daniel 7:24).

The "ten horns," then, are symbolic of ten "kings" (rulers) who will be associated with the beast. The phrase "and another shall arise after them" is taken by some to refer to the antichrist, who by intrigue will become the leader of the revived Roman Empire.

In the book of Revelation, the aforementioned "great harlot" is pictured as riding upon a beast with "seven heads and ten horns." As mentioned, the harlot is connected with "Babylon"—or Rome. Although the notion of seven heads complicates the interpretation, for many students the mention of ten horns confirms the theory that the revived Roman Empire will consist of ten member states. The text itself indicates that, as in Daniel, the horns refer to earthly potentates:

> *"And the ten horns that you saw are ten kings who have not yet received a kingdom, but they are to receive authority as kings for one hour, together with the beast. These are united in yielding their power and authority to the beast"*
>
> *(Revelation 17:12-13).*

Once again we see here the ascendancy of an antichrist-figure who assumes power over the other "kings."

These, then, are the essential reasons why many believe that in our day we are seeing the fulfillment of prophecies concerning a revived Roman Empire consisting of ten nations led by the antichrist. But as is so often the case in attempts to connect current events to biblical prophecy, tomorrow's headlines may announce new and conflicting developments that no longer support a particular speculation.

More than Ten is Too Many

And so it was with the belief that the European Community was the revived Roman Empire. Many waited with a sense of anticipation for the original six member states of the EC to expand to ten, thus becoming the "ten-nation confederacy" that would then become the tool of the antichrist.

Excitement reached fever pitch in 1973 when Ireland, Britain, and Denmark joined the EC, making a total of nine member states. Only one more state was needed for the seeming fulfillment of the prophecy.

In 1981 Greece joined, making ten. Some teachers of prophecy issued a chorus of pronouncements about the imminent rapture of the faithful (that is, those being caught up and taken to heaven), to be followed by the rise of the antichrist, who would take control of the EC. All of this would signal the beginning of the great tribulation.

Headquarters of the European Community, Brussels.

But like passengers standing agape as a train they hoped to board speeds past the station, events soon overtook the fervent expectations of the prophecy interpreters. In 1986 newspapers did not announce the rapture and the antichrist, but that Spain and Portugal had become new member states of the EC. That made 12, which exceeded the prophesied ten nations.

Adding insult to injury, the number of EC member states continued to grow to 15, with more applicants standing in the wings. The reaction of the prophecy teachers was varied: Some employed ingenious scriptural-based explanations to account for the growing number of horns on the head of the beast, while others quietly abandoned the attempt to identify the ten-horned beasts of Daniel and Revelation with the EC.

In the midst of the earlier excitement, few paid attention to the apparent discrepancies in the ten-horned beast/EC theory. The headquarters of the EC, for example, is located in Brussels, not Rome. The assurances by some popularizers of biblical prophecy that Rome would soon become the capital of the EC seems to be based on wishful thinking.

"The Seven Horns are Seven Mountains . . ."

The cryptic symbolism of the Apocalypse has engendered a vast literature of often-conflicting interpretations, with few sure guideposts to point the commentator. In the following passage, a mysterious, reprobate "great whore" who persecutes the faithful is associated with "seven mountains." While the identity of the woman remains elusive, many cite the allusion to "seven mountains" as a reference to the eternal city of Rome, which, according to tradition, was built upon seven hills:

"Then one of the seven angels who had the seven bowls came and said to me, 'Come, I will show you the judgment of the great whore who is seated on many waters, with whom the kings of the earth have committed fornication, and with the wine of whose fornication the inhabitants of the earth have become drunk.'

"So he carried me away in the spirit into a wilderness, and I saw a woman sitting on a scarlet beast that was full of blasphemous names, and it had seven heads and ten horns. The woman was clothed

The emblem of the EC, a woman riding a bull surrounded by 12 stars, was scrutinized and offered as proof of the alliance's alleged nefarious intentions. The woman was said by some to be a blatant representation of Revela-

in purple and scarlet, and adorned with gold and jewels and pearls, holding in her hand a golden cup full of abominations and the impurities of her fornication; and on her forehead was written a name, a mystery: 'Babylon the great, mother of whores and of earth's abominations.'

"And I saw that the woman was drunk with the blood of the saints and the blood of the witnesses to Jesus. When I saw her, I was greatly amazed. But the angel said to me, 'Why are you so amazed? I will tell you the mystery of the woman, and of the beast with seven heads and ten horns that carries her. The beast that you saw was, and is not, and is about to ascend from the bottomless pit and go to destruction. And the inhabitants of the earth, whose names have not been written in the book of life from the foundation of the world, will be amazed when they see the beast, because it was and is not and is to come.'

"'This calls for a mind that has wisdom: the seven heads are seven mountains on which the woman is seated; also, they are seven kings, of whom five have fallen, one is living, and the other has not yet come; and when he comes, he must remain only a little while'"

(Revelation 17:1-10)

tion's "great whore," who rides the beast. The 12 stars supposedly echoed a Satanic symbol familiar from classic occultism.

In truth, the EC symbol is derived from Greek mythology, in which the goddess Europa was abducted by Zeus, who disguised himself as a beautiful white bull (not a beast) and then swam with her to Crete. As for the crown of 12 stars, it is a Marion symbol that was nominated by Christian Democrats in Europe to be on the flag of the Council of Europe, which was founded in 1949. And in churches throughout the world, the Virgin Mary is depicted with a halo of 12 stars, each representing one of the 12 apostles.

In every generation, believers look forward to the consummation of the present evil age, and some succumb to the temptation to engage in groundless speculation. With regard to the issue at hand, many will agree that in that the coming antichrist will in some way be related to Rome. Beyond that, as the unwarranted hypotheses about the EC have shown, the question of the revived Roman Empire is perhaps best regarded as yet another prophecy wrapped in the elusive grandeur of divine mystery.

The Antichrist

Throughout the prophecies of the Bible a mysterious figure emerges, a personage of consummate evil, who holds unprecedented political and military power, and who will lead the nations of the world to Armageddon, the final battle of human history. Misery and destruction will follow in his wake. Of all those who oppose God, he is among the most brazen. Although addressed as such in the Bible only twice (1 John and 2 John), this individual has come to be known as the antichrist because he—above all others—symbolizes contempt for those who call themselves Christians.

Not surprisingly, the antichrist has been the focus of considerable attention on the part of students of biblical prophecy, with innumerable "candidates" proposed through the centuries. Today, at the end of the second millennium, speculation about the antichrist has reached fever pitch, with many lay people and some scholars convinced that somewhere on planet Earth the antichrist is waiting in the wings for his time to come. Inevitably, much of this speculation has been grounded less in biblical scholarship than in current events, imagination, and even hysteria.

In the following survey of the source texts, beginning with the Hebrew Scriptures and moving into the New Testament, the reader will note a progression toward a more complete picture of the antichrist. What is merely hinted at in earlier texts is fleshed out by the time we arrive at that culminating treatise on eschatology (the study of the end times), the book of Revelation. Still, the reader is likely to be surprised by the limited number of texts that discuss the evil personage later dubbed the antichrist—and will perhaps wonder if the mountains of paper and ink devoted to the subject are justified. We'll look first at the Old Testament source texts.

The Little Horn

As we've explored earlier, several passages in the book of Daniel are thought to have a dual reference. That is, while they describe the historical rule of the second-century B.C. Seleucid ruler Antiochus Epiphanes, they also reach far into the future to describe another, more ominous personage. One of these passages is found in chapter seven, where a "little horn" emerges from a ten-horned beast, which is the last of four beasts to emerge from the sea:

> *"I was considering the horns, when another horn appeared, a little one coming up among them; to make room for it, three of the earlier horns were plucked up by the roots. There were eyes like human eyes in this horn, and a mouth speaking arrogantly. I watched then because of the noise of the arrogant words that the horn was speaking. And as I watched, the beast was put to death, and its body destroyed and given over to be burned with fire"*
>
> *(Daniel 7:8,11).*

Here we find an initial clue as to the nature of the "little horn": He will be a man of insolent, boastful declarations. But against whom—and why? Later in the chapter we read:

> *"He shall speak words against the Most High, shall wear out the holy ones of the Most High, and shall attempt to change the sacred seasons and the law; and they shall be given into his power for a time, two times, and half a time. Then the court shall sit in judgment, and his dominion shall be taken away, to be consumed and totally destroyed"*
>
> *(Daniel 7:25-26).*

The Little Horn will speak arrogantly against the One True God. But since God is forever beyond his reach, he will direct his wrath against the saints of the Most High. This may be the meaning of the words spoken by Jesus to his disciples: "You will be hated by all because of my name" (Luke 21:17).

Significantly, the text also indicates a limited period of time during which the Little Horn will hold sway: "a time, two times, and half a time" (Daniel 7:25). If "time" here means "year," as is often interpreted, then the antichrist will persecute the saints for three and one-half years.

Here, as in virtually every biblical passage believed to refer to the antichrist, we find the

The prophet Daniel was deeply preoccupied with visions of terrible beasts, and what they portended.

announcement of his certain defeat and destruction: "[H]is power will be taken away and completely destroyed forever" (Daniel 7:26). The Bible does not allow the reader to entertain any doubts about the outcome of the final conflagration. Although persuasive, the antichrist will be vanquished.

The King of Bold Countenance

A second passage in Daniel thought to refer to the antichrist appears in chapter eight, where a ram and a goat are seen arising from the sea. As previously discussed, the text identifies a series of kingdoms, including Media, Persia, and Greece. From the goat, representing Greece, arises a ruler described as possessing a "bold countenance":

> *"At the end of their rule, when the transgressions have reached their full measure, a king of bold countenance shall arise, skilled in intrigue. He shall grow strong in power, shall cause fearful destruction, and shall succeed in what he does. He shall destroy the powerful and the people of the holy ones. By his cunning he shall make deceit prosper under his hand, and in his own mind he shall be great. Without warning he shall destroy many and shall even rise up against the Prince of princes. But he shall be broken, and not by human hands"* (Daniel 8:23-25).

Daniel is told that this vision "refers to many days from now." Once again we have a mention of the persecution of the saints as well as the contemptuous arrogance of this king. To this is added an allusion to the ruler's powers of deceit: He will be "skilled in intrigue." He will even challenge the "Prince of princes," a reference to the coming Messiah. Many have inferred that the antichrist will mount his campaign from a considerable power base that is both political and military.

As one might expect, this has encouraged speculation encompassing a dizzying array of politicians with military capabilities.

The Coming Prince

In the next chapter, the angel Gabriel appears to Daniel in a vision, in which he reveals a prophetic timetable of 70 groups of "sevens" (or years) leading up to the consummation of all things:

> *"After the sixty-two weeks, an anointed one shall be cut off and shall have nothing, and the troops of the prince who is to come shall destroy the city and the sanctuary. Its end shall come with a flood, and to the end there shall be war. Desolations are decreed. He shall make a strong covenant with many for one week, and for half of the week he shall make sacrifice and offering cease; and in their place shall be an abomination that desolates, until the decreed end is poured out upon the desolator"* (Daniel 9:26-27).

Some students of biblical prophecy believe they have gleaned several future events from this text. First, the "Anointed One" will be "cut off," or killed, an event fulfilled at the crucifixion of Jesus Christ around A.D. 30. Following this is the destruction of "the city and the sanctuary." In A.D. 70, at the culmination of the

First Jewish Revolt against Rome, Jerusalem and the Temple were destroyed, thus fulfilling of the words of Jesus: "You see all these, do you not? Truly I tell you, not one stone will be left here upon another; all will be thrown down" (Matthew 24:2).

We have already discussed how the reference to "the troops of the prince who is to come" is believed to indicate that the evil "prince"—thought by many to be the antichrist—will somehow rise from the former Roman Empire. This may be an important clue as to the origin of the antichrist.

In this passage we also learn something of the antichrist's program. It is said that the "prince" will "confirm a covenant with many for one 'seven.'" "Seven" here is often taken to mean a group of seven years. However, in the middle of that "week" he will "break" that covenant, or peace treaty. That the Jewish people are being invoked here seems clear because the evil prince will "make sacrifice and offering cease." This likely refers to the Levitical Temple sacrifices—which also indicates one more prophetic detail: At the time of the prince, the Temple will be rebuilt and sacrifices will again be offered.

Sometime after the rebuilding of the Temple this prince will perform what is known as the

The Roman practice of idol worship suggests the empire as a fertile breeding ground for the antichrist.

"abomination of desolation." There is a historical precedent to this blasphemous act. Just prior to the Maccabean Revolt in 168 B.C., the Seleucid Ruler Antiochus Epiphanes IV, as part of his drive to subjugate Judea by imposing Hellenistic religion and culture, desecrated the Temple precincts.

What this desecration entailed is not known with exactness, but it is thought that Antiochus IV sacrificed a pig on the altar of sacrifice, or erected a statue to Zeus in the Temple, or perhaps did both. Whatever the particulars of Antiochus's horrific act, the Jewish historian Flavius Josephus termed it the "abomination of desolation."

In Matthew 24:15 Jesus speaks about yet another "abomination of desolation," this time committed by the future antichrist. Just as Antiochus IV assumed the grandiose title "Epiphanes," meaning "God revealed," the antichrist will also claim divine honors for himself. This is heresy of the highest order, and sets the antichrist up not simply for repudiation, but for harsh, thorough punishment, as well. Bloated with influence and triumphs of conquest, the antichrist will aspire to godhood. This will be seen more clearly in the next passage.

The Willful King

The eleventh chapter of Daniel describes the political and military exploits of a series of "kings" identified by historians as the successors to the empire of Alexander the Great. These men, including Antiochus IV of Syria, ruled Syria and Egypt in the late fourth to the mid-second centuries B.C. As noted earlier, the first 35 verses of Daniel chapter 11 fit the historical record with such precision that Porphyry, the third-century A.D. neoplatonic philosopher and opponent of Christianity, contended that the text was a forgery.

After verse 35, however, the text diverges from the historical record as we know it, and seems to project far into the future to describe a personage of whom Antiochus IV was only a pale shadow:

> *"The king shall act as he pleases. He shall exalt himself and consider himself greater than any god, and shall speak horrendous things against the God of gods. He shall prosper until the period of wrath is completed, for what is determined shall be done. He shall pay no respect to the gods of his ancestors, or to the one beloved by women; he shall pay no respect to any other god, for he shall consider himself greater than all"* *(Daniel 11:36-37).*

This passage reveals the antichrist's villainous character, and his monstrous self-exaltation above all other gods. The phrase mentioning that he will "pay no respect" for "the one beloved of women" has been translated to read, "Neither shall he regard . . . the desire of women."

In all probability this does not, as some have supposed, refer to the antichrist's sexual orientation. Rather, it probably refers to an ancient Jewish tradition that the deepest desire of every Jewish woman was to be the bearer of the promised Messiah. Thus we learn of the antichrist's utter enmity toward Jesus Christ.

The passage continues to describe the antichrist's consummate political and military skills in creating his worldwide power base:

"He shall deal with the strongest fortresses by the help of a foreign god. Those who acknowledge him he shall make more wealthy, and shall appoint them as rulers over many, and shall distribute the land for a price" (Daniel 11:39).

In these words are concealed dark mysteries, such as the meaning of the reference to a "foreign god," which commentators have had little success in deciphering. The text continues to describe a series of fast-moving, pitched battles involving many nations:

> *"At the time of the end the king of the south shall attack him. But the king of the north shall rush upon him like a whirlwind, with chariots and horsemen, and with many ships. He shall advance against countries and pass through like a flood. He shall come into the beautiful land, and tens of thousands shall fall victim, but Edom and Moab and the main part of the Ammonites shall escape from his power. He shall stretch out his hand against the countries, and the land of Egypt shall not escape" (Daniel 11:40-42).*

One of the countries the antichrist will invade is the "beautiful land," which, as we shall presently see, refers to the land of Israel. In spite of his phenomenal success on the battlefield, forces are being arrayed against him, and the antichrist will soon be embroiled in bloody conflicts leading to his eventual downfall:

> *"But reports from the east and the north shall alarm him, and he shall go out with great fury to bring ruin and complete destruction to many. He shall pitch his palatial tents between the sea and the beautiful holy mountain. Yet he shall come to his end, with no one to help him"*
>
> *(Daniel 11:44-45).*

This ominous description of the end of the king identified by many as the future antichrist brings to an end the principal Old Testament texts dealing with this frightening figure. Let's summarize what many students of biblical prophecy believe these texts indicate about the antichrist:

- In some fashion, not explained in the text, he will be related to, or arise from, the old Roman empire.
- He will possess unparalleled skills at intrigue, which will enable his meteoric rise to the pinnacle of world power.
- The length of his rule will be limited—three and a half years according to some scholars; seven according to others. At some point

Signorelli Luca's astonishing vision of the antichrist.

during that period a decisive break with the Jewish people will cause the antichrist to repudiate his covenant with them.

- He will speak arrogant, blasphemous things against the Most High God, and will embark eventually upon a savage persecution of the saints.
- He will conquer many countries by the sword and will at some point invade the land of Israel.
- Despite phenomenal battlefield success against his enemies, the antichrist will meet his end at the height of his power through divine intervention.

The Lawless One

An important New Testament text that describes the antichrist is found in 2 Thessalonians:

"He opposes and exalts himself above every so-called god or object of worship, so that he takes his seat in the temple of God, declaring himself to be God . . . And then the lawless one will be revealed, whom the Lord Jesus will destroy with the breath of his mouth, annihilating him by the manifestation of his coming. The coming of the lawless one is apparent in the working of Satan, who uses all power, signs, lying wonders, and every kind of wicked deception for those who are perishing, because they refused to love the truth and so be saved. For this reason God sends them a powerful delusion, leading them to believe what is false, so that all who have not believed the truth but took pleasure in unrighteousness will be condemned"

(2 Thessalonians 2:4,8-12).

The passage quoted above is a particularly explicit reference to the antichrist's demand to be worshiped as God in a rebuilt Jewish Temple. The passage also reveals another mysterious aspect of the antichrist: his ability to deceive mankind with demonstrations of power, signs, lying wonders, and every kind of wicked deception. It is widely assumed that the source of these supernatural powers will be Satan himself, the evil puppeteer.

In a sobering reference to "those who are perishing," the Apostle Paul explains that many will be deceived by the delusions wrought by the antichrist because, tragically, "they refused to love the truth and so be saved." Yet this does not mean that God is cruel, for the divine intention is stated elsewhere: "The Lord is not slow about his promise, as some think of slowness, but is patient with you, not wanting any to perish, but all to come to repentance" (2 Peter 3:9).

The Blasphemer is Named

The final New Testament references to the antichrist, before the book of Revelation, occur in 1 John and 2 John, where the antichrist is identified as such for the only time.

The first and second letters of John are commonly thought to have been written by an anonymous elder who followed Johannine tradition. Both letters are essentially cautionary: The first is a sermon that warns against false teachers; the second addresses the danger faced by Christians who associate with church dissidents. The respective messages are clear:

"Do not love the world or the things in the world.... the desire of the flesh, the desire of the eyes, the pride in riches – comes not from the Father but from the world. And the world and its desire are passing away, but those who do the will of God live forever.

"Children, it is the last hour! As you have heard that antichrist is coming, so now many antichrists have come. From this we know that it is the last hour"

(1 John 2:15-18).

Later, we learn that deadly deception is afoot:

"Many deceivers have gone out into the world, those who do not confess that Jesus Christ has come in the flesh; any such person is the deceiver and the antichrist! Be on your guard, so that you do not lose what we have worked for, but may receive a full reward" (2 John vv. 7-8).

The Beast

We now come to the book of Revelation, which, although not describing the antichrist with that term, contains Scripture's most detailed discussion of this personage. These passages are remarkable both for their symbolism and sparseness of detail. The inspired writer painted his canvas with broad, vivid stokes, which has encouraged teachers of prophecy to wrangle over the smallest detail.

In chapter 13 we read about a fearsome beast with ten horns and seven heads that arises from the sea:

> *"And the beast that I saw was like a leopard, its feet were like a bear's, and its mouth was like a lion's mouth. And the dragon gave it his power and his throne and great authority. One of its heads seemed to have received a death-blow, but its mortal wound had been healed. In amazement the whole earth followed the beast. They worshiped the dragon, for he had given his authority to the beast, and they worshiped the beast, saying, 'Who is like the beast, and who can fight against it?' The beast was given a mouth uttering haughty and blasphemous words, and it was allowed to exercise authority for forty-two months. It opened its mouth to utter blasphemies against God, blaspheming his name and his dwelling, that is, those who dwell in heaven. Also it was allowed to make war*

on the saints and to conquer them. It was given authority over every tribe and people and language and nation, and all the inhabitants of the earth will worship it, everyone whose name has not been written from the foundation of the world in the book of life of the Lamb that was slaughtered"

(Revelation 13:2-8).

The picture of the antichrist in this passage, though shrouded in apocalyptic language, complements that presented in previous texts. We see more references to the beast receiving worship and blaspheming God, but here we find a curious new detail: The beast will suffer an apparently fatal wound but will somehow recover. This astounding turn of events merits two more allusions in

Acolytes of the antichrist: the seven-headed beast and the whore of Babylon.

the same chapter (vs. 12,14) as well as later in the book of Revelation (17:8,11).

It is often surmised that the antichrist's seemingly miraculous resuscitation from the dead will be the catalyst that will cement his worldwide following. But what can it mean? Some commentators have taken the position that the future antichrist will be a resurrected Judas Iscariot.

This view is based upon similarities between the two. For instance, both are called "the one destined for destruction" (John 17:12; 2 Thessalonians 2:3). In referring to Judas, Jesus said: "Did I not choose you, the twelve? Yet one of you is a devil" (John 6:70). Also, Judas was the only man, other than the antichrist, of whom it was said that "Satan entered [him]" (Luke 22:3).

Most scholars, however, prefer not to identify the antichrist with any deceased historical person brought back to life, for the simple reason that to do so grants Satan that which belongs only to God: the power to resuscitate the dead.

Others believe that the text itself provides a clue as to the probable meaning when it states that one of the heads of the beast "*seemed to have received* [emphasis added] a deadly blow."

This suggests that the "deadly wound" will be a clever subterfuge—one of the antichrist's "lying wonders and wicked deceptions," as warned about in 2 Thessalonians 2:9. Another possibility is that the antichrist will suffer a grievous wound that only appears to be fatal, and from which he recovers.

A Worldwide Rule?

In popular literature the antichrist is often portrayed as holding absolute sway over the nations of the world, who are forced to do his bidding. Indeed, Revelation states that the "beast" was "given authority over every tribe and people and language and nation"(Revelation 13:7). A careful appraisal of the evidence, however, calls into question this common assumption.

While it is undoubtedly true that the antichrist will wield unprecedented worldwide power and influence, those attributes will by no means be absolute. Terms such as "all" and "the whole world" must be taken in an appropriate context. For example, while Revelation 13:3 says that the "whole earth followed the beast," this does not mean *everybody*, because the antichrist is simultaneously (and furiously) persecuting those who refuse to worship him.

Chapter 7 describes "a great multitude that no one could count, from every nation, from all tribes and peoples and languages, standing before the throne and before the Lamb, robed in white, with palm branches in their hands" (Revelation 9). Who are these saints? John is told they are those "who have come out of the great ordeal; they have washed their robes and made them white in the blood of the Lamb" (Revelation 14). It seems clear, then, that there will be those from every corner of the globe who, at great cost, will refuse to bow before the antichrist.

Moreover, political power blocks will successfully oppose the antichrist. Daniel chapter 11, for example, notes that "tens of thousands shall fall victim, but Edom and Moab and the main part of the Ammonites shall escape from his power"(Revelation 41). Daniel also reports that the antichrist's rule will be challenged by nations opposed to him: "[R]eports from the east and the north shall alarm him, and he shall go out with great fury. . . ."(Revelation 44).

The picture is considerably more complex than many of its interpreters claim. In fact, it appears that the antichrist will fail to consolidate his rule. Formidable military alliances representing substantial areas of Earth will rebel against him. Given such concerted opposition, it is difficult to imagine how, as many claim, he is to be the political leader of the entire world.

It's obvious that popular interpreters, eager to promote their own dogma, have often read too much into the biblical texts. Such efforts, though usually springing from well-meaning desires to simplify the difficult and enigmatic aspects of biblical prophecy, only lead to more confusion. Analysts often analyze themselves into self-contradictory scenarios that, in the end, just don't make logical sense. The wisest course is to remain mindful of what the biblical texts state clearly, and to interpret modestly.

The False Prophet

The nefarious individual called the "beast" in Revelation, also known as the antichrist, does not act alone: Another mysterious personage, described cryptically as a second "beast," performs wonders on the antichrist's behalf:

> *"Then I saw another beast that rose out of the earth; it had two horns like a lamb and it spoke like a dragon. It exercises all the authority of the first beast on its behalf, and it makes the earth and its inhabitants worship the first beast, whose mortal wound had been healed. It performs great signs, even making fire come down from heaven to earth in the sight of all; and by the signs that it is allowed to perform on behalf of the beast, it deceives the inhabi-*

The "beast" (right), one of the most dangerous figures described in biblical prophecy.

tants of earth, telling them to make an image for the beast that had been wounded by the sword and yet lived; and it was allowed to give breath to the image of the beast so that the image of the beast could even speak and cause those who would not worship the image of the beast to be killed" (Revelation 13:11-15).

Later in the book of Revelation, at the second coming of Christ, this second "beast" is called the "false prophet": "And the beast was captured, and with it the false prophet who had performed in its presence the signs by which he deceived those who had received the mark of the beast and those who worshiped its image . . ." (Revelation 19:20).

The Deceivers

Above all else, the false prophet is a master of deception. Commentators note that he appears with two horns like a lamb, thus conveying a misleading impression of gentleness. The writer may be alluding to the warning of Jesus: "Beware of false prophets, who come to you in sheep's clothing but inwardly are ravenous wolves" (Matthew 7:15).

The second beast acts as minister of propaganda, and his purpose is to deceive the people of the world into worshiping the antichrist. He accomplishes this through "great signs" that mimic the miracles performed by true prophets of old. As Elijah called down fire from heaven to consume the altar of Baal on Mount Carmel, so the false prophet makes "fire come down from heaven to earth in the sight of all."

One of the most bizarre acts of the false prophet is to create an "image" of the beast—or antichrist. Through the use of magic or supernatural means the false prophet "gives breath" to the image so that "the image of the beast could even speak." While strange in the extreme to the modern mind, there are many references in ancient literature to a belief in statues that spoke and performed miracles. Some early Church Fathers believed that Simon Magus, mentioned as a sorcerer in the book of Acts, utilized his dark arts to bring statues to life. One of the first uses of ventriloquism was demonstrated by the priests of Oriental cults in Rome, who used it to create the illusion that the idols themselves were speaking.

The Telltale Mark

Whether the false prophet employs a clever magical illusion or whether some genuine spiritual manifestation is at work here is not clear. In either case, all humankind is ordered to worship the image—upon pain of death.

Determined to stamp out all opposition, the false prophet employs Draconian economic coercion to force men to worship the antichrist: "Also it causes all, both small and great, both rich and poor, both free and slave, to be marked on the right hand or the forehead, so that no one can buy or sell who does not have the mark, that is, the name of the beast or the number of its name" (Revelation 13:16-17).

The mention of people from all classes of society is designed to emphasize the fact that no one will be able to carry on normal commerce without carrying the "mark of the beast." Some believe that this mark is derived from the practice in Roman times of branding rebellious slaves or soldiers captured in battle. Also, devotees of cults in the ancient world used tattoos to signify their loyalty to a particular deity.

In recent times, popularizers of biblical prophecy have offered numerous suggestions as to the meaning of the mark of the beast. It is claimed, for example, that researchers in Sweden have tested a device that imprints an invisible laser identification mark on the back of the hand. Other devices currently being tested that "read" human fingerprints also are claimed by some to be the "mark of the beast."

According to another rumor, a massive computer called "the beast" is located at the headquarters of the European Union in Brussels. According to these rumors, this computer is "two stories high" and has the capacity to store information about every person on earth. The false prophet, it is said, will use such a computer to control the people of the world.

Such claims, however, are rarely subjected to critical analysis. Why, for example, would this computer need to be so large? Modern supercomputers occupy a much smaller space than cumbersome earlier prototypes. Also, exactly how this computer might maintain data on every human being is not explained. Many poor countries, it would seem, have little or no ability to maintain accurate records on their citizens. Other countries—such as China, with a quarter of the world's population—would presumably be reluctant to supply information about its citizens to the West.

Despite the deficiencies of current speculation regarding the mark of the beast, many people of today—like peoples of past ages—feel that the general scenario presented in Revelation has entered the realm of feasibility.

The Great Red Dragon

An evil presence lurks behind the events of the book of Revelation, plunging the world into its darkest hour:

> *"Then another portent appeared in heaven: a great red dragon, with seven heads and ten horns, and seven diadems on his heads. . . . And war broke out in heaven; Michael and his angels fought against the dragon. The dragon and his angels fought back, but they were defeated, and there was no longer any place for them in heaven. The great dragon was thrown down, that ancient serpent, who is called the Devil and Satan, the deceiver of the whole world – he was thrown down to the earth, and his angels were thrown down with him"* (Revelation 12:7-9).

Little is known about this serpentine arch-enemy of God, otherwise known as the Devil, or Satan. The name "Satan" is the English transliteration of a Hebrew word meaning "adversary." In the Hebrew Scriptures the word occurs in only three passages, including the book of 1 Chronicles, where we read, according to one interpretation of the passage, that it is Satan who "stood up against Israel, and incited David to count the people of Israel," an act that proved to have fateful consequences (1 Chronicles 21:1).

Beginnings of the Demon

While not mentioning Satan by name, two cryptic passages in the Hebrew scriptures are thought by many to address the origins of the Prince of Darkness.

Satan, supremely cocksure of his power to corrupt and destroy, is barely mentioned in the Bible by name, but his presence is inescapable.

The first of these is found in the book of Ezekiel. There we find the prophet foretelling doom for the king of Tyre. Closer examination, however, shows that the prophecy transcends any ruler; instead, it describes the casting down of a magnificent being from heaven:

> *"Thus says the Lord God: You were the signet of perfection, full of wisdom and perfect in beauty. You were in Eden, the garden of God; every precious stone was your covering. . . . On the day that you were created they were prepared. With an anointed cherub as guardian I placed you; you were on the holy mountain of God; you walked among the stones of fire. You were blameless in your ways from the day that you were created, until iniquity was found in you . . . so I cast you as a profane thing from the mountain of God, and the guardian cherub drove you out from among the stones of fire"*
>
> *(Ezekiel 28:12-16).*

This being, thought by some Bible scholars to be Satan, was evidently perfect in his original state, and occupied an exalted place on the "holy mountain of God." As the text continues we learn that pride—the desire for even greater glory—was the source of his downfall: "Your heart was proud because of your beauty; you corrupted your wisdom for the sake of your splendor. [Therefore] I cast you to the ground . . ." (Ezekiel 28:17). Pride has undone yet another biblical personage.

According to Jewish tradition and literature, Satan was originally an angel who vainly attempted to achieve equality with God. In another passage, this one from Isaiah, we find the theme expressed in the midst of a prophecy apparently directed to yet another human ruler, the king of Babylon. But as the prophecy progresses, the focus changes to an enigmatic figure who overshadows any earthly personage:

> *"How you are fallen from heaven, O Day Star, son of Dawn! How you are cut down to the ground, you who laid the nations low! You said in your heart, I will ascend to heaven; I will raise my throne above the stars of God; I will sit on the mount of assembly on the heights of Zaphon; I will ascend to the tops of the clouds, I will make myself like the Most High. But you are brought down to Sheol, to the depths of the Pit"* (Isaiah 14:12-15).

In Latin, the name "O Day Star" is rendered as "Lucifer," which became a synonym for Satan. Here is the story of a consummate pride that sought to usurp the very throne of God.

Fallen Angels

The book of Revelation adds a mysterious detail to this great rebellion: "His tail swept down a third of the stars of heaven and threw them to the earth. . ." (Revelation 12:4).

The "third of the stars" are considered to be the number of those angels who joined Satan's rebellion. Those co-conspirators, known as fallen angels and demonic spirits, remain in unholy servitude to him, and will suffer eternal damnation for their defiance: "And the angels who did not keep their own position, but left their proper dwelling, he has kept in eternal chains in deepest darkness for the judgment of the great Day"(Jude 6).

According to the book of Revelation, Satan is destined to fail in his final rebellion against God, after which he will join his evil subordinates: "And the devil who had deceived them was thrown into the lake of fire and sulfur, where the beast and the false prophet were, and they will be tormented day and night forever and ever"(Revelation 20:10).

The fearsome horned beast, an evil agent of Satan, as depicted by Giusto de Giovanni in 1393.

Although the Scriptures acknowledge that Satan and his minions possess supernatural powers beyond that of mortals, they remain created beings, and as such cannot be the equal of the Creator. One aspect of the "mystery of evil," long pondered by theologians, is that such beings were sufficiently bold to imagine they could challenge the Almighty. In the end, however, the forces of evil will know only complete and final defeat, as promised by the Apostle Paul: "The God of peace will shortly crush Satan under your feet" (Romans 16:20).

666: The Mark of the Beast

Perhaps no verses in the book of Revelation have received more attention than those describing the cryptic number "666." This enigmatic number is found in chapter 13, where the false prophet, in conjunction with the antichrist, commands an unprecedented control over the monetary systems of the world:

> *"Also it causes all, both small and great, both rich and poor, both free and slave, to be marked on the right hand or the forehead, so that no one can buy or sell who does not have the mark, that is, the name of the beast or the number of its name. This calls*

for wisdom: let anyone with understanding calculate the number of the beast, for it is the number of a person. Its number is six hundred sixty-six"

(Revelation 13:16-18).

On the basis of these verses, it is commonly assumed that the antichrist will establish a worldwide economic system, and will convert all the currencies of the world into a single denomination under his control. Only those who agree to receive an identification mark on their hand or forehead will be able to engage in commerce. To those not in league with the antichrist, these identifying marks will be anathema – visible symbols of the corruption of the godless.

This notion of a universal currency has been propagated with such fervor that many Bible students assume it is clearly taught in Scripture. However, nowhere in prophetic Scripture is this idea explicitly stated. The belief about a one-world monetary system is an inference – or, put another way, an educated guess – based upon the sparse information actually provided by the text.

Nero Unending

What seems clear is that the faithful will suffer from an economic boycott enforced by the antichrist. Moreover, some form of identification will be used to identify those eligible to engage in commercial transactions. This identification will involve the number 666 inscribed upon the hand or forehead.

In ancient times the letters of the alphabet were used also as numbers, and every name could thus be expressed, as in the oft-quoted graffito from the doomed city of Pompeii: "I love her whose number is 545." The Jews looked for esoteric meaning in the numeric values of names, and since ancient times Christians have sought to identify the personage whose numerical equivalent of his name equals 666.

Roman emperor Nero (center) was suspected of setting the fires that destroyed Rome. Some considered him the antichrist.

An amazing number of possibilities for the title of antichrist have been advanced through the centuries. For those living in the first century the most plausible candidate was the Roman Emperor Nero, who initiated the first persecution of the early Christians by blaming them for a fire that destroyed much of Rome in A.D. 64. Even though Nero was driven to suicide in A.D. 68, about 30 years before John wrote Revelation, his memory still exerted a powerful and mythical influence.

During his rule, Nero was considered to be the antichrist by Christians in Rome because of his attempts to deify himself via the enforcement of emperor worship. When Nero died in seclusion in his villa outside Rome, passing from the scene without even a state funeral, rumors began to fly that he had not actually died.

Instead, it was said that he had escaped and was living among Rome's dreaded enemies, the Parthians, who would one day furnish him with an army to wreak revenge upon Rome. These rumors continued with amazing persistency for centuries, fed on several occasions by the appearance of impostors claiming to be Nero. One such pretender managed to convince a large number of Parthians of the story and subsequently spread terror in the empire.

Many Christians came to believe that the antichrist would be a resurrected Nero, who would one day return to wage war against Rome. The legend of *Nero redivivus* (Nero resurrected) was held by Christian writers long after the first century. Jerome, writing at the end of the fourth century, affirmed that in his day the belief was still held by many Christians.

The belief that the antichrist would be a resurrected Nero was bolstered by a remarkable coincidence: The Hebrew transliteration of the Greek words "*Caesar Nero*" adds up to 666. This does not necessarily mean that the Apostle John intended to identify Nero as the future antichrist; he may simply have been indicating Nero as a forerunner of the coming antichrist—a man who exhibited many of the characteristics of the future beast of Revelation.

As the centuries passed the myth of *Nero redivivus* gradually faded, only to be replaced by other attempts to identify the personage behind the mysterious number 666.

At the time of the Reformation a new sentiment emerged, which remains strong in some quarters of Protestantism: that the antichrist will be the Pope of the Roman Catholic Church. Those opposed to the Catholic Church claim that the numerical value of the Pope's Latin title "*Vicarius Filii Dei*" is 666. But the book of Revelation does not explicitly state that the antichrist and the false prophet will be supported by any church or denomination. A more plausible scenario would place these satanically inspired individuals at the head of either a newly created cult or an existing religion opposed to Christianity. In any case, despite their theological differences with Catholicism, virtually no modern Protestants equate the Pope with the antichrist.

Führer as Antichrist?

At the time of the Second World War many wondered if Adolf Hitler was the antichrist. He had united much of Europe under his iron fist and was the single most important figure in the precipitation of a worldwide conflagration. It was pointed out by some that the name "Hitler"

Adolf Hitler

added up to 666. However, this conclusion was arrived at by a questionable methodology that assigned the letter A the value of 100, B the value 101, C the value 102, and so on, giving a value of 666 for Hitler. Although intriguing, this method of calculation appears to have been completely arbitrary.

Dark Politics

In the post-war era numerous candidates have been suggested as possible antichrist candidates. During the Jimmy Carter administration, some students of biblical prophecy observed with suspicion the meteoric rise of the Secretary of State, Henry Kissinger, to a position of great power and influence. Especially interesting to some interpreters of prophecy was his role in brokering the Israeli-Egyptian peace agreement through intensive "shuttle diplomacy." Because it was widely believed that the antichrist would be a counterfeit "man of peace" who initiates a false accord between Israel and her enemies, imaginative interpretations suggested Kissinger. Finally, ingenious (and rather labored) means were employed to "prove" the numerical value of his name as the magic number, 666.

Speculation extended as well to the Republican administration of Ronald Reagan because his full name, Ronald Wilson Reagan, consists of three groups of "six," equaling, it was claimed, 666 . . . or, doubters may be quick to note, 18.

Others took note of Reagan's partner in détente, Mikhail Gorbachev. It was suggested that the prominent red birthmark on the Soviet leader's forehead, which resembled a head wound, was the antichrist's "mortal wound which had been healed." Perhaps, some speculated, Gorbachev would arise from his political death to become the antichrist by assuming leadership of the United Nations.

In recent years it has been noted that the name of one of Reagan's successors, William J. Clinton, also can be calculated to a value of 666. This conclusion is reached by adding up the values of his name as it would appear in the Hebrew-Aramaic language. By way of justification for this novel approach, it has been pointed out that the closely related Hebrew and Aramaic languages were in use in Palestine during the time of Christ. However, that fact seems to have little relevance to our modern age, which is removed by a millennia from the first century.

Prophecy Collides with High Tech

One of the latest and most curious suggestions regarding the identity of the antichrist is grounded in the information-technology revolution of the twentieth century. Computers have brought dramatic changes to virtually every aspect of our lives, as well as considerable social, economic, and political power to its leading entrepreneurs. It's not surprising, then, that some particularly imaginative—and decidedly extreme—searchers for the antichrist cast their eyes toward cyberspace's most prominent figure, Bill Gates III. Speculation begins with his name: The industry-standard DOS (Disk Operating System) method of assigning numeric values to letters, characters, and symbols is called "ASCII"; coincidentally, the ASCII-values of "Bill Gates III" (with "3rd" assigned the value of "3") add up to 666.

Further, Gates's high profile has encouraged more speculation. The conversion of the letters of Bill Gates III (3rd) to ASCII values yields the following:

B	66
I	73
L	76
L	76
G	71
A	65
T	84
E	69
S	83
+	3
	666

This is not the only odd coincidence surrounding Bill Gates and his corporation, Microsoft: The ASCII values of "MS-DOS 6.21," a recent version of Microsoft's Disk Operating System, also add up to 666.

But not everything falls into place as neatly. Microsoft's "Windows 95," for instance, adds up to 665—a near miss, to be sure, and perhaps sufficient to convince those who are eager to be convinced. Then again, it breaks the apparent pattern.

Attempts through the centuries to decipher the meaning of the mysterious 666, although intriguing, merely serve to demonstrate the extraordinary "elasticity" of the number—and the imagination and ingenuity of those seeking to uncover the identity of the antichrist.

The Two Witnesses of Revelation

In the book of Revelation the archenemy of God, identified as the antichrist, is portrayed as exercising an unprecedented degree of power and authority over humankind. But he does not go unopposed: Two mysterious witnesses mount a determined and spectacular resistance.

Numerous possibilities regarding the identities of the two witnesses found in Revelation have been suggested. As previously discussed, some students believe one of the witnesses is the prophet Elijah, a conclusion based on the prophecy found in the book of Malachi: "Lo, I will send you the prophet Elijah before the great and terrible day of the Lord comes" (Malachi 4:5).

It is suggested that the second prophet is Moses, who appeared with Elijah when Jesus ascended a mountain with his disciples Peter, John, and James:

> *"And while he was praying, the appearance of his face changed, and his clothes became dazzling white. Suddenly they saw two men, Moses and Elijah, talking to him. They appeared in glory and were speaking of his departure, which he was about to accomplish at Jerusalem" (Luke 9:39-31).*

It is thought that Moses and Elijah will appear together again as the "two witnesses" in the book of Revelation.

Another possibility is that the second prophet will be Enoch, who lived in such close fellowship with God that he was translated into the presence of God without dying: "Enoch walked with God; then he was no more, because God took him" (Genesis 5:24). The phrase "God took him" has been taken to mean that Enoch did not experience death. If so, Enoch and Elijah have the distinction of

The prophet Enoch, who was so close to God that he was considered a logical choice to resist the antichrist.

being the only two mortals who were taken directly to heaven without dying. It is argued that they eventually will return to earth to experience the common lot of all humans and die, but not before prophesying against the antichrist.

Still others believe that the two witnesses are not literal persons but symbolic of the faithful who resist the antichrist. They are figuratively described as "the two olive trees and the two lampstands that stand before the Lord of the earth"(Revelation 11:4). In Revelation chapter one, where the seven churches are thought to symbolize the faithful of different ages, they are said to be "seven lampstands."

Holy Fire

Whether literal or symbolic, the two witnesses "are granted authority" to prophesy against the "beast" and his followers. Although isolated and threatened, the witnesses are far from impotent. Indeed, what ensues is a remarkable display of spiritual powers, as fire issues from their mouths to consume their enemies.

Although bizarre to the modern mind, the use of fire as an instrument of divine judgment occurs frequently in the Bible, as in the following encounter between Elijah and soldiers sent by his opponent, King Ahaziah:

> *"Then the king sent to him a captain of fifty with his fifty men. He went up to Elijah, who was sitting on the top of a hill, and said to him, 'O man of God,' the king says, 'Come down.' But Elijah answered the captain of fifty,' If I am a man of God, let fire come down from heaven and consume you and your fifty.' Then fire came down from heaven, and consumed him and his fifty. Again the king sent to him another captain of fifty with his fifty. He*

went up and said to him, 'O man of God, this is the king's order: Come down quickly!' But Elijah answered them, 'If I am a man of God, let fire come down from heaven and consume you and your fifty.' Then the fire of God came down from heaven and consumed him and his fifty"
(2 Kings 1:9-12).

The book of Revelation indicates that the two prophets will be protected from their enemies in similar fashion.

The witnesses have other weapons for their defense: We read, for example, that they have the power to shut the heavens so that no rain will fall for the duration of their prophesying. Here we are reminded of Elijah, who prophesied to wicked King Ahab: "As the Lord the God of Israel lives, before whom I stand, there shall be neither dew nor rain these years,

The devoutly faithful—and powerful—Elijah destroys the messengers of King Ahaziah.

except by my word" (1 Kings 17:1). A prolonged drought followed, which lasted several years and caused extreme famine in the land.

The two witnesses also will have the authority to turn the water of the earth to "blood" and to strike men and women with "every kind of plague, as often as they desire" (Revelation 11:6).

Death That Is Not Death

A great confrontation is brewing as the two witnesses complete their time of prophesying. The "beast which comes up from the bottomless pit" makes war on them and emerges victorious—or so it seems. That he emerges from the bottomless pit, the home of evil, death and destruction, indicates the demonic origin of the beast.

The two witnesses are slain by the beast, after which their bodies are left to lie in "the great city that is prophetically called Sodom and Egypt, where also their Lord was crucified" (Revelation 11:8). This reference to the place of Jesus' crucifixion would seem to identify Jerusalem as the city in question.

Some commentators, however, note that elsewhere in the book of Revelation, the great city refers to Rome. For those who accept this view, the reference to Jesus being crucified in "the great city" suggests the documented historical persecution in Rome of those who are called by the name of Christ.

The ancients considered being deprived of burial or other acceptable means of interring

Battling the Beast

Curiously, as the end-time nefarious ruler known as the "beast" of Revelation unleashes his evil program upon the planet, we find little human opposition to his machinations. That is, until "two witnesses" rise to challenge him:

"And I will grant my two witnesses authority to prophesy for one thousand two hundred sixty days, wearing sackcloth. These are the two olive trees and the two lampstands that stand before the Lord of the earth. And if anyone wants to harm them, fire pours from their mouth and consumes their foes; anyone who wants to harm them must be killed in this manner. They have authority to shut the sky, so that no rain may fall during the days of their prophesying, and they have authority over the waters to turn them into blood, and to strike the earth with every kind of plague, as often as they desire.

"When they have finished their testimony, the beast that comes up from the bottomless pit will

one's bodily remains as the ultimate indignity. The Mosaic law instructed that even those guilty of capital crimes were to be granted the basic dignity of burial: "When someone is convicted of a crime punishable by death and is executed, and you hang him on a tree, his corpse must not remain all night upon the tree;

make war on them and conquer them and kill them, and their dead bodies will lie in the street of the great city that is prophetically called Sodom and Egypt, where also their Lord was crucified. For three and a half days members of the peoples and tribes and languages and nations will gaze at their dead bodies and refuse to let them be placed in a tomb; and the inhabitants of the earth will gloat over them and celebrate and exchange presents, because these two prophets had been a torment to the inhabitants of the earth.

"But after the three and a half days, the breath of life from God entered them, and they stood on their feet, and those who saw them were terrified. Then they heard a loud voice from heaven saying to them, 'Come up here!' And they went up to heaven in a cloud while their enemies watched them. At that moment there was a great earthquake, and a tenth of the city fell; seven thousand people were killed in the earthquake, and the rest were terrified and gave glory to the God of heaven" (Revelation 11:3-13).

you shall bury him that same day, for anyone hung on a tree is under God's curse" (Deuteronomy 21:22-23).

The *Psalms of Solomon,* a Jewish document written in the first century B.C., discusses the fall of the Roman general Pompey, who was defeated by Julius Caesar and murdered in Alexandria, Egypt. The *Psalms* notes that Pompey's decapitated body lay on the seashore "with none to bury him, because God had rejected him with dishonor" (2:30-31).

Such is the popular contempt for the two witnesses that they will likewise be denied the common decency of burial. Aware of the denunciations and physical afflictions they experienced while the two witnesses were alive, "the inhabitants of the earth will gloat over them and celebrate and exchange presents" (Revelation 11:10). In a grotesque spectacle, people will come from all "tribes and languages and nations" to gaze at the bodies.

The theme of evildoers taking delight over the afflictions of believers is echoed by Jesus, who forewarned his disciples of the reaction they could expect following his crucifixion: "Very truly, I tell you, you will weep and mourn, but the world will rejoice; you will have pain, but your pain will turn into joy" (John 16:20).

The reveling, however, will be cut short. The horror of the inhabitants of the earth can scarcely be imagined when, after three and a half days, "the breath of life from God" entered the two witnesses and "they stood on their feet, and those who saw them were terrified" (Revelation 11:12).

The ultimate outrage that men can commit, murder, had failed to quell the two witnesses. An astonished world now hears a great voice summoning the pair, and in full view of their enemies they rise in a cloud to heaven.

The ascension of the two witnesses is followed by divine retribution upon the world. A great earthquake strikes, killing a tenth of the population of the city. Curiously, in view of their pronounced hostility to the witnesses, we read that "the rest [of the population] were terrified and gave glory to the God of heaven"(Revelation 11:13).

It may be that the repentance of the inhabitants of the earth was more apparent than real. Like the familiar "deathbed conversion," claims of fealty from the previously faithless is probably to be expected after people have witnessed a miracle.

We later read of their response to another supernatural event, the healing of the beast's fatal injury:

> *"One of its heads seemed to have received a death-blow, but its mortal wound had been healed. In amazement the whole earth followed the beast. They worshiped the dragon, for he had given his authority to the beast, and they worshiped the beast, saying, 'Who is like the beast, and who can fight against it?'" (Revelation 13:3-4).*

But as we have already suggested, phrases like "the whole earth" are meant to be taken in a general rather than an absolute sense. The book of Revelation portrays a titanic struggle between the forces of good and evil for the hearts of men. For those who choose to follow God in those dark days, the two witnesses will be shining examples of courageous determination in the face of overwhelming opposition . . . and ultimate victory will follow.

The Mother of All Battles: Armageddon

Anyone who has pondered biblical prophecy is bound to have asked why there are so many conflicting ideas about the timetable of future events. Popular literature on the subject reveals a multitude of opinions about the prophetic timetable—opinions often complete with dogmatically presented charts and reams of biblical references. The layperson is easily bewildered by these detailed theories and diagrams, no two of which seem to agree.

Many of the neatly laid-out blueprints for the prophetic future share a common shortcoming: Instead of focusing on the overall prophetic themes that have been held by Christians throughout history, Bible teachers compete to discover novel "truths."

We already have examined some of the common beliefs about the prophetic future held by the majority of Christians through the ages. These include a general expectation of a final spiritual rebellion against the heavenlies, which will be played out on planet earth. Jesus himself describes this grim period, which will bring persecution to the faithful:

> *"Then they will hand you over to be tortured and will put you to death, and you will be hated by all nations because of my name. Then many will fall away, and they will betray one another and hate one another. And many false prophets will arise and lead many astray. And because of the increase of lawlessness, the love of many will grow cold. But the one who endures to the end will be saved"*
>
> *(Matthew 24:9-13).*

Further, the worldwide situation will deteriorate into a dark period of human history dubbed the time of "tribulation, marked by man-made and natural disasters, as well as spiritual deception:

> *"For at that time there will be great suffering, such as has not been from the beginning of the world until now, no, and never will be. And if those days had not been cut short, no one would be saved; but for the sake of the elect those days will be cut short. Then if anyone says to you, 'Look! Here is the Messiah!' or 'There he is!' – do not believe it. For false messiahs and false prophets will appear and produce great signs and omens, to lead astray, if possible, even the elect" (Matthew 24:21-24).*

This reign of wickedness will precipitate a final confrontation between God and the forces of evil. Later, we'll examine further elements of this commonly held understanding about the prophetic future, including the Second Coming of Christ, final Judgment, and the eternal state. For now, let's take a close look at the consummate battle: Armageddon.

As previously discussed, the book of Ezekiel describes a final conflict called the battle of

Gog of the land of Magog. Scholars are divided as to whether this is the same battle described in the book of Revelation:

> *"And I saw three foul spirits like frogs coming from the mouth of the dragon, from the mouth of the beast, and from the mouth of the false prophet. These are demonic spirits, performing signs, who go abroad to the kings of the whole world, to assemble them for battle on the great day of God the Almighty. (See, I am coming like a thief! Blessed is the one who stays awake and is clothed, not going about naked and exposed to shame.) And they assembled them at the place that in Hebrew is called Harmagedon" (Revelation 16:13-16).*

The Greek form of Harmagedon is Armageddon. Those who believe that the battles of Gog of the land of Magog and Armageddon are two separate events claim that the battle of Gog of the land of Magog will occur in the middle of the period of tribulation; Armageddon at the end.

Others say that the text does not allow for such fine distinctions. They point to the fact

Scholars debate whether the climactic end-time battle described by Ezekiel (right) is the one described by John in Revelation.

that apocalyptic literature employs imagery and symbolism that are not intended to be taken literally in every detail. Because the very nature of symbolic literature defies precise interpretation, one must look for overall themes rather than attempt to dissect each phrase and word.

Accordingly, while different names and terms are used to describe the participants in Ezekiel and in Revelation, this does not necessarily mean that two separate battles are being described. After all, many scholars point out, various terms are used to describe the figure called the antichrist: In II Thessalonians 2:8-9 he is called "the lawless one"; in Revelation he is called the "beast"; and in Ezekiel he is called by the mysterious name of "Gog." Each of these names symbolizes the personified head of the forces of evil that are intent on destroying the people of God. Similarly, the prophet Ezekiel may be seen as describing the final battle, which, despite differences in detail, is essentially the same as that portrayed in Revelation.

As we have seen, the cataclysmic battle at the end of time is also connected with the "day of the Lord," as spoken of by the prophet Joel:

> *"The sun shall be turned to darkness, and the moon to blood, before the great and terrible day of the Lord comes . . . . I will gather all the nations and bring them down to the valley of Jehoshaphat, and I will enter into judgment with them there, on account of my people and my heritage Israel, because they have scattered them among the nations"* (*Joel 2:31; 3:1-2*).

Here we see the essential feature of the battle of Armageddon: the gathering of "all the nations" for a final battle against those allied with God. The name Jehoshaphat appropriately means "Yahweh judges," and a valley by that name is located outside the walls of

Jerusalem. The Valley of Jehoshaphat is believed to be the site where the nations will be judged for their transgressions against Israel.

We find the identical theme expressed in Ezekiel, where God is said to execute judgment against Gog of the land of Magog:

> *"In the latter days I will bring you against my land, so that the nations may know me, when through you, O Gog, I display my holiness before their eyes. . . . I will summon the sword against Gog in all my mountains, says the Lord God; the swords of all will be against their comrades. With pestilence and bloodshed I will enter into judgment with him; and I will pour down torrential rains and hailstones, fire and sulfur, upon him and his troops and the many peoples that are with him"*
>
> *(Ezekiel 38:16,21-23).*

This description agrees with that of the battle of Armageddon found in the book of Revelation, where demonic spirits entice the "kings of the whole world, to assemble them for battle on the great day of God the Almighty" (Revelation 16:6).

But here the waters become murky, as the texts appear to describe different locations of the great battle. Ezekiel states that Gog and his allies will descend upon the "mountains of Israel" while Joel mentions the valley of Jehoshaphat outside Jerusalem. The scholarly consensus is that the Hebrew word Harmagedon (and its Greek form, "Armageddon") literally means the mountain of Megiddo. Consequently, many scholars would place the battle of Armageddon in the Valley of Megiddo in the north of Israel, because "Har" is the Hebrew word for "mountain" and Megiddo was a city built in the hill country of the tribe of Manassch.

So where will the final battle be fought? The situation is clarified somewhat by the fact that Jerusalem is located in the central mountains of Israel. Thus there is no discrepancy between Ezekiel's "mountains of Israel" and Joel's reference to a valley outside Jerusalem: Both describe the same geographic region in Israel.

The alleged identification of Armageddon with the Valley of Megiddo has aroused much interest on the part of students of biblical

A horrifying vignette from Armageddon, as men are stung to death by monstrous locusts. Monastery art from tenth-century Spain.

prophecy. The "tel"—or mound containing the ancient archaeological remains—of the biblical city of Megiddo is situated at the north end of a major pass, the Carmel, that cuts through the mountain range of the same name.

This vital pass connects the coastal road with the valley and points eastward. In 1799, when Napoleon stood at the site during his campaign in Palestine, he was reported to have remarked that the broad valley was an ideal location for a major battle. And indeed, the valley has been the site of numerous ancient battles: It is here that Deborah and Barak defeated the Canaanite king Sisera (Judges 5); Jehu prevailed against king Ahaziah (2 Kings 9:27); and Pharaoh Neco of Egypt defeated

King Josiah in 609 B.C.

In recent years, unsubstantiated rumors designed to arouse additional curiosity have circulated. One is that a peculiar breed of buzzard was found in the valley. The claimed significance of this "discovery" is that, unlike normal buzzards that have few offspring, these unique birds produce unusually large broods, which in turn are greatly increasing the buzzard population in the Valley of Megiddo. The apparent rationale behind this rumor is that a large population of buzzards is necessary to consume the dead bodies of the armies of antichrist:

> *"Then I saw an angel standing in the sun, and with a loud voice he called to all the birds that fly in midheaven, Come, gather for the great supper of God, to eat the flesh of kings, the flesh of captains, the flesh of the mighty, the flesh of horses and their riders – flesh of all, both free and slave, both small and great.*
>
> *Then I saw the beast and the kings of the earth with their armies gathered to make war against the rider on the horse and against*

his army. And the beast was captured, and with it the false prophet who had performed in its presence the signs by which he deceived those who had received the mark of the beast and those who worshiped its image. These two were thrown alive into the lake of fire that burns with sulfur.

And the rest were killed by the sword of the rider on the horse, the sword that came from his mouth; and all the birds were gorged with their flesh" (Revelation 19:17).

However, the identification of Armageddon as the "Valley of Megiddo" is only one possible interpretation of the name. The problem is complicated by variant spellings found in different manuscripts. Suggested translations of the Hebrew Harmagedon include "city of Megiddo," "land of Megiddo," "mount of assembly," "city of desire," and "his fruitful mountain." The last translation agrees with the writings of Ezekiel and Joel, which refer to the mountains of Israel and Jerusalem.

But even if Harmagedon does refer to the Valley of Megiddo, the text may still be reconciled when it is noted that Israel is a small country about the size of New Jersey, and that the battle could easily be fought *both* at Megiddo in the north, as well as in the mountains around Jerusalem.

The distance between the Valley of Megiddo and Jerusalem is only 75 miles. Modern conflicts in the Middle East have involved fronts of greater distance. The Allies' static line of defense during the 1990 Gulf War against Iraq, for example, extended 150 miles along the Kuwaiti border, and the celebrated "left hook" of encirclement drove hundreds of miles into Iraq. Given the large numbers of combatants expected by many to descend upon the Holy Land during the final battle, it is entirely possible that the conflagration could engulf much of the land of Israel.

It appears then, that the biblical descriptions of the end-time battle between God and the forces of evil, known variously as the battle against Gog of the land of Magog, the day of the Lord, and the battle of Armageddon, all describe the same climactic struggle in which God puts an end to evil rebellion.

The Coming World Dictator

What do we know about the nefarious world leader known as the antichrist, who will lead the final revolt against God? Surprisingly, the name appears only in the Epistles of John, who warns that "every spirit that does not confess Jesus is not from God. And this is the spirit of the antichrist, of which you have heard that it is coming; and now it is already in the world"(1 John 4:3). Despite his essential mysteriousness, the antichrist figures prominently in the cosmic battle of good and evil.

According to John, the "spirit of the antichrist" already was present in his day. Scholars believe he is likely referring to teachers who had left the church and embraced heresy. John identifies the "antichrists" as those who deny the incarnation—the coming of the God-man Jesus Christ in the flesh.

Elsewhere in the New Testament a final, personal manifestation of evil is described, whom the Apostle Paul calls "the man of lawlessness," and who will appear prior to the final battle:

> *"Let no one deceive you in any way; for that day will not come unless the rebellion comes first and the lawless one is revealed, the one destined for destruction. He opposes and exalts himself above every so-called god or object of worship, so that he takes his seat in the temple of God, declaring himself to be God"*
>
> *(2 Thessalonians 2:3-4).*

We find this antichrist again in Revelation, where he is called the "beast," who, along with the "false prophet," will make war with the saints. Led by the "great red dragon," they form a Satanic trinity. The beast will command the allegiance of the nations: " . . . and all the inhabitants of the earth will worship it, everyone whose name has not been written from the foundation of the world in the book of life of the Lamb that was slaughtered" (Revelation 13:8).

As previously discussed, these passages indicate that a political leader will one day arise who will exercise unprecedented—though not complete—authority over the nations of the world. He will be demonically inspired, will appear to recover from a deadly wound, and will have the power to perform unimaginable feats. One can imagine the terri-

In the midst of Armageddon, an angel pours the contents of a holy vial upon the seven-headed beast.

ble state of confusion that will exist in the world as these spectacular events occur, especially in those of the western world who deny the existence of the supernatural.

The ultimate aim of the beast and the other members of the Satanic trinity is to draw the nations of the world into a final battle against the forces of good. To witness for the first time undeniable and terrifying paranormal phenomena will cause shock and paranoia among the masses, who will accept the beast as the only solution to the overwhelming problems facing planet Earth.

But how will this frightful hurly-burly come about? For centuries, students of biblical prophecy have attempted to envision the possible relationships between the various political and military forces that will gather for the final conflict. One valuable source of information is the Jewish rabbinic literature. The rabbis engaged in endless discussion about the prophetic books, and their insights often shed light on difficult passages.

Commenting on the battle of Gog, Magog, and company, the rabbinic sages agreed that Gog and Magog originate from the Caucasian region between the Black and Caspian seas. The Table of Nations in Genesis chapter 10 notes that Magog was the son of Japheth. The descendants of Japheth settled in the regions to the north and west of the Near East, especially Anatolia (Turkey) and the Aegean.

Some have connected the Greek mythological figure *Iapetos* with Japheth, thereby broadening the lands of Japheth to include the European heritage. The rabbis concluded that Japhethic peoples will be in the forefront of the final battle. If true, the implications are significant, for this would also include Greece and, by further implication, the civilization of Europe.

This, however, posed a problem for the rabbis, for in the Hebrew Scriptures it has always been Edom, not Japheth, that has been the one irreconcilable enemy of Israel. The Edomites are the descendants of Esau who inhabited what is now the southern Jordanian desert. The Edomites have long been associated with the Arabs, who first overran their territory in the fifth century B.C.

The rabbinic tradition had an intriguing solution to the relation of Edom to all of this: There is wide agreement in the literature that Gog himself is a descendant of Esau. He will follow in the footsteps of his ancestors, the Edomites, who have never lost their bitter enmity toward the house of Jacob. Indeed, Edom is the perennial archenemy of the children of Israel. For this the prophets foretold judgment upon Mount Seir: "As you rejoiced over the inheritance of the house of Israel, because it was desolate, so I will deal with you; you shall be desolate, Mount Seir, and all Edom, all of it. Then they shall know that I am the Lord" (Ezekiel 35:15).

So it's fitting that the leader of the final great battle should come from Edom. The rabbis also believed that this Edomite Gog would lead the Japhethic nations—which would include Europe and the western nations—to fight against God in that conflict. But how would this world leader be related to the western world?

One possibility is that he will be a Middle Eastern leader who will succeed in exercising control over the western world. One way of achieving this could be through economic blackmail. It is entirely conceivable, given the growing dependence of the West upon Middle East oil, that a powerful Middle Eastern leader could force the West to do his bidding or risk a cut-off of this vital commodity. This is precisely what was attempted in 1973, when OPEC quadrupled the price of oil virtually overnight. The reason for this decision, which caused economic depression in the economies of the West, was to force the West to adapt a more pro-Arab Middle East policy.

Will Saddam Hussein dominate the West?

The Mother of All Convoys

The rabbinic belief about a Middle Eastern leader is not the only theory about the coming evil figure. A cryptic reference in the book of Revelation is thought also to refer to the participants of a great end-time battle: "The sixth angel poured his bowl on the great river Euphrates, and its water was dried up in order to prepare the way for the kings from the east"(Revelation 16:12). This verse occurs just prior to the gathering together of the "kings of the whole world, to assemble them for battle on the great day of God the Almighty" (Revelation 16:14).

According to this commonly held theory, at some point prior to the battle of Armageddon the People's Liberation Army of China will invade the Middle East. The identification of the "kings of the east" with China is made because of an alleged connection between two distinct passages in the book of Revelation.

As seen above, Revelation chapter 16 states that the kings of the east will cross the dried Euphrates River, apparently on their way to invade Israel. There is no mention of the size of their armies, yet some interpreters of biblical prophecy are so eager to make the connection with China that they take a verse from an *earlier* chapter to prove their point: "So the four angels were released, who had been held ready for the hour, the day, the month, and the year, to kill a third of humankind. The number of the troops of cavalry was two hundred million; I heard their number" (Revelation 9:15-16). Skip back to 16:12 and put this together with the kings of the East and—*voilà*—there you have it, for the hugely populous China is the only nation that can possibly fulfill this prophecy.

But a closer look at the biblical text casts doubt on this popularly taught idea. To begin with, there is no direct relation between the two passages. Revelation 9:15-16 does not mention *any* kings, let alone kings from the east. In addition, the passage does not indicate that the 200 million horses and riders are soldiers. Rather, they appear to be fearsome demonic beings spewing "plagues of fire, smoke, and sulfur that came out of their mouths" (Revelation 9:17-18). There is, in short, no basis for identifying these creatures as the soldiers of the "kings of the east" mentioned in Revelation chapter 16.

On the practical side, the necessary logistics of such an invasion make the "Chinese invasion" theory quite unbelievable. The following calculations will demonstrate the folly of combining unrelated texts to "prove" a speculative idea. A land invasion involving 200 million troops would be beyond comprehension and virtually impossible. By comparison, in the greatest airlift of military history, the United States moved approximately one-half million troops and their equipment to the Middle East in a six-month period during 1990-1991. The American air- and sealift was carried out with the greatest expediency, using modern air and sea transport. At the rate of movement accomplished in the Gulf, 200 *years* would be needed to move a 200-million-man army from China to the Middle East.

But that's not the whole story. The "Chinese invasion" theory proposes that the kings of the east (supposedly China) will cross the Euphrates. That can mean only that they are traveling not by air or sea, but overland. Since overland transport is considerably slower than air or sea, we would need to allow even *more* time for a Chinese army to arrive in Israel.

The reader is invited to pick up a map of the world to see what would be involved here. A Chinese army of 200 million men, with numberless tons of necessary equipment and other support, would have to travel along one of the most difficult routes on the planet, traversing inhospitable Pakistan, Afghanistan, and Iran before it reached even the outskirts of the Arab Middle East.

The most direct overland route from China follows the ancient trade route known as the "Silk Road," which skirts India and the almost impassable Himalayas. That would mean that the armies of China would be traveling through the Central Asian republics, formerly part of the Soviet Union.

Here another problem arises. A commonly accepted scenario pits the 200-million-man

Chinese army led by the antichrist against the rest of the world. But if China is supposedly at war against the rest of the world at this point, are we expected to believe that they will be allowed safe passage not only through the former Soviet Union, but all the other countries along their route as well?

What country would permit a massive hostile army to pass freely through its midst? In addition to the problem of passing through hostile territory, any army would face huge difficulties caused by the geography of the region. Much of the terrain through the countries in question does not permit the construction of modern superhighways. Mountainous regions and difficult mountain passes must be crossed, requiring an endless single-lane convoy.

In fact, as we continue our critique of the "kings of the east" theory, it becomes clear that this expeditionary convoy would require literally millions of vehicles, including tank carriers and other military vehicles; trucks carrying troops, fuel, food supplies, weapons and ammunition; communications and intelligence units, and more.

Here's another fantastic calculation: Let's assume that each vehicle occupies an average of only 40 yards of road space, including the space between vehicles to the front and back. That adds up to a convoy stretching 227,272 miles, or nearly ten times around the circumference of the earth.

These calculations are obviously only crude approximations of an unimaginable scenario, but suggest nonetheless the inherent absurdity of an unquestioning acceptance of the China theory.

Now, even supposing it were somehow possible to move such a military force overland to the Middle East, our difficulties are not yet over, for we would then have to find room for the millions of hordes in the tiny land of Israel. It may safely be stated that even if all the precipitous slopes of the mountainous Holy Land were bumper to bumper with vehicles and men, there would not be nearly enough space for an army of this size.

If Not from China, Then Where?

As we have suggested, the supposed "Chinese invasion" comes from an intellectually unwise combination of two unrelated verses in the book of Revelation. Assuming that the China scenario is off the mark, what, then, do those verses mean? Regarding Revelation 9:16, one possibility is that it refers to a demonic force that rains plagues upon the earth. But even if this verse is meant to describe human soldiers, scholars question whether it denotes a force of 200 million.

The Greek words used in the passage literally mean a "double myriad of myriads," or "twice 10,000 times 10,000," and is used to signify an indefinite number too large to calculate. A similar expression is found in Genesis, where the descendants of Jacob would be "like the sand of the sea, which cannot be counted" (Genesis 32:7). The ancient world had no use for the mathematical number of 200 million. The numbers suggested in the verses simply convey "more than the eye can see."

In any event, there is no connection between this incalculable host—whether human or demonic—and the passage in Revelation 16 that speaks of the kings of the east. Assuming that the "kings of the east" are not Chinese, who might they be? A look at the map of the Middle East reveals that the Euphrates River would stand precisely in the direct path of any armies coming from the areas of Turkey, Iran, and the Central Asian republics.

As previously suggested in the book of Ezekiel, these nations are identified as the allies of Gog of the land of Magog. Ezekiel notes that these armies come from the remotest parts of the north. "But why are these lands referred to as coming from the *north* in Ezekiel and from the *east* in Revelation 16:12?

For one possible answer we must look again at the historical geography of the region. In the time of Ezekiel all major travel routes followed the Fertile Crescent as it described an enormous hook through Mesopotamia (modern-day Iraq) and around the Syrian desert. However, by the time of the New Testament, other routes had been opened up from the East. After the death of Alexander the Great in 323 B.C., the Seleucid kingdom stretched eastward to India. In the third century B.C. a major trading route to the eastern part of the kingdom was developed. Two major cities developed by the Seleucids and the Romans after them were Palmyra, in central Syria; and Dura Europos, located on the northern reaches of the Euphrates. They were major links of the new trading route connecting the Mediterranean with Parthia and points east.

At the end of the first century, when the book of Revelation was written, this eastern route was a major international highway. It had become commonplace to think of passage directly from the East; therefore, John speaks of the "kings of the east" But another look at the map of the Middle East will show that these "eastern lands" across the Euphrates comprise the very same geographical region as the lands of the "north."

In actuality, since the precise direction of the lands of Gog and Magog is neither directly north nor east but rather almost exactly northeast, the directions given in Ezekiel and Revelation can be easily correlated. It is also reasonable to assume that all available routes from that general direction would be used by the invading armies.

And there we have it. It is quite unnecessary to postulate yet more (hopelessly implausible) routes, invading armies, and battles. The kings of the east described in Revelation are likely from the same general region as Gog, Magog and company, described in Ezekiel 38 and 39.

What about the motivations of nations that participate in the great final battle? Some have suggested a common thread running through each one of the place names mentioned as allies of Gog, the great enemy of God. From North Africa to the horn of Africa to the southern Republics of the Soviet Union, each of these lands has a compelling reason for participating in an invasion of Israel: They are part of the *dar al-Islam,* the realm of Islam.

The Islamic Genie

For 13 centuries Islam has considered the land of Israel to be Muslim territory. After Muhammad's death in 632 A.D., Abu Bakr, the first caliph (successor to Muhammad), galvanized Muhammad's followers into a formidable fighting force. Brandishing the sword, nearly 20,000 faithful set out across the desert in search of conquest. In just a few years they were already in Transjordan, gazing at Palestine, the bastion of Christianity in the Middle East.

Weakened by internal divisions, and exhausted by a costly struggle with Persia, the Byzantine Empire in the Holy Land offered little resistance to the new threat from the eastern desert. The mercenary Byzantine army proved to be no match for the ferociously single-minded Muslim warriors. In 636 A.D. Jerusalem surrendered to the Caliph Omar without a struggle.

Forty thousand more soldiers of Islam then marched to North Africa, which was soon subdued by the sword. Europe was next. Crossing Gibraltar, the Muslim force swept across all of Spain. It seemed nothing could stop them. But in one of the most decisive battles of history, the armies of Islam finally met their match. In 732 during the Battle of Tours, the Christian army of Charles Martel stopped and turned back the armies of Islam.

Another eight centuries passed before Spain was released from the grip of Islam following the capture of Granada in 1492. Other Muslim armies advanced across Eastern Europe, and on several occasions nearly succeeded in capturing Vienna. Today, many extremist Muslims still have not conceded their former European territory.

But the issue that invokes the most passion among many in the Muslim world is the existence of the State of Israel, viewed as a thorn in the side of the vast Arab community. After several major Middle East wars since 1948, the Arab-Israeli conflict remains unresolved. Many wonder if this age-old struggle for control of the Holy Land, perhaps fueled by another oil crisis and joined by the distant Muslim lands mentioned in Ezekiel, will be the catalyst for the fulfillment of the biblical prophecies regarding Armageddon.

The Second Coming of Christ

Jesus predicted that one day the world would be engulfed in a cataclysm of unimaginable proportions, with effects so dire as to endanger the survival of the human species: "For at that time there will be great suffering, such as has not been from the beginning of the world until now, no, and never will be. And if those days had not been cut short, no one would be saved; but for the sake of the elect those days will be cut short" (Matthew 24:21-22).

As we have seen, during these dark days a figure of consummate evil, called the antichrist, will make his appearance and lead humankind in one last, desperate battle against the forces of good. Since God is eternally beyond his reach, the antichrist will instead direct his vengeance against the faithful. Saint Patrick is said to have been so concerned about the faithful during this perilous time that he prayed for heavenly assurances that Ireland would sink beneath the sea before the reign of the antichrist begins, lest any of the Irish succumb to the temptation to apostatize (renounce their faith).

Throughout much of John's book of Revelation the focus is upon the astonishing events occurring on earth. At times in his narrative, however, John's attention is shifted to the heavenlies. We glimpse not just inexpressible visions of the divine throne, but also a vast presence composed of those who have resisted the antichrist at the cost of their lives. This group is described as "a great multitude that no one could count, from every nation, from all tribes and peoples and languages, standing before the throne and before the Lamb"(Revelation 7:9).

One question often asked by people curious about the afterlife is whether those in heaven are aware of events on the earth. The book of Revelation indicates *yes.* We read that this "great multitude" is conscious of the continuing slaughter on the earth and anxiously concerned to see it ended:

> *"I saw under the altar the souls of those who had been slaughtered for the word of God and for the testimony they had given; they cried out with a loud voice, 'Sovereign Lord, holy and true, how long will it be before you judge and avenge our blood on the inhabitants of the earth?' They were each given a white robe and told to rest a little longer, until the number would be complete both of their fellow servants and of their brothers and sisters, who were soon to be killed as they themselves had been killed" (Revelation 6:9-11).*

In the midst of an orgy of violence and persecution, many on the earth will mock those who are looking for Jesus Christ to appear in the heavens. The Apostle Peter warns, "First of all you must understand this, that in the last days scoffers will come, scoffing and indulging their own lusts and saying, 'Where is the promise of his coming? For ever since our ancestors died, all things continue as they were from the beginning of creation!'" (2 Peter 3:3-4).

According to Peter, however, the delay in divine intervention is not due to God's impotence or inattention but rather to His mercy: "The Lord is not slow about his promise, as some think of slowness, but is patient with you, not wanting any to perish, but all to come to repentance" (2 Peter 3:9).

Divine Patience Runs Out

But the time of divine forbearance is fast coming to an end. The great multitude is comforted with the assurance that they would have to wait "a little longer" until evil reached its full measure. At that moment—and not one instant later—God will decisively intervene. Jesus describes the cosmic signs immediately preceding his return to a shattered planet: "Immediately after the suffering of those days the sun will be darkened, and the moon will not give its light; the stars will fall from heaven, and the powers of heaven will be shaken"(Matthew 24:29).

The book of Revelation portrays a similar range of disturbances in the heavens and on the earth:

> *"I looked, and there came a great earthquake; the sun became black as sackcloth, the full moon became like blood, and the stars of the sky fell to the earth as the fig tree drops its winter fruit when shaken by a gale. The sky vanished like a scroll rolling itself up, and every mountain and island was removed from its place"*
> *(Revelation 6:12-14).*

The ancients considered the order in the movement of the heavenly bodies as a token of divine providential control. The breakdown of this order was to be viewed as a grim omen of the end of the world. We would do well to keep in mind that the notion of "order" was, to the ancients, quite unlike our own. Lacking the scientific understanding we enjoy today, the ancients reasoned that order was, at best, tenuous. For the moderns as well, one can imagine such disturbances causing widespread terror of the sort foretold in the prophecy of Isaiah:

> *"Wail, for the day of the Lord is near; it will come like destruction from the Almighty! Therefore all hands will be feeble, and every human heart will melt, and they will be dismayed. Pangs and agony will seize them; they will be in anguish like a woman in labor. They will look aghast at one another; their faces will be aflame"* *(Isaiah 13:6-8).*

Jesus continues his description of his own return to earth, using the messianic title "the Son of Man":

> *"Then the sign of the Son of Man will appear in heaven, and then all the tribes of the earth will mourn, and they will see 'the Son of Man coming on the clouds of heaven' with power and great glory. And he will send out his angels with a loud trumpet call, and they will gather his elect from the four winds, from one end of heaven to the other"* *(Matthew 24:30-31).*

This passage is a major stumbling block to those who would spiritualize the Second Coming as symbolic of a nebulous enlightenment of humanity. Jesus leaves little room for doubt that his return will be highly visible and unmistakable. But how is it possible for "all the tribes of the earth" to "see the Son of Man coming on the clouds"? It has been suggested that while this would have been impossible in previous ages, with the advent of modern satellite telecommunications it is indeed possible for people around the world to view an event simultaneously. Whether the Second Coming will be a televised event remains to be seen, but there can be little doubt that such technological capacity now exists.

The Announcement

Revelation also mentions the "loud trumpet call," termed the Last Trumpet, which announces the return of Christ. In biblical times the trumpet was used to assemble armies and to sound the attack, as in the book of Joshua, which records how the walls of Jericho came tumbling down at the shout of the people and the sound of the trumpet.

The faithful remaining on earth are gathered together from the four winds to meet their Lord. In ancient Rome it was customary for senators and other notables to go a certain distance outside the city to meet visiting dignitaries and escort them into the city. The same courtesy was extended to the Apostle Paul when he was taken under arrest to Rome: "The believers from there, when they heard of us, came as far as the Forum of Appius and Three Taverns to meet us. On seeing them, Paul thanked God and took courage" (Acts 28:15).

At his first coming, Jesus fulfilled his ordained ministry as the peaceable "lamb of God" who willingly lays down his life as a sacrifice. Here we see him in another role: that of dauntless military conqueror—the warrior Messiah.

The final portion of the book of Revelation describes how, without warning, the heavens open to reveal Jesus Christ riding a white horse. His eyes are "like a flame of fire" and on his head are "many diadems" identifying him as a ruling sovereign. Accompanying him are "the armies of heaven, wearing fine linen, white and pure" (Revelation 19:14). This is the "great multitude" that had suffered ignominy at the hands of the antichrist, now in their moment of triumph.

Battle and Retribution

The heavenly army can scarcely go unrecognized by the "beast and the kings of the earth," who gather their forces to "make war against the rider on the horse and against his army" (Revelation 19:19). The contest is more than unequal, as out of the Conqueror's mouth "comes a sharp sword with which to strike down the nations" (Revelation 19:15). The leaders who have led the nations astray, the beast and false prophet, are captured and "thrown alive into the lake of fire that burns with sulfur" (Revelation 19:20), and their followers are slain with the sword. These images are sure to give pause to all but the most unrepentant sinners. The message, that earthly power is ultimately ineffectual, is clear.

While scholars disagree as to the nature of this final battle and the literalness of the details, believers of all ages have taken comfort in the assurance that an end will one day be made of evil. But while the outcome of human history is certain, the exact timetable remains shrouded from human view, as Jesus instructed his disciples: "Heaven and earth will pass away, but my words will not pass away. But about that day or hour no one knows, neither the angels in heaven, nor the Son, but only the Father. Beware, keep alert; for you do not know when the time will come" (Mark 13:31-33).

Timetables of the Faithful

Despite these words of Jesus, there has been no shortage of attempts throughout history to determine the time of his return. Such efforts at date-setting have often spread panic and confusion as well as violence and bloodshed.

Rumors were flying even before the New Testament was completed: The church at Thessalonica panicked when it was taught by a misguided zealot that it had missed the day of the Lord. The Apostle Paul sought to allay the faithfuls' concerns:

> *"As to the coming of our Lord Jesus Christ and our being gathered together to him, we beg you, brothers and sisters, not to be quickly shaken in mind or alarmed, either by spirit or by word or by letter, as though from us, to the effect that the day of the Lord is already here. Let no one deceive you in any way; for that day will not come unless the rebellion comes first and the lawless one is revealed, the one destined for destruction"*
>
> (2 Thessalonians 2:1-3).

Thomas Muntzer

Paul assured the Thessalonians that the Second Coming of Jesus Christ would not happen until after the rebellion and the revealing of the lawless one, a clear reference to the end-time revolt against God led by the antichrist. Paul's instruction on the matter, however, failed to dampen speculation about the Lord's return. As the centuries passed, fervent Christians continued to attempt to determine the exact date of their Lord's return.

Despite the absence of the antichrist, the approach of the year 1000 and a new millennium caused widespread excitement and hysteria, with many believing that Jesus would return on January 1, 1000 A.D. In December 999, some people disposed of their worldly goods and ceased their daily work in anticipation of the momentous event. Criminals were released, and groups of pilgrims traveled to Jerusalem to experience firsthand the Second Coming. Those who could not make the journey were warned to hide themselves in caves for protection when the world came to an end.

In the Middle Ages, Thomas Muntzer (1490-

1525), a firebrand leader of the Reformation, urged his followers to help him usher in a new age. Muntzer's announcement that the Lord would return after he and his men destroyed Catholicism led to open conflict with the civil authorities, and his espousal of violence precipitated the ill-fated Peasant's Revolt in Germany.

Undeterred, Muntzer joined the battle fearlessly, believing he was promised in a vision that he would catch the cannon balls of his enemies in the sleeves of his cloak. His claim of divine protection notwithstanding, Muntzer and his followers were mowed down by cannon fire in the ensuing melee.

In 1534, only a few years after the Muntzer affair, an almost identical scenario played out elsewhere in Germany. Convinced that the city of Munster would alone be spared destruction upon the imminent return of Christ, a radical Protestant by the name of Jan Matthys rallied his followers to seize control of the city. His bizarre teachings, however, only incensed Munster's inhabitants, who promptly lay siege to the city. Within a year Matthys, his followers, and all others who remained in the city were dead.

Speculation was not limited to the European continent. During political turmoil in England

This undated etching suggests the horror of the London fire of 1666. Some thought it meant the end of the world.

during the 1600s, an eccentric group known as the Fifth Monarchy Men believed that Jesus would soon return to establish a theocracy, that is, a government ruled directly by God. The group took up arms and attempted to hasten divine rule by force, but were thwarted when the British monarchy was restored in 1660.

A few years later, in 1666, London was ravaged by an outbreak of bubonic plague, which killed an estimated 100,000 inhabitants of the city. In the same year the Great Fire of London struck, causing many to wonder if the end of the world was upon them. That the year ended with the number of the beast—666—offered little to encourage the pessimistic.

Three Sixes, a Hen, and a Spiritualist

The New World was not unaffected by the ominous date of 1666. The Quaker leader George Fox remarked that every thunderstorm during that year triggered fears that the end had come. The belief that America was the "New Jerusalem" that would precede the Second Coming of Christ was a common theme among preachers and theologians. Inevitably, as the movement for independence grew, King George of England was portrayed as the antichrist. According to calculations based in Hebrew and Greek, the words "Royal Supremacy in Great Britain" totaled 666.

As the Second Coming was perceived to be tardy, speculation—much of it of dubious veracity—continued. In 1809 a fortune teller named Mary Bateman claimed to have a magic chicken that laid eggs inscribed with messages announcing the imminent return of Christ. Initial interest in her hen turned to indignation when an unannounced visitor caught Bateman forcing an egg into the bird's oviduct. She was later found guilty of poisoning a wealthy client and hanged.

Several years later, in 1814, a spiritualist named Joanna Southcott made the startling claim that, in a duplication of the Virgin Birth, she would bear the second Jesus Christ. Crowds of people gathered around as her abdomen began to swell, but alas, the appointed time came and went, no baby was born, and Southcott died shortly afterwards. An autopsy revealed that Southcott had had (or had somehow induced) a false pregnancy.

Setting a Date

One of the most illustrious Bible prophecy teachers of the nineteenth century was William Miller, who determined that the Second Coming would occur by March 21, 1844. A spectacular meteor shower in 1833 was taken as one of the signs in the heavens mentioned in the book of Revelation.

William Miller

When March 21 passed Miller was disheartened, but some of his followers rallied, recalculating the date of Christ's return to occur on October 22 of that year. When that prediction, too, failed to be fulfilled, Miller dropped from sight. One discouraged follower described public reaction to the missed predictions: "The world made merry over the old Prophet's predicament. The taunts and jeers of the 'scoffers' were well-nigh unbearable." But his followers—who came to be known as Seventh-Day Adventists—thrive to this day.

The return of Halley's Comet in 1910, during which the earth passed through its gaseous

Riding on a White Horse

The book of Revelation paints a dramatic picture of the apex of human history, when Jesus Christ returns to earth at the head of a vast heavenly host to put an end to evil:

"Then I saw heaven opened, and there was a white horse! Its rider is called Faithful and True, and in righteousness he judges and makes war. His eyes are like a flame of fire, and on his head are many diadems; and he has a name inscribed that no one knows but himself. He is clothed in a robe dipped in blood, and his name is called The Word of God.

"And the armies of heaven, wearing fine linen, white and pure, were following him on white horses. From his mouth comes a sharp sword with which to strike down the nations, and he will rule them with a rod of iron; he will tread the wine press of the fury of the wrath of God the Almighty. On his robe and on his thigh he has a

trail, signaled for many the return of Christ. At that time Charles Russell, a former drapery salesman and founder of the Jehovah's Witnesses sect, was spreading his anti-Trinitarian teachings. Russell predicted that Jesus Christ would return to earth in 1914. In a novel twist, when his hopes failed to materialize, Russell insisted that the Second Coming had indeed occurred as a "spiritual" appearance that only the faithful witnesses of Jehovah could discern.

name inscribed, 'King of kings and Lord of lords.'

"Then I saw an angel standing in the sun, and with a loud voice he called to all the birds that fly in midheaven, 'Come, gather for the great supper of God, to eat the flesh of kings, the flesh of captains, the flesh of the mighty, the flesh of horses and their riders—flesh of all, both free and slave, both small and great.'

"Then I saw the beast and the kings of the earth with their armies gathered to make war against the rider on the horse and against his army. And the beast was captured, and with it the false prophet who had performed in its presence the signs by which he deceived those who had received the mark of the beast and those who worshiped its image. These two were thrown alive into the lake of fire that burns with sulfur. And the rest were killed by the sword of the rider on the horse, the sword that came from his mouth; and all the birds were gorged with their flesh" (Revelation 19:11-21).

The establishment of Israel in 1948 led some to hope that the Second Coming of Christ (left) was imminent.

The great world wars encouraged speculative attempts to relate political and military events to the Bible. Many predicted in the summer of 1935, for instance, that Adolf Hitler (or Benito Mussolini) was the antichrist. But it was not until after World War II, when the state of Israel was proclaimed in 1948, that many students of biblical prophecy believed they had a sure sign that the return of Christ would occur in the near future. That year was widely assumed to be the end of the "times of the Gentiles," the period of foreign domination over the land of Israel.

Now another prophecy came into play: After describing the various signs that will occur in the world prior to his coming, Jesus said: "So also, when you see all these things, you know that (the Son of Man) is near, at the very gates. Truly I tell you, this generation will not pass away until all these things have taken place" (Matthew 24:33-34).

Scholars have wrestled with the meaning of "this generation will not pass away "; Jesus may simply have been referring to a rapid flow of events taking place within a relatively brief period of time. Numerous prophecy teachers, however, saw in this verse an opportunity to precisely calculate the time of the return of Christ.

Although the context does not mention political sovereignty over the land of Israel, the verse was nevertheless taken to mean that no more than one generation would pass from 1948 until the Second Coming.

All that remained was to determine the length of one generation. Eager not to let too much time transpire, some prophecy teachers confidently proclaimed that a generation was approximately 35-40 years. Indeed, the Bible indicates that a generation is approximately 40 years of adulthood between ages 20 and 60. After his tragedies, Job lived 140 years and saw four generations (Job 42:16), thus making a generation about 35 years.

One prognosticator, Edgar Whisenant, published a book in 1987, *88 Reasons Why Christ Will Return in 1988*. But as 1988 (1948 plus 40 years) approached with no sign of the end of the age, it became obvious that more time was needed to allow for the Second Coming. Hindsight suggested that the supposed answer had come in 1967 when, during the Six-Day War, Israel gained control over Jerusalem. It was pointed out that the Old City of Jerusalem was under Arab control until the Six-Day War, hence the "times of the Gentiles" ended not in 1948 but in 1967, thereby allowing several more decades until the Second Coming.

Various prognosticators have set the date of Christ's return for virtually every year during the 1980s and 1990s. As the end of the millennium approaches the speculation has reached a fever pitch, as is vividly suggested by the furor aroused in 1997 by the Hale-Bopp comet and the mass suicide of the Heaven's Gate followers.

The skeptic who, with good cause, ridicules arbitrary attempts to set dates would nevertheless do well to heed the words of Jesus: "Heaven and earth will pass away, but my words will not pass away" (Matthew 24:35).

The Millennium: A Thousand Years of Peace

With the approach of the year 2000, millennial fever is spreading, with widespread expectations of the dawn of a new age. For many, the belief that 2000 is a pivotal year is based upon a series of arguments thought to be derived from the Bible.

One key is the number seven, which is delineated in the Bible as signifying completion and perfection. God's creative work was completed in seven days, and on the seventh day humankind was likewise commanded to rest from its labors.

James Ussher

Could it be that the divine program of human history would also be completed in seven "days"—and if so, how long was a "day"? Students of the Bible have taken note of the verse: "But do not ignore this one fact, beloved, that with the Lord one day is like a thousand years, and a thousand years are like one day" (2 Peter 3:8). This has been thought to teach that one "divine" day equaled a thousand years of earthly time.

Accordingly, it was concluded that human history would be completed after seven days, each of a thousand years' duration. If the world was supposedly destined to last 7,000 years, then, when did it begin?

One answer to that question was provided by the seventeenth-century Irish bishop James Ussher, who calculated that Creation occurred at 9:00 A.M. on October 23, 4004 B.C. Ussher arrived at his remarkably precise date in a simple way: by adding up the life spans of the people listed in the biblical genealogies.

Since Ussher's time, Bible scholars have realized that the biblical genealogies contain significant gaps and thus cannot be used to determine the time of Creation. Nonetheless, prophecy enthusiasts took Ussher's calculations, added seven "days" of 1,000 years each, and concluded that the end of human history would come in 3000 A.D.

Taking the biblical week as the model, the final 1,000-year "day" was held to be one of peace and rest, and called the millennium. According to this theory, the catastrophic wars, natural disasters, and rebellion of the antichrist— as well as Christ's Second Coming—would take place by the end of the sixth day—or in 2000 A.D.

Although beguiling in its simplicity, this notion of a 1,000-year period of peace and prosperity following the return of Christ has not gained universal acceptance. One glaring weakness in the idea is the almost complete lack of biblical texts that refer to a millennium—with one exception.

Satan and the Millennium

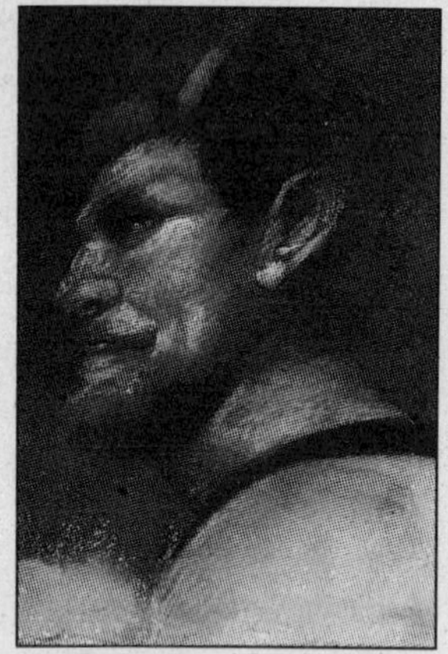
Revelation reports that Satan's allies are many.

The sole biblical mention of a 1,000-year period is found in a cryptic passage at the end of the book of Revelation. There we read that an angel descends from heaven and seizes the "dragon, that ancient serpent, who is the Devil and Satan, and bound him for a thousand years" (Revelation 20:2). Satan is thrown into the "pit" of Hell so that "he would deceive the nations no more, until the thousand years were ended" (Revelation 20:3).

However, we then read this ominous sentence: "After that he must be let out for a little while" (20:3). Once released he will "come out to deceive the nations at the four corners of the earth, Gog and Magog, in order to gather them for battle; they are as numerous as the sands of the sea" (Revelation 20:8).

This passage is taken by some to mean that after the Second Coming of Christ and the defeat of the antichrist, the devil will be in chains for the following 1,000 years—a millennium. Under the direct rule of the returned Christ, and in the absence of Satanic influence, the millennium will be a period of unprecedented peace and prosperity.

However, according to this view, the battle between good and evil is not quite over, for Satan will be released after the 1,000 years to lead yet another rebellion against God. This is the battle of Gog and Magog. Curiously, though, proponents of this view do not equate it with the battle by the same name that is described in the book of Ezekiel. The reason is because the battle of Gog and Magog in Ezekiel is thought to have taken place a thousand years earlier, during the reign of the antichrist.

It is at this point that others have questioned belief in a literal millennium, for it appears that it makes for two "final" battles: Armageddon *and* the battle of Gog and Magog at the end of Revelation. The Second Coming of Jesus Christ is portrayed as putting an end to wickedness and rebellion, as stated in the Epistle to the Hebrews: "But when Christ had offered for all time a single sacrifice for sins, 'he sat down at the right hand of God,' and since then has been waiting 'until his enemies would be made a footstool for his feet'" (Hebrews 10:12-13).

The reference to Jesus' enemies being "made a footstool for his feet" signifies the subjugation of a defeated foe. Accordingly, those who deny a literal millennium hold that Satan and his minions were utterly defeated at the Second Coming, and that the days of evil are finished.

In this view the "thousand years" in Revelation is taken to symbolically represent the time between Christ's first and second advent. So, we are living *in* the millennium today. Satan, released at the end of that period, inspires the antichrist and instigates the final rebellion known variously as Armageddon or Gog and Magog.

But there are difficulties with this view as well. In it Satan is bound during the present time, between Christ's first and second coming. However, the Apostle Peter indicates that Satan is active in the world: "Discipline yourselves, keep alert. Like a roaring lion your adversary the devil prowls around, looking for someone to devour. Resist him, steadfast in your faith"(1 Peter 5:8-9).

Still other commentators caution against

using a passage from the book of Revelation, a book filled with symbolism, as a proof text either for or against the idea of a millennium.

A Cosmic Interlude

An enigmatic passage in the book of Revelation describes the imprisonment of Satan for a thousand years. Scholars have long disputed the nature of this period; some interpret the passage literally while others hold that it is symbolic of the age separating the two advents of Christ:

> *"Then I saw an angel coming down from heaven, holding in his hand the key to the bottomless pit and a great chain. He seized the dragon, that ancient serpent, who is the Devil and Satan, and bound him for a thousand years, and threw him into the pit, and locked and sealed it over him, so that he would deceive the nations no more, until the thousand years were ended. After that he must be let out for a little while.*
>
> *"Then I saw thrones, and those seated on them were given authority to judge. I also saw the souls of those who had been beheaded*

*for their testimony to Jesus and for the
word of God. They had not worshiped the
beast or its image and had not received its
mark on their foreheads or their hands.
They came to life and reigned with Christ
a thousand years. (The rest of the dead did
not come to life until the thousand years
were ended.) This is the first resurrection.
"Blessed and holy are those who share in the
first resurrection. Over these the second
death has no power, but they will be
priests of God and of Christ, and they will
reign with him a thousand years.
"When the thousand years are ended, Satan
will be released from his prison and will
come out to deceive the nations at the four
corners of the earth, Gog and Magog, in
order to gather them for battle; they are as
numerous as the sands of the sea. They
marched up over the breadth of the earth
and surrounded the camp of the saints
and the beloved city. And fire came down
from heaven and consumed them"*

(Revelation 20:1-9).

The Dead Shall Rise: The Resurrection

The Gospel of Matthew records a bizarre event that took place in Jerusalem after the crucifixion, an event believed by Christians to be a foretaste of what would occur at the Second Coming of Christ:

"Then Jesus cried again with a loud voice and breathed his last. At that moment the curtain of the temple was torn in two, from top to bottom. The earth shook, and the rocks were split. The tombs also were opened, and many bodies of the saints who had fallen asleep were raised. After his

resurrection they came out of the tombs and entered the holy city and appeared to many" *(Matthew 27:50-53).*

It is thought that those who were raised from the dead following Christ's crucifixion were the "first fruits"—or vanguard—of a massive resurrection destined to take place in the future.

All three monotheistic faiths (those believing in one God)—Judaism, Christianity, and Islam—have a belief in the resurrection of the body. The idea, however, is unheard of in the Hindu faith, where the human body is regarded as merely one of innumerable outer shells to be discarded as the soul—the spiritual aspect of existence—progresses up the ladder of reincarnation. Existence is indeed a journey to the devout Hindu, and the body merely the vehicle that allows one to do dharma—duty to divine law—and advance to transcendent conciousness by adhering to the sacred Hindu texts, the Vedas. In Hindu lands, the body is typically disposed of through cremation and the ashes scattered. The soul, simply, has no more use of it.

Here Today, There Tomorrow

Human personality, likewise, is transient, with the soul adopting a separate individuality with each incarnation. According to Hindu mysticism the *telos,* or goal, of human existence is to finally lose all pretense of personality as one attains Nirvana and merges with ultimate reality—or "Brahman." Similarly, the Greeks held to the dichotomy of body and soul, with the body being merely the temporary receptacle of the immortal soul.

The religions of the ancient Near East appear to have had a concept of individual personality surviving death. Thus in Egypt, for example, great care was taken to embalm the

High-ranking deceased in ancient Egypt were sent on their journeys into the afterlife expertly embalmed.

bodies of Pharaohs and other high-ranking officials. Royal tombs were filled with the accoutrements of everyday life, including personal items, furniture, food, and the personal servants of the deceased, who were executed in order to accompany their master. The purpose of all this, however, was to aid the individual in his or her passage through the underworld, and not because it was expected that they would one day rise from the dead.

Intimations of belief in the bodily resurrection of the dead appear in the later books of the Hebrew Scriptures. While not clearly defined, the souls of the departed are said to pass into Sheol, or the underworld. There the wicked are without hope: "Such is the fate of the foolhardy, the end of those who are pleased with their lot. . . . Like sheep they are appointed for Sheol; Death shall be their shepherd; straight to the grave they descend, and their form shall waste away; Sheol shall be their home"(Psalms 49:13-14).

Redemption

Still, the Psalmist expects to be delivered from the world of shadows: "But God will

Redemption: Christ in glory among the saints, as depicted by fifteenth-century Florentine painter Domenico Ghirlandaio.

ransom my soul from the power of Sheol, for he will receive me" (Psalms 49:15). While the meaning of "he will receive me" is uncertain, it is apparent that the writer hopes for a future beyond the grave. The same expectation is found more clearly expressed in the book of Job, who in the midst of his sufferings stated confidently, "For I know that my Redeemer lives, and that at the last he will stand upon the earth; and after my skin has been thus destroyed, then in my flesh I shall see God" (Job 19:25-26).

At the conclusion of Daniel's prophecy we find yet another reference, this time to a resurrection of both the righteous and wicked at the end of time, "when [m]any of those who sleep in the dust of the earth shall awake, some to everlasting life, and some to shame and everlasting contempt. Those who are wise shall shine like the brightness of the sky, and those who lead many to righteousness, like the stars forever and ever"(Daniel 12:2-3).

As related in the New Testament, Jesus was opposed by the Sadducees, the aristocratic party of the Jews that did not believe in a resurrection. Jesus, being challenged by them on one occasion, replied, "And as for the dead being raised, have you not read in the book of Moses, in the story about the bush, how God

The World of Shadows

In Hebrew thought, *Sheol* is the abode of the dead, a shadowy place where both the righteous and the wicked await final judgment. It is pictured as a dark, gloomy region deep within the earth, reached by crossing a river. Elsewhere it is described as a city entered through gates, a place of ruins, or a prison.

The Hebrews conceived of the individual as a unity of body and spirit, and believed that the existence of the soul outside the body was incomplete and temporary. The inhabitants of Sheol are called "shades," or spirits of the dead. The dead are said to exist in a state of helplessness: "For in death there is no remembrance of you; in Sheol who can give you praise?"(Psalms 6:5); "Are your wonders known in the darkness, or your saving help in the land of forgetful-

said to him, 'I am the God of Abraham, the God of Isaac, and the God of Jacob'? He is God not of the dead, but of the living; you are quite wrong" (Mark 12:26-27). That is, rather than perish in Sheol, the Hebrew patriarchs will be "eternally present" with God.

The writers of the New Testament viewed the resurrection of Jesus as the indisputable proof that one day believers would likewise be raised from the dead. The Apostle Paul challenged those who doubted this truth:

ness?" (Psalms 88:12).

There is no labor in Sheol, yet it is described as a troubled, dreamlike state. When the prophet Isaiah foretells the end of the king of Babylon, he writes, "Sheol beneath is stirred up to meet you when you come; it rouses the shades to greet you, all who were leaders of the earth; it raises from their thrones all who were kings of the nations" (Isaiah 14:9).

Though Sheol is grimly portrayed, the omnipresent God, nevertheless, is there: "Where can I go from your spirit? Or where can I flee from your presence? If I ascend to heaven, you are there; if I make my bed in Sheol, you are there" (Psalms 139:7-8).

God also is capable of ransoming souls from the depths of the earth: "For great is your steadfast love toward me; you have delivered my soul from the depths of Sheol" (Psalms 86:13).

> *"Now if Christ is proclaimed as raised from the dead, how can some of you say there is no resurrection of the dead? If there is no resurrection of the dead, then Christ has not been raised; and if Christ has not been raised, then our proclamation has been in vain and your faith has been in vain. We are even found to be misrepresenting God, because we testified of God that he raised Christ – whom he did not raise if it is true that the dead are not raised . . . . If Christ has not been raised, your faith is futile and you are still in your sins"*
>
> (1 Corinthians 15:12-15,17).

As well as being the consummate proof for the Christian faith, for Paul the resurrection was the final event needed to usher the faithful out of the present age into the glory that will accompany Jesus' Second Coming.

The Great White Throne Judgment

"Then I saw a great white throne . . ." begins one of the most ominous passages in the book of Revelation, marking the terminus of human history. Most peoples of the ancient Near East as well as the Greeks had a cyclic view of time based on the endless repetition of the four seasons. There was little room for genuine progress, for in time the great cycle of life would return again to the same point. Time had neither beginning nor end, and all things were destined to continue as they had from time immemorial.

In sharp contrast to this, the Bible presents a linear view of time, which begins with the creation of the world and proceeds toward its end point. And that end point, it must be emphasized, is not random, but carefully ordered and predestined. History is thus viewed as the record of dynamic change and progress through time, culminating in the day of judgment.

Patience Has Its Limits

The Hebrew Scriptures present God as the merciful judge of the world, as depicted by Abraham's plea to spare the city of Sodom:

> *"Then Abraham came near and said, 'Will you indeed sweep away the righteous with the wicked? Suppose there are fifty righteous within the city; will you then sweep away the place and not forgive it for the fifty righteous who are in it? Far be it from you to do such a thing, to slay the righteous with the wicked, so that the righteous fare as the wicked! Far be that from you! Shall not the Judge of all the earth do what is just?' And the Lord said, 'If I find at Sodom fifty righteous in the city, I will forgive the whole place for their sake'"* (Genesis 18:23-26).

This remarkable exchange continues when Abraham asks if the Lord would spare the city if a slightly lower number of righteous men, 45, were found. The Lord agrees, and Abraham continues to reduce the number to 40, 30, and 20. Finally, he dares to makes one last appeal: "Then he said, 'Oh do not let the Lord be angry if I speak just once more. Suppose ten are found there.' He answered, 'For the sake of ten I will not destroy it'" (Genesis 18:32).

Alas, even ten worthy could not be found, and the city suffered a catastrophic destruction. This story illustrates the nature of God as supremely merciful to those who repent. But for those who continue in their rebellion there is no escape. While there is in the Hebrew Scriptures the expectation that rewards and punishments will

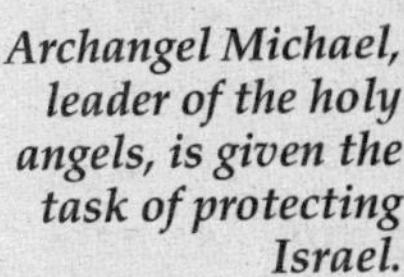

Archangel Michael, leader of the holy angels, is given the task of protecting Israel.

occur in this life, some passages also hint of a final judgment at the end of time.

At the conclusion of his prophecies about the final rebellion, Daniel speaks of a resurrection and judgment:

> *"At that time Michael, the great prince, the protector of your people, shall arise. There shall be a time of anguish, such as has never occurred since nations first came into existence. . . . Many of those who sleep in the dust of the earth shall awake, some to everlasting life, and some to shame and everlasting contempt. Those who are wise shall shine like the brightness of the sky, and those who lead many to righteousness, like the stars forever and ever"* (*Daniel 12:1-3*).

Here we see the promise of eternal glory for the faithful, and the warning of "shame and everlasting contempt" for the wicked. The archangel Michael is thought to be the head of the holy angels who, in the Hebrew Scriptures, is given the special responsibility of protecting Israel. Earlier in the book Michael is seen engaging in warfare against the evil forces that were preventing an angelic messenger from reaching Daniel. At the end of time Michael will again be sent to render assistance in the time of tribulation.

Fire and Decay

The book of Isaiah describes the two fates of mankind in the eternal kingdom of God:

> *"For as the new heavens and the new earth, which I will make, shall remain before me, says the Lord; so shall your descendants and your name remain . . . . And they shall go out and look at the dead bodies of the people who have rebelled against me; for their worm shall not die, their fire shall not be quenched, and they shall be an abhorrence to all flesh"* (Isaiah 66:22,24).

In Jesus' day, this vivid image of continual decay was associated with the valley of Hinnom, which marked the southwest border of Jerusalem. The valley acquired an evil reputation as the location of the cultic shrine of Topheth. The prophet Jeremiah denounces the abominations committed there by his countrymen: "And they go on building the high place of Topheth, which is in the valley of the son of Hinnom, to burn their sons and their daughters in the fire—which I did not command, nor did it come into my mind" (Jeremiah 7:31).

The Hebrew prophets engaged in a long and largely unsuccessful struggle against the Topheth, an Aramaic term meaning "hearth" or "fireplace." The Topheth was a shrine probably created to offer human sacrifices to the Semitic god Moloch. However, some scholars argue that the practice of burning sons and daughters in the fire was a symbolic act of initiation for the children rather than human sacrifice. Others believe that the reference to burning should be interpreted literally, especially in the light of the known practice of human sacrifice by the Canaanites, Phoenicians, and others. If so, the Topheth in the Valley of Hinnom may well have been a "high place," an area considered to be sacred and where human sacrifices were offered.

Another ominous association with the Valley of Hinnom is that of Gehenna, which is the Greek form of the Hebrew word for Valley of Hinnom. In the New Testament and rabbinical literature, Gehenna is the place of judgment and punishment after death. It is a place of permanent abode, while Hades (perhaps more familiar to modern readers) was thought to be a temporary abode of the dead.

Jesus, quoting Isaiah, spoke of Gehenna as the destiny of the wicked, "where their worm never dies, and the fire is never quenched" (Mark 9:48).

In New Testament times the Hinnom valley was the (literal) garbage dump for Jerusalem. The mention of worms and undying fire refers to the maggots and continual burning that characterized the valley, and that, symbolically, suggest corruption and suffering.

The book of Hebrews states that "it is appointed for mortals to die once, and after that the judgment" (Hebrews 9:27). The awesome scene of final judgment is described at the end of the book of Revelation, where God is seated on a "great white throne." Before him are assembled "the dead, great and small" (20:12), indicating that no one, regardless of status in life, is exempt.

Judgment will be based upon open "books" that, apparently, contain records of the deeds of all people. Jeremiah speaks of this divine examination: "I the Lord test the mind and search the heart, to give to all according to their ways, according to the fruit of their doings" (Jeremiah 17:10).

The judgment, however, will not be concerned solely with external deeds. The Apostle Paul speaks of the day when God "will judge the secret thoughts of all": "Therefore do not pronounce judgment before the time, before the Lord comes, who will bring to light the things now hidden in darkness and will disclose the purposes of the heart. Then each one will receive commendation from God" (Romans 2:16; 1 Corinthians 4:5).

The passage in Revelation states that "Death and Hades" are "thrown into the lake of fire" (Revelation 20:14), where the beast, the false prophet, and the devil are already in torment. Paul affirms that the "last enemy to be destroyed is death" (1 Corinthians 15:26).

The lake of fire is called the "second death" because it indicates everlasting spiritual separation from God. Jesus told his disciples that the eternal fire was prepared for the devil and his angels. However, their dreadful abode is shared by all those who have served the devil, and whose names are not written in "the book of life" (Revelation 20:14).

Torment and eternal fire await mortals who dare to serve Satan. Painting by Pedro de Rubiales.

This, however, is not the

divine intention, as the Apostle Peter indicates: "The Lord is not slow about his promise, as some think of slowness, but is patient with you, not wanting any to perish, but all to come to repentance" (2 Peter 3:9).

All Eyes on the Book

According to the book of Revelation, men's fates will be determined by mysterious books to be opened at the great white throne judgment of God. Mention is made of books containing the record of the deeds of men, as well as the "book of life," in which are found the names of those who will spend eternity with God in heaven.

In biblical times a "book" was actually a scroll made either of papyrus or animal skins. It was not until the second century A.D. that the bulky scrolls were replaced by sheets of writing stacked and sewn together. Important documents were secured with a wax seal certifying that the contents had not been tampered with.

Numerous scrolls are mentioned in the book of Revelation, including one that Jesus Christ alone can open: "You are worthy to take the scroll and to open its seals, for you were slaughtered and by your blood you ransomed for God saints from every tribe and language and people and nation" (Revelation 5:9).

The idea of a divine register is found elsewhere in the Bible. While pleading on behalf of the children of Israel, Moses asks the Lord to forgive their sin: "but if not, blot me out of the book that you have written." But the Lord said to Moses, "Whoever has sinned against me I will blot out of my book" (Exodus 32:32-33).

The Heavenly Tribunal

In an awe-inspiring passage, the book of Revelation describes the gathering together of all mankind to give an account at the last judgment:

"Then I saw a great white throne and the one who sat on it; the earth and the heaven fled from his presence, and no place was found for them. And I saw the dead, great and small, standing before the throne, and books were opened. Also another book was opened, the book of life. And the dead were judged according to their works, as recorded in the books. And the sea gave up the dead that were in it, Death and Hades gave up the dead that were in them, and all were judged according to what they had done. Then Death and Hades were thrown into the lake of fire. This is the second death, the lake of fire; and anyone whose name was not found written in the book of life was thrown into the lake of fire"

(Revelation 20:11-15).

The Lord himself records the names of the faithful: "Then those who revered the Lord spoke with one another. The Lord took note and listened, and a book of remembrance was written before him of those who revered the Lord and thought on his name" (Malachi 3:16).

When his disciples returned, excited about the demonstrations of spiritual power they had witnessed, Jesus admonished them: "Nevertheless, do not rejoice at this, that the spirits submit to you, but rejoice that your names are written in heaven" (Luke 10:20).

The book of Revelation calls this record "the book of life of the lamb," a reference to the sacrificial death of Christ (Revelation 13:8). During the period of tribulation at the end of time the "inhabitants of the earth" will follow after the beast, "and all the inhabitants of the earth will worship it, everyone whose name has not been written from the foundation of the world in the book of life of the Lamb that was slaughtered" (Revelation 13:8).

Faithful believers who endure sufferings during the tribulation will be vindicated. In describing the glories of heaven the reader is told," But nothing unclean will enter it, nor anyone who practices abomination or falsehood, but only those who are written in the Lamb's book of life" (Revelation 21:27).

THE ELEMENTS SHALL MELT: A NEW HEAVEN AND EARTH

Heaven is often portrayed as a place somewhere in space where white-robed saints pluck harps as they perch on fluffy clouds. This image, endemic to Christian popular culture, brings innocent comfort to some. Life in Heaven, it seems to say, is innocuous and remote. The Bible, however, paints a quite different picture. The *earth* is described as the dwelling place of God, and it is on earth that the faithful will spend eternity, enjoying its beauty and exploring its resources and treasures.

Heaven on Earth

A remarkable divine promise closes the book of Isaiah: "For I am about to create new heavens and a new earth; the former things shall not be remembered or come to mind" (Isaiah 65:17). The first indication of this extraordinary transformation occurs during the final judgment, as related by John: "Then I saw a great white throne and the one who sat on it; the earth and the heaven fled from his presence, and no place was found for them" (Revelation 20:11).

Some believe that the phrase "heaven and the earth fled from his presence" is only poetic imagery expressing the fear of the created order in the presence of God. Others believe it signals the beginning of the dissolution of the physical universe in preparation for the new heavens and the new earth.

The dramatic metamorphosis of the planet is made necessary, the Bible claims, because all of creation has been corrupted by the existence of sin, which has affected not only the human race but the world itself. According to the book of Genesis, the "curse" of sin threw the entire natural world into disorder. Childbirth was changed to a painful experience; the soil no longer freely produced its abundance, and human toil became necessary for the production of crops; and above all, creation was cursed with the process of disintegration that leads to death.

Accordingly, attention in both heaven and earth remains fixated upon the evil scourge that is bringing ruin to the planet. The entire universe awaits deliverance, as indicated by the Apostle Paul: "We know that the whole creation has been groaning in labor pains until now" in anticipation of being "set free from its bondage to decay" (Romans 8:21,22). The "decay" was part of the curse leveled against both humankind and creation itself after the disobedience in the Garden of Eden. Just as the distress of labor precedes the joy of birth, the growing difficulties of this present era signal the dawn of a new age.

The Heavens Set Ablaze

Further details regarding this universal baptism of fire are found in the second Epistle of Peter: "But the day of the Lord will come like a thief, and then the heavens will pass away with a loud noise, and the elements will be dissolved with fire, and the earth and

The climactic last days of the world will be heralded by angels of the Apocalypse.

everything that is done on it will be disclosed" (2 Peter 3:10).

Some modern-day analysts have suggested that this cataclysmic dissolving of the world by fire will be triggered by the detonation of the world's stockpiles of nuclear weapons. However, as frightening a possibility as that may be, it does not approach the magnitude of the awesome event described in the Bible. Something more would have to be involved: perhaps the ignition of the earth's molten core—a dismaying event that would make the biblical conflagration entirely possible.

Others prefer to interpret these passages symbolically, in an attempt to describe the glorious presence of God, before whom nothing unholy can stand. Still, Peter seems to be insisting on an actual event as he continues to speak of "the coming of the day of God, because of which the heavens will be set ablaze and dissolved, and the elements will melt with fire" (2 Peter 3:12).

No Sea to See

The final chapter of the book of Revelation adds one more intriguing detail: "Then I saw a new heaven and a new earth; for the first heaven and the first earth had passed away, and the sea was no more" (Revelation 21:1). Various explanations have been offered to explain the lack of oceans on the new earth. Some explain the omission as the result of the ancients' fear of the sea, a vast expanse that symbolized danger and the great unknown.

Intertwined with early notions about the sea is a preoccupation with order and its opposite, chaos. In Babylonian mythology, for instance, the dragon of chaos, Tiamat, battles Marduk, the god of order. Similarly, the Bible contains descriptions of mythological sea monsters that represent the forces of chaos and evil, and who exist in clear opposition to the creative and redemptive work of God. One serpentine creature, Leviathan, is called "the dragon that is in the sea"—a foe too formidable for mortals. Similarly, the mysterious beasts of

Daniel's visions are seen arising from the sea, as does the evil beast of Revelation. The lack of a sea in the new heavens and earth, then, is taken by some to indicate that nothing will remain to strike fear in the hearts of men.

There may also be a practical reason for the absence of seas. Oceans cover 71 percent of the earth's surface, making for a vast area that is essentially uninhabitable. The removal of the seas would greatly increase the available land area.

Other geological changes are also thought to enhance human habitation, such as described in the prophecy of Isaiah: "Every valley shall be lifted up, and every mountain and hill be made low; the uneven ground shall become level, and the rough places a plain" (Isaiah 40:4).

Some believe that references to the elimination of the oceans and mountains speaks of the removal of all barriers,

Phoenicians (left) and others believed the sea held numberless terrors.

natural or otherwise, that have contributed to the separation, segregation, and hostility of nations. Indeed, in a passage thought to speak of this future state, Isaiah indicates that the peace that pervades the new heaven and new earth will extend to all of creation:

> *"The wolf shall live with the lamb, the leopard shall lie down with the kid, the calf and the lion and the fatling together, and a little child shall lead them. The cow and the bear shall graze, their young shall lie down together; and the lion shall eat straw like the ox. The nursing child shall play over the hole of the asp, and the weaned child shall put its hand on the adder's den. They will not hurt or destroy on all my holy mountain; for the earth will be full of the knowledge of the Lord as the waters cover the sea"* (Isaiah 11:6-9).

The City of God: A New Jerusalem

Appropriately, the concluding vision in the Bible concerns the age to come, when time shall be no more and the faithful enjoy eternal bliss. True to the fascination evoked by the study of prophecy, this final glimpse into the future is apt to exceed the reader's wildest imagination.

The book of Revelation describes the appearance of a "new heaven and a new earth" following the great conflagration, in which the first heaven and earth are said to pass away. Scholars disagree as to whether the New Jerusalem should be taken as a literal city or symbolic of the community of believers. Whatever the case, the writer of the Epistle to the Hebrews indicates that the heavenly city to come is more enduring than any earthly city: "For here we have no lasting city, but we are looking for the city that is to come" (Hebrews 13:14).

A City for the Ages

The vision described in Revelation is of a magnificent city descending from heaven, which will be the "home of God . . . among mortals" (Revelation 21:3). The presence of God had been provisionally represented by the Ark of the Covenant, which the children of Israel carried with them in their wilderness wanderings, and later by the divine presence in the Holy of Holies of the Temple. But in the New Jerusalem, God in His glorious presence comes to dwell with His people throughout eternity. In the heavenly city the deepest aspirations of humankind are at last met; it is a place where "death will be no more" and all "mourning and crying and pain" will have ceased (Revelation 21:4).

The description of the New Jerusalem is so fantastic as to lead some interpreters to suspect that John is not intending to portray a literal

The New Jerusalem will be "prepared as a bride adorned for her husband."

city. The dimensions are indeed daunting, forming a colossal cube of unimaginable proportions: "The city lies foursquare, its length the same as its width; and he measured the city with his rod, fifteen hundred miles; its length and width and height are equal" (Revelation 21:16). The city's exact symmetry and its hugeness are thought to comprise a symbolic expression of the perfection and greatness of God.

If intended to be taken literally, a city of such proportions could only have a divine origin. The patriarch Abraham anticipated the New Jerusalem: "For he looked forward to the city that has foundations, whose architect and builder is God" (Hebrews 11:10).

Not only are the dimensions of the New Jerusalem beyond human comprehension, but so too are the materials used in its construction. It is described as a "very rare jewel" and "clear as crystal," which likely refer to the luminescence that emanates from it. The city is surrounded by walls, the foundations of which are adorned with every kind of precious jewel.

Here we find the single most oft-quoted description of the heavenly city: "And the twelve gates are twelve pearls, each of the gates is a single pearl, and the street of the city is pure gold, transparent as glass" (Revelation 21:21). Some have suggested that John was alluding to the memory of Herod's temple, with a golden facade that gleamed in the sun. According to the Jewish historian Josephus, the brilliant effect in the first rays of the morning sun on the temple was such that all those looking at it had to shield their eyes from its "fiery splendor." The roots of this idea, however, undoubtedly go back to the prophet Ezekiel, whose vision of a glorious Temple and city of Jerusalem included 12 gates inscribed with the names of the 12 tribes (Ezekiel 48:31-34). Too, the city gates described by John are inscribed with the names of the 12 tribes (Revelation 21:12), and the foundations of the gates are described as having been named for the 12 apostles (Revelation 21:14).

The mention of gold "transparent as glass" refers to the metal's lack of impurity. Such a pure form of gold is exceedingly rare, but not unattested. One earthly parallel to this unalloyed state is found in rare crystal glass, which, like the streets of the city, has no opaqueness.

The mind-boggling description of the 12 gates, each made from a single pearl, corresponds to a rabbinic prophecy that God will set huge pearls in the gates of Jerusalem. Each of these pearls is said to be 30 cubits (45 feet) in circumference, with hollow passageways measuring 10 cubits (15 feet) wide by 15 cubits (23 feet) high. The mention of pearls completes the picture of unsurpassed wealth and glory. A pearl was a mark of affluence, as reflected in Jesus' parable about the merchant who sold all his possessions to obtain a "pearl of great value."

The Safety of Divine Illumination

There will be no need of sun or moon in the New Jerusalem for "the glory of God is its light, and its lamp is the Lamb" (Revelation 21:23). Some take this to refer symbolically to the divine splendor of Jesus, who, as the Lamb of God, is called "the true light, which enlightens everyone" (John 1:9) and "the light of the world" (John 8:12).

Perceived literally, however, the absence of sun or moon indicates the fundamental restructuring of the universe spoken of by John: "Then I saw a new heaven and a new earth; for the first heaven and the first earth had passed away" (Revelation 21:1). The "new heavens" of the eternal state will apparently not include the solar system as we know it, in which the planets revolve around the sun.

The prophet Isaiah spoke in similar terms:

> *"For darkness shall cover the earth, and thick darkness the peoples; but the Lord will arise upon you, and his glory will appear over you. Nations shall come to your light, and kings to the brightness of your dawn"* *(Isaiah 60:2-3).*

And, again Isaiah:

> *"Your sun shall no more go down, or your moon withdraw itself; for the Lord will be your everlasting light, and your days of mourning shall be ended"* *(Isaiah 60:20).*

Cities in the ancient Near East relied upon strong walls and fortified gates to protect against attack. It was common practice to secure the gates of the city at nightfall for safety. However, since there will be no night in the New Jerusalem, the gates of the city are said to remain open at all times.

The perpetually open gates also indicate the absence of any threat, a great comfort to those who had suffered through the evil dangers and attacks of the tribulation. This unthreatening atmosphere is reflected in the city's ill-proportioned walls, which were only "one hundred forty-four cubits" (75 yards) in height and width, surrounding a city 1500 miles in height, length, and width. (Revelation 21:17.) In stark contrast to the oppressive rule of the antichrist, who demanded that all take his mark, those dwelling in the New Jerusalem will dwell in safety with God's name "on their foreheads" (Revelation 22:4).

Reward and Redemption

The vision of John continues to describe a "river of the water of life, bright as crystal, flowing from the throne of God and of the Lamb" (Revelation 22:1). This image of life-giving water would hold special appeal for those living in the hot and arid climate of Palestine, where, save for a few sluggish coastal tributaries, such rivers are unheard of.

The sides of the crystal river are bordered by

The "river of the water of life" will flow "from the throne of God and of the Lamb."

"the tree of life, with its twelve kinds of fruit" (Revelation 22:2). The imagery recalls Genesis and the "tree of life" (Genesis 3:24). After disobeying the Lord by eating from the "tree of the knowledge of good and evil" (Genesis 2:17), Adam and Eve were cast out of the garden lest they obtain immortality in their sinful state:

> *"Then the Lord God said, 'See, the man has become like one of us, knowing good and evil; and now, he might reach out his hand and take also from the tree of life, and eat, and live forever' – therefore the Lord God sent him forth from the garden of Eden, to till the ground from which he was taken. He drove out the man; and at the east of the garden of Eden he placed the cherubim, and a sword flaming and turning to guard the way to the tree of life"*
>
> *(Genesis 3:22-24).*

I Saw a New Heaven . . .

The wondrous description of heaven found in the last chapter of Revelation is an exalted one that remains as gloriously impenetrable today as when the words were first penned:

"Then I saw a new heaven and a new earth; for the first heaven and the first earth had passed away, and the sea was no more. And I saw the holy city, the new Jerusalem, coming down out of heaven from God, prepared as a bride adorned for her husband. . . . Death will be no more; mourning and crying and pain will be no more. . . .' And the one who was seated on the throne said, 'See, I am making all things new. . . .'

"And in the spirit he carried me away to a great, high mountain and showed me the holy city Jerusalem coming down out of heaven from God. It has the glory of God and a radiance like a very rare jewel, like jasper, clear as crystal. It has a great, high wall with twelve gates, and at the gates twelve angels, and on the gates are inscribed the names of the twelve tribes of the Israelites. . . .

"And the city has no need of sun or moon to shine on it, for the glory of God is its light, and its lamp is the Lamb. The nations will walk by its light, and the kings of the earth will bring their glory into it. Its gates will never be shut by day—and there will be no night there. People will bring into it the glory and the honor of the nations"

(Revelation 21:1-5,10-12, 23-26).

In the eternal state, however, those dwelling in heaven have been redeemed by the blood of the Lamb, and there is no longer any restriction on eating from the tree of life. The leaves of the tree "are for the healing of the nations" (Revelation 22:2), indicating the absence of any physical or spiritual want, thus completing a picture of abundance and perfection.

This picture of abundance appears also in Ezekiel, in which it is declared, "Wherever the river goes, every living creature that swarms will live, and there will be very many fish. . . . everything will live where the river goes" (Ezekiel 47:9).

Scholars continue to disagree as to the literalness of the vision of the New Jerusalem in the book of Revelation. That a great deal of symbolism is employed in the fantastic portrayals of the future life can scarcely be denied. Whether literal or symbolic, there seems little doubt that John is attempting to describe with the frailty of mortal language an incomprehensibly glorious reality beyond the grasp of the human mind.

DARK SECRETS

The curious often wonder why, given the intense scrutiny devoted to the interpretation of biblical prophecy, many of the cryptic visions remain maddeningly difficult to comprehend. A possible clue is given at the conclusion of the prophecy of Daniel, where the prophet is told to "keep the words secret and the book sealed until the time of the end" (Daniel 12:4).

Some take this verse to mean that the interpretation of certain biblical prophecies will remain shrouded in mystery until the last days of human history. Then, the meaning will be revealed to those who remain alive, and who presumably will have an immediate need for insight into the prophecies. This point of view regards biblical prophecy as a key part of a sort of handbook, designed to guide the faithful in the end times.

Safety and Faith

Some clerics regard the prophecies as a sort of "resistance literature" designed to bolster the courage and faith of persecuted peoples. According to this view, if one stands firm in the face of evil and adversity, the power of God, expressed through Christ, will triumph over evil.

Another benefit of advance understanding of the tribulations about to descend upon the planet is found in Jesus' discourse about the end of time, where he warns those who hear his words:

> *"So when you see the desolating sacrilege standing in the holy place, as was spoken of by the prophet Daniel (let the reader understand), then those in Judea must flee to the mountains; the one on the housetop must not go down to take what is in the house; the one in the field must not turn back to get a coat. . . . For at that time there will be great suffering, such as has not been from the beginning of the world until now, no, and never will be"*
>
> *(Matthew 24:15-18, 21).*

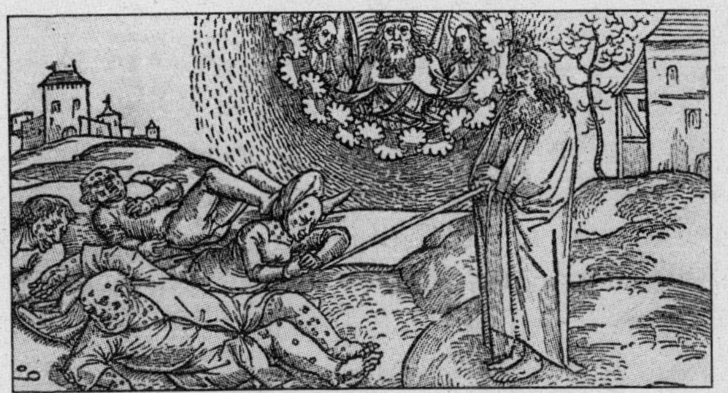

Biblical prophecy does not merely foretell dark terrors, but prepares the devout for ways to avoid them.

One practical advantage of understanding what is looming ahead, then, is to *escape* the coming terrors. The early Church bishop and historian Eusebius records that during the revolt against Rome in A.D. 66-70, the early Christians in Judea became convinced that Jesus' prophecy was meant for them. Accordingly, the Christians of the city heeded Jesus' admonition, "then those in Judea must flee to the mountains" and fled *en masse* to Pella in Trans-Jordan, where they lived in safety while Judea was ravaged by the Roman armies.

Biblical prophecy, then, is not simply a series of intriguing tales, but, according to many, the foundation of a practical guide to living, and how to achieve the ultimate reward.

How Close Are We?

Woody Allen once commented, "More than any time in history mankind faces a crossroads. One path leads to despair and utter hopelessness, the other to total extinction. Let us pray that we have the wisdom to choose correctly."

This comic summation of the dilemma facing humankind reflects the growing expectation that—for better or worse—the planet is on the threshold of unparalleled transformation. A number of widely varied sources are converging to indicate the dawn of a new age. Things seem to be in flux. Many observers are concerned about changes in the earth itself, such as environmental pollution, holes in the ozone layer, global warming, and deforestation. In recent years a number of self-proclaimed psychics and visionaries have predicted that a planetary realignment will take place, triggering major earthquakes, coastal flooding caused by the melting of the polar icecaps, and other global upheavals.

Warnings and Transformation

Looming threats to the environment are accompanied by a heightened interest in the paranormal. Recent polls indicate that for the first time a majority of Americans believes in the reality of UFOs—spacecraft piloted by beings who are not of this earth. Curiously, a recurring theme in many of the alleged "contacts" with space aliens is concern about the ominous changes

Since 1947, people have been fascinated by UFOs. Do the pilots wish to warn us?

taking place on earth. If such reports are to be believed, even creatures from other solar systems are worried about the future of our planet.

Warnings about the future are apparently originating not only in outer space but in inner space, as well. One psychologist specializing in dreams reported discovering a startling phenomenon while giving a series of radio interviews across the United States: Listeners from vastly different backgrounds and geographic locales called in to give accounts of dreams that bore frightening similarities. Many were visions of planetary doom and the end of the world, complete with hideous images of burning cities, tidal waves, earthquakes, and floods.

Though differing in details, the evolution of a belief in the radical transformation of the planet can be traced in cultures and religions around the world. Hopi and Mayan cultures recognize that we are approaching the end of a decisive World Age. The former offer no time limits, but the latter have a calendar system whose cycle will end in 2011-2012. At that date, the Mayans believe, hideous events will occur, including the transport of humankind to a new galactic state of consciousness.

One sect of Hindus anticipates the beginning of the Kalki avatar (an incarnation in